The population of the European Community will fall by 2% from its current level by the year 2025, while the total population of Eastern and Western Europe taken together will increase by 3.4%. Between 1960 and 1990, the EC population grew by 17%. This contrast reflects both the dramatic growth of the population of pensioners in the total population and also the rapid ageing of the Community's working population.

In this volume, based on a CEPR conference held in Munich on 23–25 April 1992, demographers and labour economists assess recent demographic and labour market developments in Western and Eastern Europe. They compare them with developments in the USA and Japan and assess the effects of ageing on European productivity, earnings, and human capital formation. They consider the relationships between ageing, unemployment, labour mobility and migration and investigate the policy implications of ageing for productivity, wages, mobility, unemployment and educational activity. They consider possible policies to improve the quantity or quality of the labour force, including incentives to female labour participation, selective immigration policies, 'pronatalist' family policies, and measures to improve human capital formation through schooling and further education.

T0312090

Labour markets in an ageing Europe

Centre for Economic Policy Research

Labour markets in an ageing Europe

Edited by

PAUL JOHNSON

and

KLAUS F. ZIMMERMANN

CAMBRIDGE
UNIVERSITY PRESS

CAMBRIDGE UNIVERSITY PRESS
Cambridge, New York, Melbourne, Madrid, Cape Town, Singapore, São Paulo

Cambridge University Press
The Edinburgh Building, Cambridge CB2 8RU, UK

Published in the United States of America by Cambridge University Press, New York

www.cambridge.org
Information on this title: www.cambridge.org/9780521443982

First published 1993
This digitally printed version 2008

A catalogue record for this publication is available from the British Library

ISBN 978-0-521-44398-2 hardback
ISBN 978-0-521-05760-8 paperback

Contents

Figures

Tables

Preface

This book is the outcome of a conference on 'Labour Market Implications of European Ageing', held at the University of Munich on 23–25 April 1992. The conference was made possible by a grant from Directorate-General V (Employment, Industrial Relations and Social Affairs) of the Commission of the European Communities.

We would like to thank the University of Munich for hosting the conference, David Guthrie and Kate Millward at CEPR for guiding this volume to press, and John Black of the University of Exeter for his work as Production Editor.

Paul Johnson
Klaus F. Zimmermann
October 1992

Conference participants

Rudolph Andorka *University of Economic Sciences, Budapest*
Didier Blanchet *Institut National d'Etudes Démographiques, Paris*
Axel Börsch-Supan *Universität Mannheim and CEPR*
Kenneth Burdett *University of Essex*
Paul Chapman *National Economic Development Office, London*
John De New *Universität München*
John F. Ermisch *University of Glasgow and CEPR*
Christopher Flinn *New York University*
Knut Gerlach *Universität Hannover*
Stanislawa Golinowska *Institute of Labour and Social Studies, Warsaw*
David Guthrie *CEPR*
Joop Hartog *Universiteit van Amsterdam*
Olaf Hübler *Universität Hannover*
Paul Johnson *LSE and CEPR*
Heather Joshi *London School of Hygiene and Tropical Medicine and CEPR*
Anders Klevmarken *Gothenburg University*
Anja Koch *Universität München*
Walter Krämer *Universität Dortmund*
Gerhard Kühlewind *Institut für Arbeitsmarkt und Berufsforschung, Nürnberg*
Sergio Perelman *Université de Liège*
Gerd Ronning *Universität Konstanz*
Winfried Schmähl *Zentrum für Sozialpolitik, Bremen*
Christoph Schmidt *Universität München and CEPR*
Coen Teulings *Universiteit van Amsterdam*
Rainer Winkelmann *Universität München*
Robert Wright *University of Glasgow*
Naohiro Yashiro *Japan Center for Economic Research, Tokyo*
Klaus F. Zimmermann *Universität München and CEPR*

1 Ageing and the European labour market: public policy issues

PAUL JOHNSON and
KLAUS F. ZIMMERMANN

1 Introduction

The population of Europe is ageing. By the early decades of the next century this process is likely to lead to a decline in the population of the 12 countries of the European Community, with the number of EC citizens being 2 per cent less in 2025 than it is today. This fundamental demographic restructuring is a consequence of the generally low and declining fertility rates over the last twenty years which have produced small cohorts of children and young adults while the large post-war 'baby-boom' cohort has moved into middle age. There has, of course, been considerable variation among EC countries in the scale and timing of this demographic change because of their different population structures and histories, and yet wider variation among Eastern European countries, several of which still have fertility rates above the replacement level. Figures 1.1(a) and (b) show that whereas in Western Europe the economically active population will reach a peak in several countries between 1990 and 2000, in Southern and Eastern Europe, as in Ireland and the US, the economically active population will continue to expand, though at a declining rate, into the third decade of the 21st century. Nevertheless, the demographic trend is common to all countries – Europe, the 'Old World', is becoming older.

Knowledge about this ageing of the European population is no more recent than the process itself, which began in the early years of the twentieth century as a consequence of a general fall in fertility rates from the very high levels of the nineteenth century. Political concern about the long-run consequences of this demographic trend has been a recurrent theme in the public policy of European nation states for over a century. There has been much discussion and hand-wringing over the fear of population decline, and particularly over how this might jeopardise a country's economic and military potential (Teitelbaum and Winter, 1985;

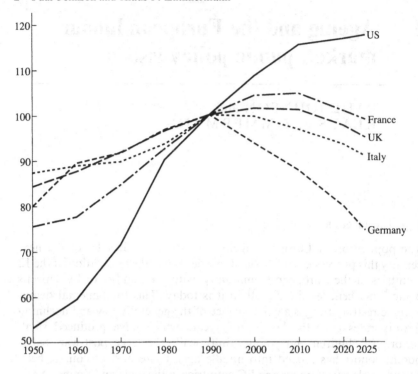

Figure 1.1(a) Index of economically active population, 1950–2025 (1990 = 100)
Source for Figures 1.1(a) and (b); International Labour Organisation (1986)

Zimmermann, 1989). Pronatalist policies ranging from exhortation through economic incentives to forcible restriction of contraception and abortion have been variously implemented in different European countries over the last hundred years, with consistent lack of success, in an attempt to reverse the long-run decline in the population growth rate (Höhn, 1987).

Public policy interest in the more specific issue of population ageing, which is itself an inevitable consequence of a long-term fall in the rate of growth of the population, is, however, a much more recent phenomenon. An ageing population implies an increase in the number of older persons to be supported and cared for by public pensions and medical services, and it is these public expenditures and their associated tax liabilities that have dominated public discussion of ageing in the 1980s (for instance, OECD, 1988a, 1988b). Considerable economic and political concern has been expressed over projections that by 2030 the necessary social security tax rate in countries such as Germany and France might have to rise to

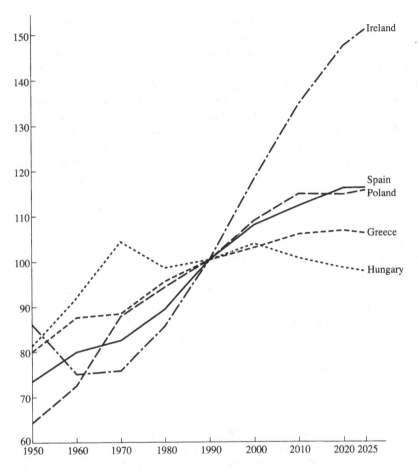

Figure 1.1(b) Index of economically active population, 1950–2025 (1990 = 100)

over 40 per cent, or around twice its current level, in order for a shrinking workforce to pay for the public pensions of an expanding elderly population (Schmähl, 1989; Vernière, 1990).

But as a socio-economic phenomenon population ageing affects much more than just the social security system, and it affects the current and future welfare of all age groups, not simply that of the elderly. This is particularly the case in the labour market where the effects of population ageing are already being felt in terms of a decline in the number of juveniles entering the labour force in Europe and an increase in the number of workers in middle age. So far, however, there has been little systematic and detailed analysis of how the ageing of the European labour

market will affect the performance and potential of the European economies, or of the role for public policy intervention in this economic-
demographic system. Previous work on the inter-relationship between age
structure and the labour market has focused on the declining employment
prospects of older workers during the economic downturns of the later
1970s and mid-1980s and on the way public authorities have used early
retirement schemes to reduce the size of the workforce and scale down the
problem of recorded unemployment (Laczko and Phillipson, 1991; Kohli
et al., 1991). In this background paper we want to consider not how
economic performance affects the employment chances of older workers,
but the more general issue of how the changing age structure of the
workforce in Europe over the next three decades is likely to affect
economic performance, and how and whether public policy needs to
respond to this demographic change.

It may be the case that substantial changes in the age structure of the
workforce in Europe will have only a minimal economic impact if age is
an insignificant variable in labour force performance, and even if the
economic consequences of an ageing workforce are substantial, it may be
concluded that supply and demand will adequately respond to the new
labour market circumstances without any public policy intervention.
However, the strong role age appears to play in, for instance, the determination of remuneration, and the prominence of public policy in most
countries in determining the type and level of education and training, in
setting minimum employment conditions and in regulating migration, all
suggest that there are strong a priori grounds for believing both that the
ageing of the labour force will have noticeable economic effects and that
there will be both scope and pressure for public policy responses. In this
paper we propose to do no more than sketch some of the possible public
policy areas that will be affected by the ageing of the labour force in the
1990s and beyond. The inter-related nature of economic and demographic
systems makes any identification of specific areas somewhat arbitrary and
artificial, but it is helpful for purposes of exposition. In the next four
sections we will consider how the ageing of the European labour force
may affect labour costs and productivity, training and skill, retirement
behaviour, and labour mobility and migration, and how public policy
may interact with these economic effects.

2   Labour costs and productivity

The ageing of the labour force in Europe is certain to put upward pressure
on labour costs, and may have a negative effect on productivity. There is,
in the majority of employments, a positive relationship over the life-cycle

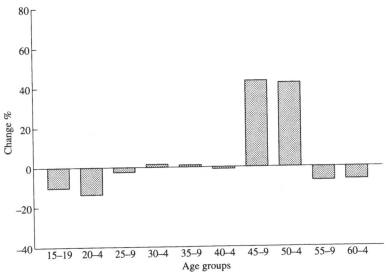

Figure 1.2(a) Changes in French population, 1990–2000 (percentage change in size of age groups)
Source: for Figures 1.2(a)–(f), *World Population Projections* (World Bank, 1990)

between age and earnings. In many countries, as in Britain, this relationship is stronger for male than for female workers, and stronger in non-manual than in manual jobs, but it seems to be deeply-entrenched and of long standing, particularly in larger organizations with bureaucratic personnel management structures (House of Commons, 1988). Wage growth tends to be faster for workers aged 20–45 than for those aged 45–65, so the individual age-earnings profile flattens out in middle age. This pattern is often obscured in cross-sectional age-earnings data, which normally show a hump-shaped profile resulting from general increases over time in real earnings for all age groups, and higher levels of skill for each generation of new labour market entrants. However, since it is the labour force aged 35–50 – the post-war baby-boomers – which will see the fastest relative growth in most European countries in the 1990s (see Figures 1.2(a)–(f), it is clear that overall labour costs will rise if current earnings differentials by age are maintained.

Will this increase be significant or trivial? This depends on how both the age structure of the workforce and the age structure of earnings change over time. Positive age-earnings profiles are a function of positive returns to both age *and* work experience, and demographic change will increase the average level of both. An estimate made for Japan (Ono, 1989–90) of the economy-wide effect of ageing on labour costs up to the end of the

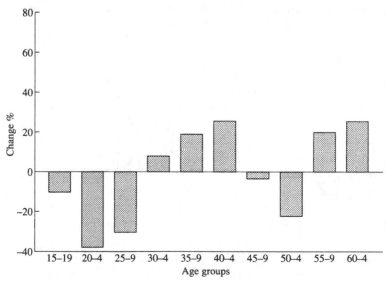

Figure 1.2(b) Changes in German population, 1990–2000 (percentage change in size of age groups)

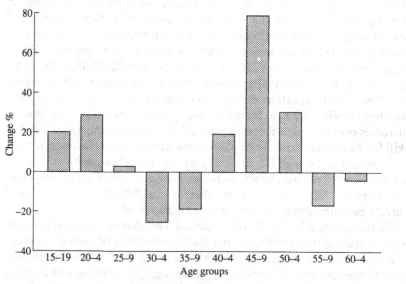

Figure 1.2(c) Changes in Polish population, 1990–2000 (percentage change in size of age groups)

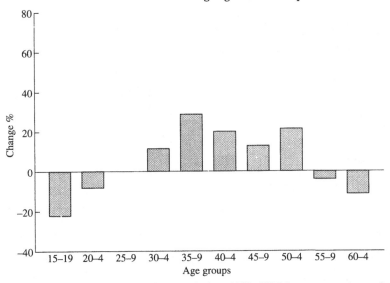

Figure 1.2(d) Changes in Spanish population, 1990–2000 (percentage change in size of age groups)

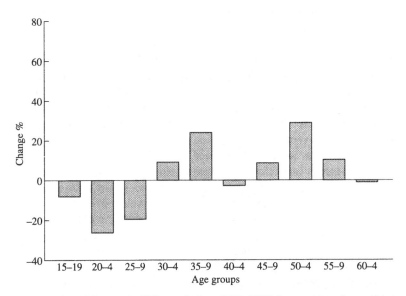

Figure 1.2(e) Changes in UK population, 1990–2000 (percentage change in size of age groups)

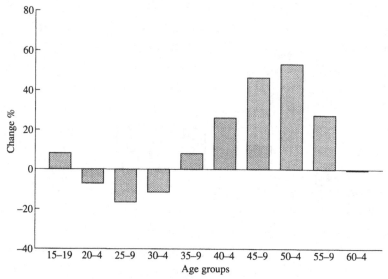

Figure 1.2(f) Changes in US population, 1990–2000 (percentage change in size of age groups)

century produces a figure of only 0.9 per cent for the pure age effect, and of 4.2 per cent for the age and experience effects combined. This is a much lower figure than was feared when the cost-push effects of an ageing labour force were discussed by the Japanese Ministry of Labor in 1976. The impact for particular firms with an age mix significantly different from that of the total labour force could, of course, be much larger. A cross-section survey of earnings in Britain in 1987 showed, for example, that average earnings of male non-manual workers aged 30–39 were 25 per cent higher than for workers aged 25–29 (*New Earnings Survey*, 1987), so young firms of the late 1980s (for instance in the information technology sector) face above average demographic wage push in the 1990s.

Future labour costs will be determined not only by changes in the age structure, but also by any changes to the existing relationship of earnings to age. In the absence of other determining factors, it might be expected that the decline in the number of young workers would drive up juvenile wage rates, while remuneration for the growing pool of workers in their 40s and 50s would suffer a relative decline. It is clear, however, that other factors are important; juvenile wages may be affected by minimum wage regulations, by restrictions on hours and type of work, and through an interaction with public and privately provided education and training. The salaries of older workers in large firms may be determined more by their position within an internal labour market than by the balance of supply and demand in a global labour market (Doeringer and Piore, 1971). How far seniority wage systems can respond to an increase in the relative supply of older workers by flattening the earnings/promotion ladder remains to be seen; too shallow an earnings gradient would undermine the system of deferred pay on which internal labour market management depends.

Empirical research provides no clear guidance on future trends in the relationship between age and earnings. Easterlin (1980) has proposed that members of large birth cohorts suffer reduced life-time earnings because of the greater labour market competition they face from their multitudinous peers. Attempts to test this hypothesis, mainly with US data, have produced mixed but on balance supportive results: the large youth cohorts that entered the labour market in the 1970s suffered both low relative earnings and high unemployment rates (Bloom *et al.*, 1987; Ermisch, 1988). This was, however, a period of considerable macroeconomic turmoil in the wake of the 1973 oil price shock, and some of the perceived earnings effect undoubtedly derives from general labour market dislocation. Furthermore, the baby-boomers were the first generation to benefit fully from the great expansion of higher education in the 1960s, so any perceived fall in income in early working life may be no more than a deferment due to a change in lifetime earnings *profiles* rather than a change in the *level* of lifetime earnings (Riboud, 1987). Easterlin himself has noted that the income of the baby-boomers has been high and rising rapidly for much of the 1970s and 1980s, though he ascribes this to changes in their lifestyle relative to earlier cohorts – fewer children, and more dual-income households (Easterlin *et al.*, 1990). Whether these behavioural changes are a *response* to the costs of belonging to a large cohort is likely to remain an open question for some time. The Easterlin hypothesis has also received mixed evidence in Europe: Wright (1989) finds no support in a comparative study for 16 Western European countries, but Ermisch (1988) and Wright (1991) support the Easterlin hypothesis on the basis of British data. Zimmermann (1991) uses West German data to show that there is no sufficient evidence that young cohorts experience higher unemployment rates if their cohort size is relatively high.

Even if it is the case that large cohort size has depressed earnings for baby-boomers on entry to the labour market, we cannot be confident that this cohort effect will continue to apply over the next two or three decades. As cohorts mature they become much more 'mixed-up', so in employment terms a five-year age difference between a 19 and a 24 year old is likely to be of much greater significance than that between a 44 and a 49 year old. Moreover, as people age their remuneration is more likely to be determined by the operation of internal labour markets than by more general competitive pressures. The apparent trend in recent years to a clearer distinction in many European countries between core and peripheral workers could produce in the future divergent trends in age-earnings profiles, with only a small group of full-time long-term employees continuing to enjoy higher income as they age. There is, however, a substantial obstacle to such a trend in the form of existing earnings-related pension arrangements, a subject we will return to in section 4 below.

If the impact of ageing on future earnings and labour costs is difficult to estimate, then the impact of ageing on productivity is almost impossible to calculate. The widespread existence of seniority wage systems and other customary determinants of worker remuneration makes it generally inappropriate to use earnings as a proxy for productivity. Only in strict individual piece-work systems does the wage equal the marginal product; elsewhere time-rates, bonus schemes, group work and age differentials complicate the relationship. Most employers (and probably most employees) seem to believe in a rule of thumb that average labour productivity declines after some age between 40 and 50 (Staehle, 1989). This belief (which is qualified in United Nations, 1988) is used by both employers and trade unions to justify ageist hiring and firing policies. The assumption about a decline in productivity with age is so common that few attempts have been made to gather supporting evidence – why bother to prove the obvious?

If this common assumption is correct, then any age structure-induced rise in European labour costs will be exacerbated by a fall in average labour productivity as the European workforce grows older. The research of industrial and social psychologists, however, indicates that the relationship between age and productivity is certainly complex, and not necessarily supportive of popular beliefs (Rabbit, 1992; Warr, 1992). Laboratory tests reveal a clear decrement with age in average scores on complex memory and physical reaction tests, but no simple inferences about workplace performance can be drawn from experimental results, for four reasons. First, the types of tasks performed in laboratory tests – for instance memorizing lists of numbers and recalling them in reverse order – have little in common with most workplace duties. In many jobs the verbal reasoning and social skills with which older workers are better endowed are more important than quick mental recall. Second, older people can substantially improve their performance on many of the laboratory tests through practice, so training can be used to counter any age-related productivity effects, a point returned to in section 3 below. Third, although average test scores decline with age from some point in the 30s, the variance around this average does not contract, so some 60 year olds will gain test results better than the average for 40 year olds. Since the variance in performance is commonly greater within age groups than between age groups, age alone is found to be a poor predictor of individual performance. Finally, and perhaps more importantly, the measurable age decrement in performance in most laboratory tests is extremely small, at least up to age 60.

The relatively small number of workplace studies collectively show no general relationship between age and productivity, either positive or negative, although individual studies produce results across a very broad spectrum (McEvoy and Cascio, 1989). It is, of course, very difficult to know what exactly is being measured. Attitudinal surveys typically find higher levels of job satisfaction and commitment among older workers, and lower levels of overall absenteeism, so the total performance being measured is some combination of ability and application. Nevertheless, the implication of these psychological studies is that the ageing of the European workforce will not have the depressive effect on productivity that popular beliefs might indicate.

It should be clear from the foregoing discussion that the consequence of population ageing for pay and productivity in Europe is very much a matter for discussion and further investigation. Uncertainty about the justification for and working of age-related promotion and remuneration systems prevents any direct inferences being drawn from either simple human capital theory or from internal labour market/efficiency wage theories (Bellmann, 1989). On the other hand, the practical difficulties involved in directly measuring individual productivity preclude a purely empirical resolution of the issue. Despite these many uncertainties, there is scope for public policy intervention. Current age-specific rates of pay and labour force participation indicate that an increase in the average age of the population will tend to decrease overall labour supply and increase labour costs. Future movements in average labour productivity are less clear cut, though a substantial age-induced rise seems unlikely. Many of the specific policy areas relate to training, retirement and mobility, and so are dealt with in the following three sections, but a general policy goal must be a flexible labour market in which human resources are used to greatest effect. It may be that labour market pressures will lead to less overt ageism in hiring and firing decisions, but the extent of age prejudice about worker performance makes it likely that age-neutral employment policies will take many years to emerge. Some legislative impetus could be given by taking action against age discrimination in the work place, following the model set by anti-sex discrimination laws. Not only would this be a first step in responding to the demographic pressures on current and future labour supply, but it would also contribute further to the creation of a unified EC labour market by standardizing policy and practice towards older workers across the twelve member states.

3   Training and skill

The implicit assumption underlying the structure and performance of public education and training systems in almost all European countries is that general learning stops when full-time work begins. Education and training for children and young adults is supposed to create an endowment of attributes and skills sufficient to sustain the individual through a lifetime's employment. Only in the case of those who fail before the age of 50 or 55 to sell their labour services is any significant public attempt made to update and enhance the stock of individual skills, and much of this public effort is, in practice, targeted on unemployed workers in their late teens and early 20s. Training provided by employers for their own workforce – whether through on-the-job learning or through formal training programmes – continues to update the stock of skill of individual workers, but tends to make these skills more specific. In a free market, employers will pay only for firm-specific training, since they can be sure of capturing returns only to firm-specific skills. An employer who pays for general skills training will effectively be providing a resource for competing employers to the extent to which recently-trained workers move between jobs; very high rates of labour mobility necessarily imply very low rates of employer-financed general training.

Extensive and growing public provision of general education up to the age of 18 or 20, and private provision of further job-specific training, has been an effective and efficient way of enhancing the quality of human capital in Europe since the Second World War. Demographic change and new economic circumstances, however, now threaten this established pattern of skills creation. The ageing of the workforce means that the stock of general skills in the workforce is also ageing. At the same time it is argued that the pace of technological change, and so the speed with which general skills become obsolescent, is increasing. These twin forces imply that a growing proportion of the ageing workforce possess outdated general skills.

This proposition is very difficult to demonstrate or test. It is certainly true that older workers bore the brunt of the recession of the early 1980s, particularly in Britain and France, and this may have been due to their functional obsolescence. Equally it may have been due to some combination of ageism on the part of employers and trade unions, together with publicly provided early retirement schemes which were designed to replace older workers by the young unemployed. The psychological studies discussed above do not show a clear inverse relationship between age and productivity, as might be expected if the average stock of general skills depreciates with age.

It is possible, however, that the productivity of the total labour force is in some way determined by the relative size of different age groups. If, for instance, old and young workers are complements rather than substitutes, then the economy will perform best when the workforce contains an optimal blend of youth and experience. An ageing of the workforce might well have a detrimental effect on this age balance, particularly if new knowledge is embodied in recently educated cohorts of young adults. In this case a declining proportion of younger people would produce a less technologically up-to-date workforce and so might reduce (or slow the rate of growth of) the productivity of workers of all ages (van Imhoff, 1988). The workplace training of older workers in job-specific skills would not overcome this age mismatch unless it could exactly replicate in older workers the embodiment of period-specific technical know-how acquired by juveniles in the normal course of their education, and this seems most unlikely. To give a specific example, the socialization and acculturation processes experienced by children today, both at home and at school, means that they grow up using and identifying with computer technology and so develop a competence which is unlikely to be achieved by more than a handful of 50 or 60 year olds.

Nevertheless it is clear that older workers can be trained in the use of new technology, and although their knowledge of the technology may be more instrumental and less encompassing than is the case with younger people, it is not necessarily any less useful in the workplace. Psychological tests show that although older people may take longer to learn new techniques than the young (it is often so long since they were last taught that they have to re-learn how to learn), they forget no more rapidly than do younger workers (Warr, 1992). Many negative workplace attitudes towards the re-training of older workers seem to rest more on age prejudice than on evidence, and pioneering companies have found that age need be no barrier to learning. When the Travelers Insurance Company in the US decided to retrain older workers beyond retirement age in new technologies they found great enthusiasm on the part of these mature trainees, and according to a senior vice-president of the company: 'the return on our training investment has been substantial. Far from being wasteful – the common attitude towards spending money to train older workers – this programme has yielded a productive group of people not otherwise available to us at any cost' (Libassi, 1988). Any such return on training for older workers is likely to be amplified by their much lower turnover rates compared with the young. A home improvement company in Britain which decided to employ only people over 50 in one of its stores (a response to a shortage of young adult workers) found that profits were 18 per cent higher, absenteeism 39 per cent lower, and turnover six times lower than in comparable stores (*The Independent*, 2 Oct. 1991).

Case studies show that firm-specific training or re-training of older workers can pay. As the pace of technological change increases and the rate of depreciation of specific skills increases in parallel, so it may become more sensible to retrain older workers. If the depreciation period of a new skill is anticipated to be, say, ten years, then a 50 year old is likely to provide almost as good a return as a 20 year old; indeed, the lower turnover rate may raise the average return on training for 50 year olds above that for 20 year olds. Generalizing to the economy, an increase in training and retraining of older workers would seem to be one way of compensating, at least partially, for the decline in the number of recently trained new labour market entrants. How much of this training should be general rather than firm-specific is an open question, the answer to which depends upon relative costs and returns. It seems probable, however, that governments will need to initiate new laws and regulations about in-service training if they wish comprehensive training schemes for older workers to be established. In the absence of compulsion and regulation, the tendency of unscrupulous employers to free-ride on the training expenditure of others will tend to undermine the whole basis of a general retraining scheme.

4   Retirement

Retirement practices and norms have a substantial impact on overall labour market performance. Participation rates for older male workers have fallen in all European countries almost continuously throughout the twentieth century, with ever younger age groups moving out of the labour force and into retirement or early retirement. Around 1900 approximately three-quarters of all men aged 65 and above in France, Germany and Britain were engaged in the labour force, but by the late 1980s considerably fewer than one in ten men over 65 were in work in these three countries. Furthermore, participation rates for men 60–64 have declined sharply since the early 1970s, and for 55–59 year olds they began to fall in the mid-1980s (Guillemard, 1989). The quantitative effect of this development has been substantial; for instance, if the participation rate in Britain for men over 65 had remained constant throughout the century, Britain's male labour force today would be greater by 1.9 million, or by 14 per cent.

The reasons for this restructuring of the employment life-course are complex and will not be discussed here (for a review see Laczko and Phillipson, 1991; Johnson and Falkingham, 1992, chapter 4); instead we will confine our attention to the interaction between trends in retirement behaviour and population age structure. The International Labour Office has developed projections of the economically active population on the basis of current and anticipated age- and sex-specific participation rates (ILO, 1986). These projections show that ever-earlier retirement combined with ageing population structures has already inaugurated a decline in the size of the economically active population in Germany, Italy, Austria and Switzerland, with the UK, Belgium, the Netherlands and the Scandinavian countries to follow in the next decade. These developments pose a dual problem – how to pay for transfers to the growing proportion of the population not in the labour force, and how to overcome potential labour shortages.

A shortage of labour can be met by resort to external sources of supply through a positive immigration policy (see section 5 below), but an alternative approach is to raise the domestic participation rate. There is some scope for further increasing the labour force participation rate of women, although in countries such as Britain and Denmark women already have virtually the same participation rate as men, except for the five years or so when they have pre-school children to care for. Much more could be done, however, to reverse the decline in the average age of retirement; this would simultaneously boost labour supply and reduce the financing burden of retirement pensions. Fundamental changes in retirement behaviour and retirement expectations would require substantial public policy intervention because governments currently play a major role in determining the course of labour force withdrawal. So far there have been enthusiastic references to flexible retirement and productive ageing, but little by way of action (DHSS, 1985; Butler *et al.*, 1990).

Public policy affects retirement behaviour, and so the overall size and age structure of the labour force, in two distinct ways. First, and most obvious, is the qualification age for a public pension. This is a major inducement to give up work, especially if pension deferral is not compensated for by actuarially fair adjustment. Second comes the array of labour market management policies that have evolved, particularly in the 1980s, in order to curtail the problem of recorded unemployment. Many programmes have been implemented to encourage or facilitate the early exit of older workers, both formally through publicly-funded early-retirement provisions, and informally through increased provision of disability benefits to unemployed workers close to the normal age of retirement (Casey and Bruche, 1983). A reversal of current retirement trends would require an explicit re-thinking of these public policies towards older workers. Yet public pension rules are not the only structural determinants of retirement behaviour; equally important are earnings profiles and private pension scheme regulations.

In Britain and the United States in particular, where the majority of earnings-related pension saving is carried out via tax-privileged occupational pension schemes run by employers, flexible retirement is typically precluded by the accrual rules of the schemes. The majority of occupational pensions are paid on a defined benefit basis, with the pension related to some proportion of salary earned in the last year (or the last few years) of employment. By directly relating pensions to pay levels at the end of a career rather than to lifetime contributions the rules give a very strong incentive to workers to retire when their earnings are at their maximum (Kotlikoff and Wise, 1987, 1989). These final salary pensions dove-tail very nicely with positive age-earnings profiles, but they are a major barrier to greater labour market flexibility which might include a shift to less demanding and lower paid employment at older ages. The provision of more employment opportunities for workers beyond their late 50s or early 60s would be an effective way of increasing the labour supply and making greater use of the stock of skills in the population, but it is not compatible with today's typical career and earnings profiles. On the other hand, a move to a more hump-shaped age-earnings profile is not compatible with current final-salary pension systems. Before new and more flexible forms of career and earnings progression can be introduced, rigid final salary pension contracts will need to be reformed.

5   Migration and mobility

In the 1950s and 60s, and to a lesser extent in the 1970s, a number of West European countries responded to general labour shortages by allowing or promoting substantial immigration – most notably from Turkey to West Germany, from North Africa to France and from the Caribbean and the Indian sub-continent to the United Kingdom. Future general or skill-specific labour shortages that may be induced by population ageing could again be met by migration from outside Europe, but the collapse of the Soviet satellite states in Eastern Europe and the establishment of a unified labour market among the twelve members of the European Community together create new opportunities for increased labour mobility and migration within Europe. It would be possible, for instance, for young workers from high-fertility Ireland to fill job vacancies in low-fertility Denmark, particularly if public policy initiatives were taken to facilitate such movement.

The substantial ageing of the European labour force will significantly alter the wage and employment structure. It will then also likely affect labour mobility, and with open borders, also induce immigration. In an equilibrium framework, labour markets tend to equalize real wages and labour productivity. If there are age-dependent productivities, there will be an adjustment of wages as soon as the age-composition of the labour force is altered. Although it has been found that the effect of age is marginal in comparison to other factors and that productivity variations within age groups are more significant than variations across age groups, there seems to be evidence that productivity increases over the work-life as, for instance, would be predicted by human capital theory. (See OECD, 1988a, and the literature cited there.) However, the necessary adjustment relies on the flexibility of the labour force and may cause unemployment, at least in the short run.

It was argued in the literature that an increase in the age of the active population will reduce labour mobility and increase absenteeism and might also adversely affect productivity through the poorer health conditions of older workers. (More detailed surveys of the arguments are given in OECD, 1988a, and United Nations, 1988. See also for the effects on labour mobility Ashenfelter, 1982; Clark and Spengler, 1980.) Efficiency losses in the allocation of labour have to be expected if the aged labour force is less willing to change jobs, industries or regions. It would then be necessary to create specific labour market policies to maintain the average level of labour flexibility and to fight a potential increase in unemployment. There is also the fear that the duration of unemployment will increase, as older workers face a longer average duration of unemployment. It is also unclear to what extent older workers can replace younger workers, which will depend on the degree of substitutability and complementarity between the age groups. In any case it is likely that the degree of mismatch between labour demand and supply will increase, either because of immobility, inappropriate skills or the unwillingness of the old to accept wage cuts and take over the jobs of the young.

A larger amount of immigration might be a reasonable policy to account for the decline in the labour force and its ageing. Because of a positive selection process, migrants tend to be more mobile than natives. However, one has to account for the fact that these people also are ageing over time and that they may also adjust their flexibility to the level of the host country. A larger stock of foreign labour may also cause an increase of native unemployment as it allows natives to become less flexible. There are two aspects of labour mobility that are of interest: the first issue is flexibility, the ability (and the willingness) to change jobs when there are economic gains from doing so. This is a virtue in a market system. The second problem is unemployment, which is related to the inflexibility of labour and is a bad. Both the positive and the negative aspects of immigration have to be considered.

6   Overview of the book

The next three chapters of the book provide an overview of recent and projected demographic and labour market developments in Western and Eastern Europe and in the US and Japan. They also investigate the causes of these changes and their interpretation in the context of behavioural theories. It is discussed that the fertility decline and the increase in life expectancy which are driving the ageing process are themselves endogenous to the economic system. In Western Europe, high unemployment rates and low female participation rates in some countries indicate labour market reserves. In Eastern Europe, the end of active population policies will enhance the ageing process.

The first chapter by Paul Johnson, *Ageing and European Economic Demography*, summarizes the demographic trends in Europe. Total fertility has fallen dramatically since the 'baby boom' of the 1950s to well below replacement levels; child and adult mortality rates have also declined, while average life expectancies have risen by up to ten years. The richer countries of Northern and Western Europe tended to lead their Southern and Eastern neighbours in these changes, but this distinction is much less clear-cut than between Europe as a whole and its near neighbours. Turkey and Morocco have fertility rates well above replacement levels, with less than 4% of their populations over 65. Johnson argues that traditional fertility models based on the need for old-age security are not relevant to post-war Europe, while economic explanations based on increased female participation cannot fully account for such non-marginal changes. Existing explanations of mortality trends are also inadequate: economic growth appears to raise life expectancy, but the relationship is weak and may operate through improvements in long-term environmental and nutritional conditions or better access to health care in old age. While these trends have major implications for social security systems and hence public finance, the existing general equilibrium attempts to model their interactions with labour markets depend critically on assumptions that have little empirical support.

The second chapter by Klaus Jacobs and Martin Rein, *Ageing and Employment Trends: A Comparative Analysis for OECD Countries*, examines employment trends for men aged 55–64 in Western Europe, the US and Japan. The recently observed decline in employment in this age group can be seen as one of the most dramatic economic transformations in the labour markets, a phenomenon called 'early retirement'. With the ageing labour force, this issue will become even more important in the future. During 1970–90, inter-country differences tended to increase; France, Germany and the Netherlands were characterized by the lowest participation rates (23–34%), Sweden, US and UK formed an intermediate pattern (54–63%), and Japan exhibited the largest participation rates (73%). In the 'high early exit countries', older men mostly move from full-time work to full-time retirement often supported by public and/or private programs. In Sweden, the US and Japan, at least a substantial minority of older men combine work and retirement. Japan has low and strict mandatory retirement ages, but retirees are often rehired by the same or an affiliated firm on less secure employment contracts. In Sweden, a system of partial pension arrangements allows retiring wage and salary recipients to recoup much of their 'lost' income by continuing to work part-time. In the US, early retirees are left to their own initiative, but poor public pension provision obliges many to work to cushion the effects of abrupt exit on earnings.

The next chapter, by Stanislawa Golinowska, is *Ageing and the Labour Market in Poland and Eastern Europe*. Eastern Europe's socialist governments used a wide range of family policy instruments to promote fertility, which in Poland were supplemented by 'pro-natalist' pressure from the church. The trend towards lower fertility first emerged in the 1970s. Therefore, the process of ageing has not yet affected Central and Eastern Europe, with the sole exception of Hungary. In 1990–2010, Central and Eastern Europe will experience the highest rate of growth of the productive-age population, which will grow by 9.1%, and in the territories of the former Soviet Union by 16.5%. The Polish economy faces the problem of absorbing some 1.7 million additional productive-age people and of reducing employment in the state sector by 2 to 4 million people. The productive-age populations in these countries will start to age only by the turn of the century. In Western Europe, this process will already be well-established by the mid-1990s, indicating that the labour market consequences of population ageing are substantially different in East and West. The interaction of demographic change and economic transformation in Central and Eastern Europe will induce real labour market and public policy problems. In the 1990s the coincidence of a rising number of young and mobile workers and increased unemployment raises pressure for publicly-funded job creation at a time when governments are trying to scale down intervention and induces also emigration pressure. In the next century, the challenge will come from the rapidly ageing labour force.

The effects of ageing on productivity, earnings and human capital formation are discussed in the next four chapters. The first, contributed by Christopher Flinn, is *The Implications of Cohort Size for Human Capital Investment*. He examines the effects of cohort size changes on the on-the-job human capital investment of young labour market participants in the US over the past 50 years and the wealth levels achieved by the various cohorts. The analysis is based on a perfect foresight partial equilibrium model in which rental rates on human capital and the investment decisions undertaken by all cohorts arc uniquely determined. Then it is possible to determine the size of the direct effects of changes in the cohort size sequence on the distribution of welfare across cohorts and the size of those effects which result from changes in equilibrium human capital investment levels. It is found that cohort wealth is quite insensitive to levels of human capital investment, which is itself somewhat responsive to changes in the cohort size sequence. A companion model based on static expectations provides similar inferences concerning wealth and human capital investment.

Didier Blanchet's chapter *Does an Ageing Labour Force Call for Large Adjustments in Training or Wage Policies?* provides an answer to this question concentrating on two particular points, the link between productivity and training, and the relationship between productivity and wages. It is often observed that on-the-job training increases productivity in the later stages of a worker's career, so ageing due to lower population growth makes schooling and on-the-job training more attractive. Schooling is costly and relatively unrewarding when younger cohorts dominate, but its collective cost diminishes in an ageing society and allows a longer initial period of human capital accumulation. Ageing can therefore be a positive factor rather than a problem for productivity, and the remaining issue is how to determine the amount of human capital investment that maintains a relatively constant total life-cycle production. As the population ages, career profiles also change; if the labour hierarchy is linked to age and seniority, workers will reach the higher levels later in life than in a growing society. Blanchet simulates a reduction in the population's growth rate from + 1% to − 1% and first finds that changes in the population structure are not likely to affect average productivity significantly. Second, if wages exceed productivity at later stages of the career, an ageing labour force will impose several financial constraints on firms. This may create incentives for an increase in early retirement of workers, which would clearly contradict the current needs of the pension system.

The chapter by N. Anders Klevmarken, *On Ageing and Earnings*, provides evidence using Swedish micro panel data. It first summarizes some important findings from human capital theory on age-earnings profiles but emphasizes that alternative interpretations of empirical findings suggested in the literature are not invalid. The second step is to allow age-earnings profiles to shift and change in shape as a result of general productivity increases and changes in the demand and supply of labour. There follows an empirical investigation of the effects of cohort size on Swedish earnings together with the standard variables education, experience, age and seniority. No support is found for the hypothesis that cohort size influences the dynamics of Swedish earnings profiles, which is also consistent with the Dutch results reported below. Klevmarken argues that changes in supply other than cohort size changes, for instance increased immigration, and major demand changes could make the age-earnings profiles shift and change in shape in a different way; demand changes tend to dominate any effects of cohort size. Finally, Klevmarken finds that because the group of earnings profiles radiates with increasing age, there is mobility away from the average earnings profile. Hence, there is in general no reason why the degree of earnings mobility should increase with age.

Age, Wage and Education in the Netherlands is the contribution written by Joop Hartog, Hessel Oosterbeek and Coen Teulings. It first provides a brief history of Dutch labour market developments and then presents a decomposition of the labour force by education and age. During the last three decades, the average age and educational level of the Dutch labour force have increased substantially and both these trends have been stronger for females than for males. The observed increase in the demand for education was not associated with any substantial changes in the expected structure of earnings and cannot therefore be explained by human capital theory alone; it may be attributed to increasing parental incomes or government subsidies. The estimated wage equations display a declining return on human capital from about 13% in 1962 to 7% in 1985 and stability thereafter, whereas there is a constant return on experience. It is not clear why the rate of return stabilized after 1985, because there was no indication of a slowdown in the growth of human capital. The age structure of the labour force has also changed continuously, but the impact on earnings is found to be quite modest. Only the youngest group of the labour force experienced reduced starting salaries in the eighties. These findings are consistent with an apparent irrelevance of cohort size for earnings.

The final two chapters investigate how the ageing process is affecting unemployment and job mobility, and how this is related to immigration. The chapter by Christoph M. Schmidt, *Ageing and Unemployment*, contains a time-series analysis to study the effects of changes in the age composition of the German population on the incidence of unemployment in different sex-age groups. The German population has aged substantially in recent decades, both as a result of declining fertility and of a cessation in guestworker recruitment. The German wage-setting process appears to be characterized by the presence of a strong union movement that hampers flexible wage adjustments. Thus, age-structure variations can be expected to lead to fluctuations in age-specific unemployment rates. In general, this intuition is confirmed in Schmidt's estimations. However, a strong positive relationship between the size of a cohort and its relative unemployment experience can only be estabished formally for a few sex-age groups.

The final chapter by Rainer Winkelmann and Klaus F. Zimmermann, *Ageing, Migration and Labour Mobility*, notes that there are currently some 20% more younger than older workers in the German (and the European) labour force, but these proportions are expected to reverse in the next 30 years. The share of foreigners in the German labour market is around 8%, comparable to that of foreign-born workers in the US, so that the German experience may serve as a useful case-study for Europe. Central to the investigation is labour mobility – defined as frequency of job changes and unemployment spells – for Germans and foreigners separately using a vast German micro data set. First, a theoretical model is outlined that covers the demand for quantity and quality of labour and its implications for relative wages, unemployment and direct job changes. The empirical evidence shows that foreign labour is more flexible to change jobs in the average, but these workers are also more frequently unemployed, especially when older. Robust Poisson estimates indicate that there is a U-shaped relationship between age and frequency of unemployment for both German and foreign workers, but that foreigners have lower unemployment risks in early stages of their work career and higher risks in later stages of their work career than natives. Direct job changes of natives decline with age for natives and with duration of stay in Germany for foreigners. The negative effect of the foreign labour share in Germany is a higher unemployment rate, the positive effect is greater labour mobility. Simulations with the predicted age structures for Germany and the EC from 1995–2020 show that the age structure induces first a decrease and then an increase of both measures of labour mobility, but the EC structure leads to a flatter development. Again, an increase in the stock of foreign labour will probably cause an increase in the frequency of unemployment which is not of negligible size.

7   Conclusions

This paper has shown that the ageing of the European labour force, which will continue rapidly over the next twenty or thirty years, could have a considerable effect on pay, on productivity, on mobility and so on the international competitiveness of the European economies. Other things being equal, ageing will increase labour costs, reduce labour supply and reduce the endowment of modern skills in the workforce. A variety of potential public policy responses to these circumstances have been discussed – the development of recurrent training throughout life, flexible retirement, less rigid pension systems, increased labour mobility and migration. On most of these issues, however, both the scale of any future problems and the effectiveness of any policy initiatives remain uncertain. It is only through careful analysis of the complex interactions between economic and demographic systems that we can develop a clear understanding of the potential benefits or pitfalls of age-specific public policy intervention in European labour markets.

REFERENCES

Ashenfelter, O. (1982) 'The economic impact of an older population: A brief survey', in A.J.J. Gilmore, A. Svanborg and M. Marois (eds.), *Ageing: A challenge to science and society*, Oxford: Oxford University Press, pp. 333–40.

Bellmann, L. (1989) 'Seniority-based wage system and postponed retirement', in W. Schmähl (ed.), *Redefining the process of Retirement*, Berlin: Springer-Verlag, pp. 151–62.

Bloom, D.E., R.B. Freeman and S.D. Korenman (1987) 'The labour market consequences of generational crowding', *European Journal of Population* **3**, 131–76.

Butler, R. L., M. Oberlink and M. Schechter (eds.) (1990) *The Promise of Productive Ageing*, New York: Springer.

Casey, B. and G. Bruche (1983) *Work or Retirement? Labour Market and Social Policy for Older Workers in France, Great Britain, the Netherlands, Sweden and the USA*, Aldershot: Gower.

Clark, R.L and J.J. Spengler (1980) *The economics of individual and population ageing*, Cambridge: Cambridge University Press.

Doeringer, P.B. and M.J. Piore (1971) *Internal Labour Markets and Manpower Analysis*, Lexington, MA: D.C. Heath.

DHSS (1985) *Reform of Social Security*, Cmnd 9518, London: HMSO.

Easterlin, R.A. (1980) *Birth and Fortune*, New York: Basic Books.

Easterlin, R.A., C. Macdonald and D.J. Macunovich (1990), 'How have American baby-boomers fared? Earnings and economic well-being of young adults, 1964–1987', *Journal of Population Economics* **3**, 277–90.

Ermisch, J.F. (1988) 'Fortunes of birth: the impact of generation size on the relative earnings of young men', *Scottish Journal of Political Economy* **35**, 266–82.

Guillemard, A.-M. (1989) 'The trend towards early labour force withdrawal and the reorganisation of the life course: a cross-national analysis', in P. Johnson, C. Conrad and D. Thomson (eds.), *Workers versus Pensioners*, Manchester: Manchester University Press, pp. 164–80.

Höhn, C. (1987) 'Population policies in advanced societies: pronatalist and migration strategies', *European Journal of Population* 3, 459–81.

House of Commons (1988) 'Select Committee on Employment; Enquiry into the Employment Patterns of the Over 50s', HC41–iii.

International Labour Organisation (1986) *Economically Active Population*, Geneva: ILO.

Johnson, P. and J. Falkingham (1992) *Ageing and Economic Welfare*, London: Sage.

Kohli, M., M. Rein, A-M. Guillemard and H. van Gunsteren (eds.) (1991) *Time for Retirement: Comparative Studies of Early Exit from the Labour Force*, Cambridge: Cambridge University Press.

Kotlikoff, L.J. and D. Wise (1987) 'The incentive effects of private pension plans', in Z. Bodie, J. Shoven and D. Wise (eds.), *Issues in Pension Economics*, Chicago: Chicago University Press, pp. 283–336.

(1989) 'Employee retirement and a firm's pension plan', in D. Wise (ed.), *Economics of Aging*, Chicago: Chicago University Press.

Laczko, F. and C. Phillipson (1991) *Changing Work and Retirement*, Milton Keynes: Open University Press.

Libassi, P.F. (1988) 'Integrating the elder in the labor force: consequences and experience for insurance', *Geneva Papers on Risk and Insurance* 13, 350–60.

McEvoy, G.M. and W.F. Cascio (1989) 'Cumulative evidence of the relationship between employee age and job performance', *Journal of Applied Psychology* 74, 11–17.

New Earnings Survey (1987) London: Department of Employment.

OECD (1988a) *Ageing Populations: The Social Policy Implications*, Paris: OECD.

(1988b) *Reforming Public Pensions*, Paris: OECD.

Ono, A. (1989–90) 'Labour Cost in an Ageing Economy', *Japanese Economic Studies* 18, 30–57.

Rabbit, P. (1992) 'Some issues in cognitive gerontology and their implication for social policy', in W.J. van den Heuvel, R. Illsley, A. Jamieson and C.P. Knipscheer (eds.), *Opportunities and Challenges in an Ageing Society*, Amsterdam: North Holland, pp. 233–74.

Riboud, M. (1987) 'Labour market responses to changes in cohort size: the case of France', *European Journal of Population* 3, 359–82.

Schmähl, W. (1989) 'Labour force participation and social pension systems', in P. Johnson, C. Conrad and D. Thomson (eds.), *Workers versus Pensioners*, Manchester: Manchester University Press, pp. 137–61.

Staehle, W.H. (1989) 'Employment of Older Persons from a Management Point of View', in W. Schmähl (ed.), *Redefining the Process of Retirement*, Berlin: Springer-Verlag, pp. 163–73.

Teitelbaum, M.S. and J.M. Winter (1985) *The Fear of Population Decline*, Orlando: Academic Press.

United Nations (1988) 'Economic and social implications of population ageing', in *Proceedings of the international symposium on population structure and development, Tokyo, 1987*, New York: United Nations.

van Imhoff, E. (1988) 'Age structure, education and the transmission of technical change', *Journal of Population Economics* 1, 167–81.

Vernière, L. (1990) 'Retraites: l'urgence d'une reforme', *Economie et Statistique* 233, 29–38.

Warr, P. (1992) 'Age and Employment', in M. Dunnette, L. Hough and

H. Triandis (eds.), *Handbook of Industrial and Organizational Psychology*, volume 4. Palo Alto: Consulting Psychologists Press (forthcoming).

Wright, R.E. (1989) 'The Easterlin Hypothesis and European Fertility Rates', *Population Development Review* **15**, 107–22.

——— (1991) 'Cohort Size and Earnings in Great Britain', *Journal of Population Economics* **4**, 295–305.

Zimmermann, K.F. (1989) 'Optimum Population: An Introduction', in K.F. Zimmermann (ed.), *Economic Theory of Optimal Population*, Berlin: Springer-Verlag, pp. 1–16.

——— (1991) 'Ageing in the Labor Market: Age Structure, Cohort Size and Unemployment', *Journal of Population Economics* **4**, 177–200.

2 Ageing and European economic demography

PAUL JOHNSON

This paper provides an overview of recent and projected demographic developments in Europe in order to establish a context for the more detailed discussion, presented in other papers, of the interaction between the population age structure and the labour market. The first part of this paper reviews data on European fertility and mortality and discusses their joint impact on the evolving age structure of the population. The second section considers whether or to what extent the fertility and mortality patterns are endogenous to the economic system and can be explained by economic factors. The third section then reverses the line of explanation and examines how the performance of the European economies may in the future be conditioned by population pressures.

1   The ageing of Europe

The population of Europe has been ageing throughout the twentieth century, and this process will continue well beyond the year 2000. Yet the continuity is associated with an important change; whereas ageing in this century has been associated with almost uninterrupted population growth, in the next century ageing will coincide with stagnation and then decline in the total European population. Table 2.1 presents the basic data, as compiled by the United Nations. There is, necessarily, some uncertainty about the future population projections since they are contingent on the accuracy of assumptions about fertility and mortality trends. In this table, medium variant projections have been selected. These assume that the total fertility rate (average number of births per woman of child-bearing age) will rise to around 1.85 by 2025, and that life expectancy at birth will continue to rise, but at a decreasing rate as expectation of life at birth in each country approaches 85 years.[1]

Table 2.1 shows that the proportion of the European population aged over 65 has increased from 8.7 per cent to 13.4 per cent in the forty years

Table 2.1. *The population of Europe, 1950–2025*

	1950	1960	1970	1980	1990	2000	2010	2020	2025
Total (m)	392	425	459	484	498	510	515	516	515
% 0–14	25.4	25.8	24.9	22.3	19.5	18.5	17.6	16.7	16.5
% 65+	8.7	9.7	11.4	13.1	13.4	14.9	16.0	18.6	20.1
Dependency ratios (%)									
Total	51.7	55.0	57.2	54.9	49.2	50.2	50.6	54.5	57.7
Young	38.5	40.0	39.2	34.6	29.2	27.8	26.5	25.8	26.0
Old	13.2	15.0	17.9	20.3	20.0	22.4	24.2	28.7	31.7
Total fertility rate/woman	2.59	2.63	2.19	1.81	1.72	1.74	1.81	1.84	1.85
Infant mortality/1000 births	62	37	24	15	11	8	7	6	6
Expectation of life at birth (years)									
Males	63.6	67.2	68.3	70.1	72.0	72.9	74.5	75.7	76.3
Females	68.0	72.4	74.5	76.8	78.5	79.3	80.5	81.7	82.2
Total	65.8	69.9	71.5	73.5	75.3	76.1	77.5	78.7	79.2

Source: United Nations (1991).

since 1950, and over the next 35 years this elderly population will continue to expand its relative share to account for a fifth of the European population by 2025. The median age in Europe, which was 30.5 years in 1950 and 35 in 1990, will increase to 42.9 by 2025. At the same time the proportion of children in Europe has fallen and is expected to decline further. In consequence, the crude demographic dependency ratio (the number of people under 14 and over 65 per 100 people aged 15–64) follows a cyclical path, only regaining its high 1970 level around 2025. This total dependency ratio is frequently taken to indicate the 'burden' of social and economic support that is borne by people of working age (though as will be discussed in section 3, this is an overly simplistic interpretation). Within the overall dependency ratio, the share of children has fallen while that of older people has grown – the support ratio of older people to workers is projected to reach twice its 1960 level by 2025.

How has this ageing of the European population come about? The age structure of a population in any period is the result of a complex inter-action between fertility, mortality and migration. Age structure at time t is affected by age structure in the previous period $t - 1$ as peaks and troughs in the age distribution move forward in time, so changes in any or all of the vital rates in the past will influence present and future age distri-butions. Conventional demographic wisdom has it that (in the absence of significant migration) it is the fertility rate which dominates changes in the age structure of a population (United Nations, 1956). Fertility determines the number of persons feeding into the population pyramid at its base. As each cohort moves up through the pyramid with time, the size of the cohorts influences the overall age structure. Unless mortality levels are very unstable they will affect each cohort in turn in a similar fashion, shaving off the sides of the pyramid but leaving the underlying age structure relatively unchanged. The most important factor determining the proportion of elderly people in the population in the past has not been the capacity to survive to pension age but rather changes in the size of each generation available to survive.

Table 2.1 shows that the total fertility rate (TFR) in Europe has declined sharply from the baby-boom levels of 1950, to fall below the population replacement level of around 2.1 in the 1970s. European ageing is in part, therefore, a consequence of twenty years of 'baby bust' which has starved the population pyramid of inputs at the bottom, while the large cohorts of the early twentieth century – the tail-enders of the demographic transition – have moved into old age. But Table 2.1 also shows that fertility has not been the only force driving the ageing process; mortality has also had a role to play. Average life expectancy at birth for both men and women in

Europe has risen by about ten years since 1950, and some further improvement is expected into the 21st century. Some of this gain has come from a dramatic decline in the average level of infant mortality since 1950, but reductions in adult mortality have also been important.

The recent rise in the number of very old people (those over 85) has been larger than expected because of unanticipated falls in mortality among the elderly (Preston, 1984). In the United States, for instance, it has been estimated that about two-thirds of the increase in the mean age of the population between 1980 and 1985 can be attributed to mortality decline alone (Preston *et al.*, 1988). In the world's most rapidly ageing country, Japan, recent improvements in life expectancy at older ages have been dramatic – for 65-year old men a rise in life expectancy from 13.72 years in 1975 to 16.22 years in 1989, for women from 16.56 to 19.95 years (Japan, Ministry of Health and Welfare, 1992: 339). It is now recognized that these changes in mortality at older ages may influence both the size and the age structure of the elderly population. Bourgeois-Pichat (1979) has suggested that, if fertility is at or below replacement level, mortality changes can cause population ageing from the apex rather than the base of the population pyramid.

A recent attempt to assess the relative role of fertility and mortality changes in the ageing of the Italian and French populations has produced some striking results. Caselli and Vallin (1990) used past and projected mortality probabilities and birth rates by cohort and calendar year to decompose the projected growth rate of the population up to 2040 into fertility and mortality effects. For France they worked with the assumption that fertility would remain at 1.8, and that life expectancy at birth would increase slowly from 71.5 to 74.0 years for men and from 79.7 to 82.4 years for women by 2020, and then remain constant. For Italy they assumed that fertility would remain at the low rate of 1.4 and that life expectancy by 2038 would increase modestly from 72.0 to 76.3 years for men and from 78.6 to 83.7 years for women. Their results are presented in Table 2.2. While below-replacement fertility contributes significantly to population ageing, especially in Italy, the role played by mortality trends is even greater, despite the relatively modest assumptions about future increases in life expectancy. Although falls in infant and child mortality earlier in the century have made a significant contribution to this mortality effect, it is at adult ages that the current cohorts of older people have benefited from the major health improvements of the post-Second World War period. We will return to this issue of mortality improvements in the next section; for the moment we should bear in mind that the stagnant or declining population growth rates of many European countries means that they are ageing rapidly from the apex as well as the base of the

Table 2.2. *Decomposition of ageing in France and Italy into fertility and mortality effects*

	France		Italy	
	Males	Females	Males	Females
Total population				
in 1986 (000)	26,948	28,330	27,792	29,410
in 2040 (000)	26,725	28,930	22,120	23,972
Proportion 60–99 years				
in 1986 (%)	15.34	21.14	16.15	21.14
in 2040 (%)	26.10	33.41	35.84	43.23
Difference	10.76	12.27	19.69	22.09
Contributions of:				
fertility (% points)	3.75	4.23	9.69	10.80
mortality (% points)	7.01	8.04	10.00	11.29

Source: Caselli and Vallin (1990), p. 22.

population pyramid, and even rapid and abrupt increases in fertility rates will do nothing to alter this fact.

There is, of course, considerable variation between European countries in vital rates and population age structures. Table 2.3 shows, for a broad range of European countries, the actual or projected timing of the most recent fall in the total fertility rate below 2.1, and of the rise in female life expectancy at birth beyond age 75. The classificatory thresholds selected in Table 2.3 are arbitrary, but several points emerge from the table. First, the fertility decline came in two distinct waves in the early 1970s and early 1980s, affecting more economically advanced Northern and Western countries before those in the East and South. The only significant outlier is Ireland, which today maintains an above-replacement fertility rate which is projected to continue into the next century.

Second, improvements in female life expectancy are temporally more dispersed, though again tending to occur first in northern European countries and last in Eastern Europe. There is, however, no direct link between the timing of fertility and mortality changes even in countries in the same region of Europe (compare, for instance, Iceland and Finland, or Hungary and Poland). Moreover, while life expectancy at birth has followed a secular downwards trend throughout Europe, fertility rates have shown considerable shorter-run variability. In Poland and East Germany, for example, the total fertility rate rose slightly in the early 1980s, though in Hungary and Czechoslovakia it declined. This may

Table 2.3. *The timing of fertility and life-expectancy transitions in Europe*

Date of reduction of total fertility rate below 2.1

1955–60	1960–65	1965–70	1970–75	1975–80	1980–85	1985–90	1990–95	1995–2000
		Finland	Austria	France	Bulgaria	Iceland	Romania	Poland
			Belgium	Italy	Czechoslovakia			
			Denmark	Norway	Greece			
			Germany (E)		Hungary			
			Germany (W)		Portugal			
			Luxemburg		Spain			
			Malta		Yugoslavia			
			Netherlands					
			Sweden					
			Switzerland					
			UK					

Date of attainment of life expectancy at birth for females of 75 years

1955–60	1960–65	1965–70	1970–75	1975–80	1980–85	1985–90	1990–95	1995–2000
Iceland	Netherlands	Denmark	Finland	Austria	Germany (E)	Bulgaria	Albania	Romania
Norway	Sweden	France	Italy	Belgium	Ireland	Czechoslovakia	Hungary	
		Switzerland	Spain	Germany (W)	Portugal	Yugoslavia	Malta	
			UK	Greece				
				Luxemburg				
				Poland				

reflect behavioural and policy differences, but more likely it is a function of changes in the cohort composition of the female population of child-bearing age.[2]

A third feature emerging from Table 2.3 is that the developmental course of demographic events within European countries is sufficiently similar and closely-timed to cause a very similar process of population ageing in all countries over the next three decades, regardless of the current age structure of their populations. This European demographic regime is very different from that in the nearest non-European countries, Morocco and Turkey, which currently have TFRs of 4.2 and 3.28 respectively, and female life expectancy at birth of 65.0 and 68.1 years. Their populations are still growing at annual rates of over 2 per cent, with the consequence that people over 65 account for around only 4 per cent of the total.

The low fertility-low mortality demographic regime is equally apparent in non-European industrialized countries, including some with distinctively different cultural and religious norms (Preston, 1987), and it is conceivable that economic development around the European periphery could induce a rapid fall in population growth rates in these neighbouring countries. However, as the next section of this paper will show, the causal connections between the level of economic development and rate of population growth are unclear. It is possible, for instance, that Turkish membership of the EC and a rapid rise in average income might reduce the fertility rate in Turkey, but there can be no certainty about this. Meanwhile in the shorter run it is clear that the rapidly growing population of the European periphery could compensate for any labour shortfall in the ageing economies of Europe – the migration networks and traditions already exist. Whether such migration will be desired or allowed depends both on whether the human capital endowments of potential migrants fit with future European labour market requirements, and on the political inclinations of European governments.

2   Fertility and mortality patterns

The course of fertility decline in Europe is well documented, but comprehensive explanations of the data remain elusive. The extent to which the fall in fertility has an economic explanation, and so is endogenous to the process of economic development, is a particular source of contention. While economists have developed rationalistic micro-economic models of fertility decisions, other social scientists have stressed the importance of social and cultural factors in determining individual attitudes towards family formation. Explanations of the mortality patterns are even more contentious, and because the major improvements in life expectancy at older ages are of recent origin, little work so far has been undertaken to determine the relative role of economic, social, medical and environmental factors in the overall improvement.

Economic interpretations of the fertilty decline which derive from the methodological individualism of neo-classical economics are not easily reconciled with macro-sociological explanations which prioritize the role of ideational change. The micro-economic theory of the family (pioneered by Becker, 1960; 1981) assumes that decisions about family formation and the number and timing of births are taken by a maximizing couple who will trade-off the utility gained from children against the costs in terms of lost time and income and additional expenditure. Most of the elaboration and econometric assessment of this theory has focused on the costs rather than the benefits of child-rearing, but the hypothesized utility gains deserve as much attention.

Children may be desired for their purely economic returns in generating income or providing services, or for the less concrete psychic satisfaction they bring their parents. One of the main income and service functions of children may be to support their parents in old age. There is a large literature on the security motive for fertility in historical European and contemporary less-developed societies (Smith, 1981; Nugent, 1985), but empirical evidence of the existence or strength of this motive is inconclusive, and in the post-war European economies it would appear to be of little relevance. Although the average age of consumption is higher than the average age of production in the countries of Northern and Western Europe, indicating a net transfer of resources from younger to older generations, the bulk of this intergenerational transfer is channelled through the public sector (Ermisch, 1989: 23). This is not a new phenomenon; in Britain, for example, the share of pensioner income received from children has been minimal since at least the 1930s (Falkingham and Gordon, 1990). A decline in the economic returns to child-rearing could in theory account for a decline in fertility, but there is little evidence to suggest that the economic returns to parents of children were significant in Europe at any time in the post-war period, or that they have declined sharply since the 1970s.

The psychic satisfaction parents derive from their children cannot be defined or measured in an unambiguous manner; the impossibility of falsifying propositions about the psychic returns to child-rearing renders the concept practically useless in positivistic research. But to leave one side of the cost-benefit equation completely blank is procedurally unsatisfactory, so attempts have been made to fill it, at least for theoretical purposes. Many assumptions can be made about the marginal psychic returns obtained from an extra child, about whether there is a child quantity-quality trade-off, and about whether returns to children have changed over time. Any or all of these assumptions, however, sit uneasily with the atomistic principles of the microeconomic theory of the family, in which *individuals* maximize their utility. However, if the utility functions of parents and children are considered to be interdependent, then familial altruism can be reconciled with an individualistic model. If this type of altruism is placed within a multi-generational (rather than life-cycle or short-term) planning model, then the utility of parents will depend on the utility of all future generations – a 'dynastic' utility function, in the terminology of Becker and Barro (1987). Such a model can be used to explain the phenomenon of intergenerational transfers (bequests, education, resource preservation or depletion), as well as incorporating the effect of social security and economic growth on fertility decisions.

Becker-Barro dynastic families are heuristic devices rather than reduced-form behavioural models, and they are undoubtedly helpful in focusing attention on the issue of the returns to child-rearing. How far they are consistent with the underlying methodological individualism depends upon the reasonability of the restriction that utility-interdependence relates only to immediately descendant kin. As Paul David (1987) has pointed out, real-world families have the annoying habit of inter-marrying; if lineages recognize their eventual mutuality of interests, the atomistic premise of the theory collapses into a messy and (probably) indeterminate social relativism. Even if this is not the case, and despite the elegance of the theory, we still know next to nothing about how parents value children.

Much more is known, however, on the cost side of the equation. Children are expensive to feed, clothe, care for, entertain and educate, and the opportunity cost of children has increased in the post-war period because of changes in parental and social expectations about the 'quality' of childhood and because of developments in the labour market. An increase in women's employment opportunities and a rise in the net female wage relative to the net male wage both increase the expected cost of child-rearing if birth necessitates the temporary withdrawal from the labour force of the mother, and so will tend to reduce fertility. This negative income effect, however, may be balanced by a wealth effect which increases the reservation wage, reduces the likelihood of employment, and so tends to increase fertility. The overall impact is theoretically indeterminate (for a brief review, see Ermisch, 1990) and will depend upon the specific wage and employment conditions in each country, but the data for the UK show that higher female earnings made a significant contribution to the decline in fertility in the 1970s (Ermisch, 1988a).

The mechanics of fertility decline have not been as simple as this finding might suggest – as if couples regularly assessed the relative costs and benefits of a return to (or continuation of) work as against another birth. There has been a very pronounced trend since the mid-1970s throughout the developed economies towards later marriage and child-bearing, higher divorce rates, and higher rates of cohabitation (Westoff, 1987). These trends are closely associated with an improvement in the economic status and independence of women through better labour market prospects. There is, however, no direct and automatic relationship over time or place between levels or rates of change of female labour force participation and the fertility rate. In West Germany in the 1970s, for instance, the fertility rate fell very rapidly despite a level of female employment low by European standards. And fertility rates can decline rapidly quite independently of female labour market opportunities – as was the case in Britain between the wars (Thane, 1990).

This variety of possible labour market and fertility regimes makes it clear that other factors are also important determinants of fertility. Technological developments (the contraceptive pill), the liberalization of abortion law, and changes in attitudes and power relationships inaugurated by the feminist movement, coincided with the fertility decline in the 1970s and 1980s and can be thought of as co-determinants of this new demographic regime. But they are also themselves related to changing rates of female labour force participation, and the direction of causality cannot readily be discerned. The uncertainty is sufficient to allow quite different emphasis to be placed by different commentators on the importance of social, economic and technological factors. For those with a more sociological bent, social values, expectations and aspirations are the key factors which determine the overall fertility regime and changes from one regime to another. Economic variables may be significant at the margin, but when the margins of fertility change as much as they have done in Europe since the mid-1970s, macro-sociological interpretations are required (Lesthaeghe and Surkyn, 1988). From this perspective, the individualistic tenets of neo-classical economic analysis necessarily preclude a proper appreciation and assessment of ideational change.

Yet economic variables need not work just at the margin; in Richard Easterlin's model of birth and fortune, large birth cohorts beget small birth cohorts for strictly economic reasons (Easterlin, 1980). The economic competition of members of large cohorts with their multitudinous peers drives down their rate of return to human capital, and this leads to lower earnings, delayed marriage and lower fertility – all of which have been observed as the baby bust has followed the baby boom. The theory was developed in the light of US demographic experience and most of the empirical testing has been carried out on US data (Bloom *et al.*,

1987). Although some European data appears to support the proposition that large cohorts experience reduced labour market income relative to small cohorts (Ermisch, 1988b; Wright, 1991), so far there has been no European confirmation of the fertility propositions of the theory (Wright, 1989).

We cannot conclude, therefore, that the level or rate of change of fertility in Europe has been either wholly endogenous or wholly exogenous to the economy since the Second World War. In truth we know rather less about the underlying determinants of fertility than is often pretended. This means that the issue continues to be an important area of research, but it also means that we should be judiciously sceptical about long-term demographic projections that depend upon linear extrapolations of current fertility trends. The twentieth century experience of fertility in Europe has been one of abrupt and substantial cyclical movement – it was in the trough of one of these cycles in the 1930s that Keynes and others raised the spectre of the British population fading away in the foreseeable future (Keynes, 1937). Cyclical movements in fertility rates have certainly not faded away – in Sweden the TFR, which touched 1.6 in 1978 had climbed back to 2.1 by 1990 (Hoem, 1990).

Equal imprecision pertains to mortality projections. At first sight this is surprising – whereas fertility is largely a matter of choice, and so subject to a wide variety of economic, social and cultural factors, mortality appears to be simply a matter of biological chance, and so scarcely amenable to economic or social analysis. However, as the data in Figure 2.1 show, this biological chance does not appear to have been randomly distributed in post-war Europe, either between countries or over time (World Health Organisation, 1980). Male life expectancy at age 65 for the countries in panel (a) of Figure 2.1 (Japan, US, France, Italy, Spain and the UK) has risen more-or-less consistently over the period from 1950 from an average level of around 12 years in 1950–55 to 15 years in 1989. Within this overall pattern, increases in life expectancy have been fastest in Japan (from 11.4 to over 16 years) and slowest in the UK (11.9 to 13.9 years. The countries in panel (b) of Figure 2.1 display a much more diverse pattern. Greece has experienced erratic and very modest improvements in life chances at older ages, starting in the 1950s from a position well above the countries in panel (a), but converging to their 1989 level. Both East and West Germany experienced a fall in male life expectancy at age 65 from the mid-1950s to 1975, but thereafter West Germany followed the improving pattern of other West European countries, whereas East Germany, along with Poland and Hungary, only regained its 1955 life expectancy level at the end of the 1980s.

The disparate trends shown in the two panels of Figure 2.1 immediately

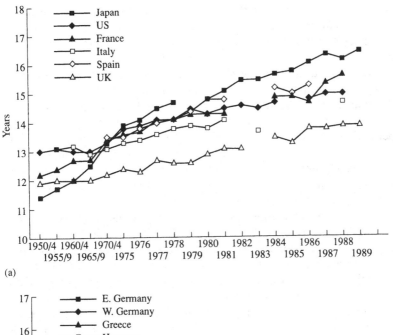

(a)

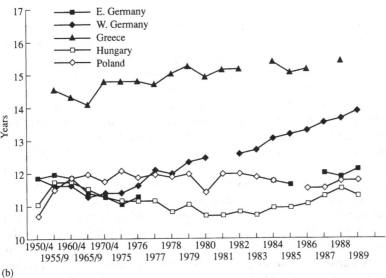

(b)

Figure 2.1 Male life expectancy at age 65

suggest that mortality gains at older ages may be causally connected to
econmic growth, but how the mechanics of such a connection might
operate is obscure. The much-researched decline in mortality in nineteenth century Europe still has no agreed explanation (Schofield *et al.*,

1991), and the aetiology of the diseases of old age today is still more guessed at than understood. There is considerable disagreement among bio-medical gerontologists over the extent to which degenerative conditions of old age arise from long-term environmental or nutritional conditions, over the extent to which improvements in life expectancy are a function of medical intervention, over the degree to which increases in life expectancy have extended active life or increased the number of years of old-age morbidity, and about whether the human life-span has a natural upper limit or whether it can continually be extended (Rogers *et al.*, 1990; Fries, 1983, 1989). The basic ignorance about the proximate causes of the recent mortality improvements at older ages necessarily makes discussion of trends even more speculative than is the case for fertility, yet some inferences can be drawn from the data.

The case of the two Germanies is particularly revealing, since it seems clear that their divergent paths since the early 1970s in male life expectancy at age 65 cannot be explained by different economic or environmental conditions for the members of these populations in their first four decades of life. Detailed examination of disease-specific morbidity and mortality data would be required to draw firm conclusions, but since adults are much more resistant to environmental and nutritional insults than are infants and children, and given the fact that from the mid-1960s to the mid-1980s the infant mortality rate in East Germany was below that in the West, it would seem that differential access to and quality of medical services in old age could be an important explanatory factor. In the state-administered health-care systems common in European countries, the share of expenditure devoted to health care is a function of both macroeconomic performance and political decision-making, so it cannot be assumed that any medically-induced increase in life-expectancy is itself a function of economic growth. Taking the periods 1975–80 and 1980–86 and all 26 European countries, there is a very weak positive relationship between the rate of growth of per capita national income and improvement in life expectancy for older men in the first period, and no relationship in the second period. Whether mortality improvements are endogenous to the economy must, therefore, remain an open question. It is a question that urgently needs to be addressed, given the prospective role of mortality changes in the ageing of the European population. For the moment, however, no firm conclusions can be drawn about the economic endogeneity of either mortality or fertility experience in post-war Europe.

3   Population and economic performance

Can stronger conclusions be drawn about the impact of population change on the economy? Is it the case that the size, or rate of growth, or age structure of the population determines or significantly affects economic performance? In the last decade there has been a growing recognition that prospective changes in the age structure of developed countries may affect the economy through the operation of social security systems. Most public social welfare expenditure is directed towards the young and the old in the form of education, pension and health care provision (the elderly are the major consumers of health services; in the major OECD countries public health expenditure per capita for the over-65 population is more than four times that for the 0–64 population). As Table 2.1 shows, the decline in fertility and increase in life expectancy has already changed the proportionate shares of the young and the old in the European population, and by 2020 it is projected that the over-65s will outnumber children. Even though the total dependency ratio in Europe is expected to be no higher in 2020 than it was in 1980, the change in the age structure will increase public expenditure because average per capita outlay on the old is so much higher than on the young – by a ratio of 2.7:1 across the major OECD countries in 1980 (OECD, 1988: 34). Static projections indication that demographic change in the period up to 2040 will increase the financing burden of social expenditure – the average cost per person of working age – by over 50% in the case of Germany and Japan, by 39% in Italy and 32% in France (OECD, 1988: 41).

These projections in turn indicate that the necessary tax rate required to finance social expenditure may need to rise from 18.5% to 41% of wage costs in Germany, and from 16.3 to 40% in France (Schmähl, 1989: 141; Vernière, 1990: 33). Significantly higher social insurance contributions or taxes would put upward pressure on labour costs and reduce the relative international competitiveness of these high-tax countries, as well as creating potentially unfair intergenerational transfers. These funding projections are, however, highly contingent on two key assumptions about labour force participation and benefit levels.

Demographic dependency ratios that compare the size of different age groups in the population will not follow the same path as *economic* dependency ratios if age- and sex-specific participation rates change over time. Activity rates for older men, and for women of all ages, have changed dramatically in Europe in the post-war period, and they may continue to change in the future. Although there has been some convergence, particularly towards very low rates for men over 60, and increasing rates for women, there are still large differences. Between 1950 and 1980, for instance, activity rates for women aged 40–44 in East Germany rose from 62% to 83%, whereas in West Germany they increased from 37% to 56%. If all women in Germany today were to participate in paid employment to the same degree as had been common in East Germany in the 1980s, then the *economic* dependency ratio would immediately fall, at least in the short run. Likewise, if benefits and services do not expand in line with average earnings in the future, then social expenditure growth will be less than projected, and pessimistic expectations will prove to be ill-founded.

This relationship between the age structure of the population and systems of public transfers has attracted and continues to attract much academic attention, but it is not the only, or even the most important, locus for interaction between economic and demographic forces. Many other elements of the economic system – the scale and structure of demand, the creation and use of human capital, the savings and investment rate, the direction of international capital flows – may all in some ways be affected by changes in the age structure of the population. The papers in this volume analyse labour market issues, but the labour market will itself be affected by demographically-induced changes in macroeconomic performances.

Since Malthus it has been recognized that population change can affect the rate and direction of economic growth, though it does not do so in an unambiguous way. There is a much-debated tension between orthodox theory which postulates that rapid demographic growth reduces the achievable rate of economic growth and leads to underdevelopment, and empirical evidence which fails to reveal a systematic negative relationship across time or place between the growth rates of population and of income (Simon, 1989). Blanchet has recently shown that the theoretical impact of changes in the size or rate of growth of the population on the level or rate of growth of income per capita can be positive or negative, depending on the assumptions made about the endogeneity of technical progress and the possibility of disequilibrium in the labour market (Blanchet, 1991).

Most discussion of economic and demographic interaction has focused on the overall size or rate of growth of the population, but the more important phenomenon in Europe over the next 30 or 40 years will be a change in the age structure within a largely static total population. Detailed analysis of the economic effect of changing age structures in developed countries is still in its pioneering stage (see, for instance, Lee et al., 1988), but the issue is now being addressed by macroeconomic modellers. Auerbach et al. (1989), Masson and Tryon (1990) and Masson (1991) have all explored the macroeconomic effects of population ageing in a number of developed countries using general equilibrium models, the first looking at four unlinked economies, the other two using the IMF's multi-region econometric model. In all three cases demographic variables are determined exogenously, and the aim is to gauge the effect of ageing on saving propensities, government revenue and expenditure, real wages, real interest rates, exchange rates and international capital flows. Ageing is taken to affect macroeconomic variables in three main ways – through a change in consumption propensities as the population ages and the dependency ratio rises, through a decline in potential output as the labour force shrinks, and through an increase in government expenditures as pension and medical benefits increase.

The simulation results indicate that ageing could have a significant effect on rates of national saving, on real wages, and on the current account and net foreign asset position. The authors of all three studies, however, stress that the results depend critically on key assumptions in the models, and that the relatively simplistic nature of the models means the simulations should not be taken as projections of the actual course of development of the major industrial economies.

The results of any model will only be as plausible as are its underlying assumptions, and one of the key assumptions in these models is that savings rates decline with age – Auerbach *et al.* model this explicitly in an overlapping generations model, whereas the IMF models introduce it in a more ad hoc way by incorporating a dependency ratio variable into the consumption equation. The underlying theoretical justification for this assumption derives from a life-cycle model of individual behaviour in which saving rates decline with age after some mid-point in the life-cycle, but its empirical foundations are shaky. Analysis of US longitudinal panel data has shown, for instance, that elderly people do not decumulate housing wealth as they age (Venti and Wise, 1989). Aaron *et al.* (1989) point out that savings rates for the retired population in America are little below those for people aged 45–64, and clearly above those for the 25–44 age group, something which cannot be captured in any model merely by introducing the age dependency ratio as a separate variable. In Germany many old people save substantial proportions of their annuity income, a finding which runs counter to the life-cycle model, although this may be because their opportunities to increase consumption expenditure have been constrained by infirmity (Börsch-Supan, 1991).

Given these unexpected results from individual-level data, it is perhaps not surprising to find that in the IMF model the dependency ratio in the consumption equation can only be made significant by introducing a further ad hoc variable, a dummy for 1980 and subsequent years. Although other international cross-section studies have found a significant negative relationship between the elderly dependency ratio and the savings rate, Graham (1987) has suggested that female labour force participation is a more important demographic influence on savings rates than is the dependency rate, and Koskela and Virén (1989) argue that when demographic variables are introduced into conventional life-cycle savings models the results they produce are not robust to changes in the sample size or the time period. Even if the results were robust, they would not demonstrate that *age* is a significant determinant of savings behaviour, since changes in age dependency ratios conflate separate age, period and cohort effects which may work in different directions. Laurence Kotlikoff, in a review of his own and other's work on the determinants of savings, has concluded that 'too little is known at an empirical level about the true causes of savings. As is often the case in economics the theory seems to have advanced well beyond empirical research' (Kotlikoff, 1989: 34). Different assumptions about savings rates in the general equilibrium models of population ageing would produce very different outcomes; the empirical uncertainty must reduce the plausibility of the results.

The general equilibrium simulations are pioneering attempts to gauge the economic impact of demographic change in advanced economies, and they are successful in demonstrating the complexity of the linkages, in a three-sector model, from the population age structure to overall economic performance. They are, inevitably, somewhat less successful in indicating the scale of likely effects. Assumptions about savings rates are crucial, as also are assumptions about the scale of international capital flows. But one assumption probably dominates all others, and that is how (if at all) demography affects the rate of technological progress. Over a forty or fifty-year period small differences in initial assumptions over the cumulative rate of technological progress can produce very large differences in outcomes. In consequence the simulation exercises cannot, as yet, produce strong conclusions about the impact of population change on economic growth and performance.

4   Conclusions

This paper has presented a brief review of what is and is not known about ageing and European economic demography; in many respects our ignorance is more apparent than our understanding. The population of Europe is ageing from the apex as well as the base of the population pyramid, and the process of ageing will therefore continue even if other countries in the 1990s follow the path of Sweden back to replacement level fertility. Hoem (1990) believes that the rise in the Swedish birth rate is a response to social policies that reduce the costs of child-rearing to parents; the lack of equally generous maternity/paternity leave entitlements and public child-care facilities in most other European countries makes similar reversals of the baby-bust appear unlikely. If, however, ideational factors are crucial underlying determinants of fertility, then it could be that major political and cultural changes now taking place in many European countries will affect future fertility trends. A future in which fertility rates fluctuate widely from one decade to the next would, on past experience, seem to be the most reasonable expectation. Mortality experience at older ages is even less well understood than is fertility, but the rapid improvements in life chances beyond age 65 experienced in many developed countries in the last fifteen years show no sign of tailing-off.

These demographic developments will have economic effects on individuals, employers and governments, but it is very difficult to determine how important these effects will be. General equilibrium models recognize the complexity of interactions between the population and the economy, but small changes in initial assumptions produce widely differing simulation results. Partial analysis of single sectors such as the labour market cannot capture this overall complexity but may be more useful in terms of policy analysis.

NOTES

1 For details of the assumptions on which the projections are based, see United Nations (1989), pp. 13–19 and United Nations (1991).
2 The TFR is calculated by summing age-specific fertility rates for a given year, and so averages across 35 adjacent cohorts (women aged 15–50). If different cohorts of women time their births differently, this will cause fluctuation in the TFR, even if the completed fertility of all birth cohorts is identical. For a review of cohort effects on fertility rates see Hobcraft et al. (1982).

REFERENCES

Aaron, H.J., B.P. Bosworth and G. Burtless (1989) Can America Afford to Grow Old?, Washington, D.C.: Brookings Institution.
Auerbach, A.J., L.J. Kotlikoff, R.P. Hagemann and G. Nicoletti (1989) 'The Economic Dynamics of an Ageing Population: The Case of Four OECD Countries', OECD Economic Studies 12: 97–130.
Becker, G.S. (1960) 'An economic analysis of fertility' in Demographic and Economic Change in Developed Countries. Princeton: Princeton University Press.
    (1981) A Treatise on the Family, London: Harvard University Press.
Becker, G.S. and R. Barro (1987) 'Altruism and the Economic Theory of Fertility', in K. Davis, M.S. Bernstam and R. Ricardo-Campbell (eds.), Below-Replacement Fertility in Industrial Societies, Cambridge: Cambridge University Press.
Blanchet, D. (1991) Modélisation démo-économique, Paris: INED/PUF.
Bloom, D.E., R.B. Freeman and S.D. Korenman (1987) 'The labour-market consequences of generational crowding', European Journal of Population 3, 131–76.

Börsch-Supan, A. (1991) 'Aging populations: problems and policy options in the US and Germany', *Economic Policy* **6**, (12), 103–31.

Bourgeois-Pichat, J. (1979) 'La transition démographique' in *Population Science in the Service of Mankind*, Liege: IUSSP.

Caselli, G. and J. Vallin (1990) 'Mortality and Population Ageing', *European Journal of Population* **6**, 1–25.

David, P. (1987) 'Comment' on Becker and Barro in K. Davis, M.S. Bernstam and R. Ricardo-Campbell (eds.), *Below-Replacement Fertility in Industrial Societies*, Cambridge: Cambridge University Press.

Easterlin, R.A. (1980) *Birth and Fortune*, New York: Basic Books.

Ermisch, J.F. (1988a) 'Economic influences on birth rates', *National Institute Economic Review* **126**: 71–81.

(1988b) 'Fortunes of birth: the impact of generation size on relative earnings of younger men', *Scottish Journal of Political Economy* **35**: 266–82.

(1989) 'Demographic Change and Intergenerational Transfers in Industrialised Countries' in P. Johnson, C. Conrad and D. Thomson (eds.) (1989), *Workers versus Pensioners*. Manchester: Manchester University Press.

(1990) 'European women's employment and fertility again', *Journal of Population Economics* **3**, 3–18.

Falkingham, J. and C. Gordon (1990) 'Fifty years on: the Income and Household Composition of the Elderly in London and Britain', in B. Bytheway and J. Johnson (eds.), *Welfare and the Ageing Experience*, London: Avebury.

Fries, J.F. (1983) 'The Compression of Morbidity', *Millbank Memorial Fund Quarterly* **61**, 397–419.

(1989) 'The Compression of Morbidity: Near or Far?', *Millbank Quarterly* **67**, 208–32.

Graham, J.W. (1987) 'International differences in saving rates and the life cycle hypothesis', *European Economic Review* **31**, 1509–21.

Hobcraft, J., J. Menken and S.H. Preston (1982) 'Age, period and cohort effects in demography: A Review', *Population Index* **48**, 4–43.

Hoem, J.M. (1990) 'Social Policy and Recent Fertility Change in Sweden', *Population and Development Review* **16**, 735–48.

Japan, Ministry of Health and Welfare (1992) *Annual Report on Health and Welfare 1990–91*, Tokyo: Japanese International Corporation of Welfare Services.

Keynes, J.M. (1937) 'Some economic consequences of a declining population', *Eugenics Review* **29**, 13–18.

Koskela, E. and Virén, M. (1989) 'International differences in saving rates and the life cycle hypothesis: a comment', *European Economic Review* **33**, 1489–98.

Kotlikoff, L.J. (1989), *What Determines Savings?*, Cambridge, MA: MIT Press.

Lee, R.D., W.B. Arthur and G. Rodgers (1988) *Economics of Changing Age Distributions in Developed Countries*, Oxford: Oxford University Press.

Lesthaeghe, R. and J. Surkyn (1988) 'Cultural Dynamics and Economic Theories of Fertility Change', *Population and Development Review* **14**, 1–46.

Masson, P.R. (1991) 'Effects of Long-Run Demographic Changes in a Multi-Country Model', IMF Research Department Working Paper 91/123 (December).

Masson, P.R. and R.W. Tryon (1990) 'Macroeconomic Effects of Projected Population Ageing in Industrial Countries', *IMF Staff Papers* **37**, 453–85.

Nugent, J.B. (1985) 'The old-age security motive for fertility', *Population and Development Review* **11**, 75–97.

OECD (1988) *Ageing Populations: the social policy implications*, Paris: OECD.

Preston, S.H. (1984) 'Children and the elderly: divergent paths for America's dependents', *Demography* **21**, 435–57.

—— (1987) 'The Decline of Fertility in Non-European Industrialized Countries' in K. Davis, M.S. Bernstam and R. Ricardo-Campbell (eds.), *Below-Replacement Fertility in Industrial Societies*, Cambridge: Cambridge University Press.

Preston, S.H. C. Himes and M. Eggers (1988) 'Demographic conditions responsible for population aging', Paper presented at the annual meeting of the Population Association of America, New Orleans.

Rogers, A., R.G. Rogers and A. Belanger (1990) 'Longer Life but Worse Health? Measurement and Dynamics', *The Gerontologist* **30**, 640–9.

Schmähl, W. (1989) 'Labour force participation and social pension systems' in P. Johnson, C. Conrad and D. Thomson (eds.), *Workers versus Pensioners*, Manchester: Manchester University Press.

Schofield, R., D. Reher and A. Bideau (1991) *The Decline of Mortality in Europe*, Oxford: Oxford University Press.

Simon, J. (1989) 'On Aggregate Empirical Studies Relating Population Variables to Economic Development', *Population and Development Review* **15**, 323–32.

Smith, R.M. (1981) 'Fertility, Economy, and Household Formation in England over Three Centuries', *Population and Development Review* **7**, 595–622.

Thane, P. (1990) 'The debate on the declining birth rate in Britain: the "menace" of an ageing population', *Continuity and Change* **5**, 283–305.

United Nations (1956) *The Aging of Population and its Economic and Social Implications*, New York: United Nations.

—— (1989) *World Population Prospects 1988*, New York: United Nations.

—— (1991) *World Population Prospects 1990*, New York: United Nations.

Venti, S.F. and D.A. Wise (1989) 'Aging, moving and housing wealth', in D.A. Wise (ed.), *The Economics of Aging*, Chicago: NBER/University of Chicago Press.

Vernière, L. (1990) 'Retraites: l'urgence d'une réforme', *Economie et Statistique* **233**, 29–38.

Westoff, C.F. (1987) 'Perspectives on Nuptiality and Fertility' in K. Davis, M.S. Bernstam and R. Ricardo-Campbell (eds.), *Below-Replacement Fertility in Industrial Societies*, Cambridge: Cambridge University Press.

World Health Organisation (1980 and other years) *World Health Statistics*, New York: World Health Organisation.

Wright, R.E. (1989) 'The Easterlin Hypothesis and European Fertility Rates', *Population and Development Review* **15**, 107–21.

—— (1991) 'Cohort size and earnings in Great Britain', *Journal of Population Economics* **14**, 245–76.

Discussion

RUDOLF ANDORKA

Hungary was a forerunner of the postwar baby-bust in Europe, as fertility rates declined below the level needed for simple replacement 10–15 years earlier than in other European societies (TFR = 2.08 in 1959, net reproduction rate = 0.973 in 1958). In the mid-1970s period fertility rates, calculated from the age-specific fertility rates for the given year, increased temporarily above the replacement level for 4 years, but declined again at the end of the 1970s and seem to have stabilized around TFR = 1.8. The cohort fertility rates display a more continuous and smooth decline: the completed total cohort fertility rate first declined below 2.0 in the birth cohort 1936–40 and seems to have stabilized more or less on the level of 1.95. Therefore Hungary was faced by the problems caused by the ageing of the population about 10–15 years earlier than other European countries. In consequence it might be interesting for the conference to have the comments on the paper by Paul Johnson of a Hungarian sociologist and demographer.

1   Economic consequences of the ageing of the population

Youth dependency is 28.9% and old-age dependency is 20.3% in 1990. These will change to 27.9% and 31.6% in 2020 according to Hungarian population projections (Kopits et al., 1990, and Kopits, 1992).[1] The unfavourable developments of the dependency rates coupled with the irrational pension system (statutory retirement age 60 for men and 55 for women, with possibilities of earlier retirement and a generous formula for calculating the starting pension) result on the one hand in the impossibility of indexing pensions to the inflation rate (causing the pauperization of each individual pensioner from year to year) and on the other hand threaten the bankruptcy of the whole pension system (Kopits et al., 1990; Andorka et al., 1992). The imminent danger of bankruptcy might be postponed by thoroughgoing reforms of the system, like an increase in the age of retirement, a modified version of the formula for calculating the pensions and an increase in the contributions to social security of active earners (the rate of these contributions is already very high). In the long term, however, only changes in the age structure of the population seem to promise a solution to these problems of the pension system.

Other economic consequences of the ageing of the population, like increasing health care expenditures, and the increasing need for daily care and human contacts (Andorka, 1988), etc., might only be mentioned in this discussion, but should not be neglected.

It might be asked why the growth of old-age dependency need cause such problems, when it will be compensated by a decline in youth dependency, if fertility continues to remain low. Here the simple fact has to be pointed out that in our European advanced societies the sustenance of the elderly is predominantly provided collectively, by the welfare state institutions, while the predominant part of the sustenance of children is shouldered by individual families. Pensions are supposed to provide a decent standard of living for the elderly, while it is usually considered that the costs of bringing up children have to be carried by their families, family allowances covering only a relatively small part (maximum 20–25 per cent on the average in a given society) of these costs.[2]

Three long-term policy responses are possible to the problems caused by ageing: increasing the labour force participation of the adult population, increasing immigration of young adults and a pronatalist or family policy (Andorka, 1989). The increase of labour force participation has obvious limits, as has an increase in the retirement age because of the decline of health with age, and the participation of women is in some countries approaching the saturation level. Therefore in the following only the other two policy responses are treated.

2   Immigration

Immigration from less developed societies to the advanced societies of Europe seems to be unavoidable. Immigration from poorer areas to mature advanced societies seems to have been happening at least since ancient Greece and the Roman Empire (McNeill, 1984). Immigration seems also to be a basic characteristic of the last phase of the demographic transition (Chesnais, 1986). Anti-immigration policies seem to be rather inefficient, as immigration inhibited in legal ways easily turns to illegal ways. On the other hand, the inflow and presence of large immigrant masses apparently might produce grave social tensions. It might make a difference, therefore, whether immigrants and the descendants of immigrants amount to 5–10 per cent or to 30–40 per cent of future young adult age groups. In other words, the problems caused by immigrants originating from more or less alien cultures could be much less severe if the level of European fertility were to increase in future to the level of simple replacement. I therefore would agree with Lesthaeghe that European societies 'would be ill-advised to rely solely on immigration to solve their demographic problems, because immigration is an inefficient counter to the problems posed by the current low fertility levels' (Lesthaeghe, 1988, p. 33). I would like nevertheless to emphasize that I would prefer an open and generous immigration policy in all European countries, including Hungary.

3   Theories of fertility

Paul Johnson in his paper briefly presents two opposite theoretical explanations of the level of fertility: an economic explanation based on the benefits and costs of children for their parents, and sociological theories based on values and norms concerning the number of children. I would propose a combination of these two theoretical schools (Andorka, 1978).

The number of children in families is, indeed, one of the recurrent problems of each society; therefore most societies develop some normative solution, expressed in terms of the number of children considered to be the best or the ideal in the families of the given society. Only a minority of families is usually willing to deviate from these values and norms concerning the number of children.

It seems, however, that these values and norms are not very exact or strict. In advanced societies the ideal number of children seems to be 1–2, 2–3 or 1–3. Only couples having more than 3 children, or no child at all, face any social disapproval for deviating from the values or norms of the society. Within the limits set by the values and norms of the society, i.e. within the range of 1–3 children, economic considerations play a role in the decisions of couples concerning the planned number, i.e. in the number of second and third children born.

I would also assume that macroeconomic conditions have some influence on societal values and norms. More favourable economic conditions, most of all for young couples, might shift the ideal number of children somewhat upwards, while serious economic difficulties, most of all for young adults, might depress the ideal number of children.

The consideration of these theories of fertility provides the background for my advocacy of pronatalist policies, more exactly of monetary allowances given to families having children, in order to alleviate the economic burden caused by the existence of children.

4   Considerations based on public choice theory

The justification of pronatalist monetary benefits might be interpreted in terms of the theory of public choice and of public goods. Children in advanced societies might be considered public goods, as the generation of children produces the national income from which the pensions of the generation of parents are paid and in the present system no former active earner can be exluded from pension rights. In consequence the children of parents having larger families contribute strongly to the payment of the pensions of childless and one-child pensioners. Thus children are 'produced' individually (by their families), but they (more exactly, the national income they produce as adults) are utilized collectively. In the case of public goods there is a well-documented tendency for them to be produced in less than optimal quantity (Demény, 1986a, 1986b). Potential parents are stimulated to behave as 'free riders', i.e. to expect that other members of their generation will be willing to shoulder the costs of the children who will later contribute to their pensions.

This argument does not hold for less developed societies having no extensive pension system. It would not hold either for any pension system based on the funding principle. But at present essentially all pension systems in advanced societies are based on the pay-as-you-go system and it does not seem probable that they could go over easily and rapidly to the funding principle.

5   The impact of pronatalist allowances in Hungary

Hungary has been experimenting since 1965 with social benefits provided to families with children, with an explicit pronatalist aim. Family allowances have been increased from time to time since 1965, attaining in 1988 30 per cent of the average wage for a 2-parent, 2-child family (the per child allowances were somewhat differentiated by the number of children in the family and by one- and two-parent families). It was estimated in 1987 that the family allowances covered about 20 per cent of the costs of children in 2-parent, 2-child families. The so-called child-care allowance was introduced in 1967 and provided an allowance more or less equivalent to the minimum wage to previously employed mothers until the third birthday of a child, if they interrupted their employment and cared for the child at home. In 1987 the child-care allowance was equivalent to 19 per cent of the average wage (earlier it attained 32 per cent of the average wage). In 1985 an additional child-care benefit was introduced which provided a sickness-benefit type allowance to mothers until their children were 2½ years old. In 1987 its average amount was at the level of 44 per cent of the average wage.

Altogether these monetary benefits given to families with children (including maternity benefit given during the 5 months before and after birth) amounted in 1988 to 3.5 per cent of GDP. Thus the efforts of the state to help families with children and to increase fertility were substantial.

Did all these efforts have any impact on fertility? It is not easy to measure their impact exactly.[3] First, it has to be decided whether the impact should be measured by period or cohort rates of fertility. The period rates influence the ageing of the population directly and they tend to react more strongly to population policy measures. On the other hand, the reproduction of the population really depends on the cohort rates. I therefore base my argument here on the cohort rates (see also Andorka, 1991a, 1991b).

Cohort rates of fertility stopped declining after the cohort born in 1936–40, i.e. in the cohorts which entered their twenties in the 1960s and later. In fact, a slight increase can be observed. It ought to be added that in these cohorts fertility declined rapidly in most Western European societies. It might be assumed that the stoppage of the decline in Hungary was due to the pronatalist policy.

Parallel to the stabilization of average cohort fertility two shifts occurred in the distribution of married women by their number of children. On the one side there was a shift from childless and one-child marriages to 2-child marriages. On the other side the percentage of married women having more than 3 children declined sharply. Thus a concentration towards 2-child families could be observed. It might be assumed that in the absence of the pronatalist policy the shift from 0–1 child marriages towards 2-child marriages would not have occurred.

Parallel to these developments, the number of children born to married women having different educational levels all increased, but at the same time the composition of married women in the procreative age groups shifted towards the higher educational categories, who had lower fertility. These two opposite changes compensated each other. It might be assumed that in the absence of the pronatalist policies, the shift towards higher educational levels of married women would have resulted in lower overall fertility.

I therefore feel justified in hypothesizing that *the pronatalist policies had indeed a modest, but nevertheless important impact on fertility.*

It might be added that Swedish (Hoem, 1990; Näsman, 1991) and French (Calot, 1991) demographers similarly showed that the recent increases of fertility rates in Sweden and France were due to pronatalist policies.

In conclusion, therefore, I would like to express the opinion that the economic consequences of ageing ought to be countered by an open immigration policy and by provision of generous social benefits to families with children.

NOTES

1 Youth dependency: population aged 0–14 over population aged 15–64. Old age-dependency: population aged 65 + over population aged 15–64.
2 One consequence of the generous provision of pensions and of the much less generous provision of family allowances is the improvement of the living conditions of the elderly and the pauperization of children in the United States (Preston, 1984) and other advanced societies (Smeeding and Torrey, 1988).
3 Measurement of the impact of the monetary benefits is made difficult by the fact that in the past decades the regulations on induced abortions were changed several times (strict enforcement of prohibition in 1953, gradual liberalization in 1955–56, slight restriction in 1973, gradual liberalization after the second half of the 1970s), and these changes might be assumed to have had an influence on fertility. Abortion policy is neglected in this discussion, as the author believes he has proved elsewhere (Andorka, 1978) that abortion policies have no lasting impact on cohort fertility.

REFERENCES

Andorka, R. (1978) *Determinants of fertility in advanced societies*, London: Methuen.
— (1988) 'Daily life of elderly persons in Hungary', in K. Altergott (ed.), *Daily life in later life: comparative perspectives*, Newbury Park: Sage, pp. 83–97.
— (1989) 'Policy responses to population decline in the twenty-first century: pronatalism, migration policy, growing labour force participation or other alternatives?', in *International Population Conference, New Delhi*, Liège: IUSSP, pp. 303–13.
— (1991a) 'Politiques démographiques natalistes et leur impact en Hongrie', *Politiques de Population, Études et Documents* 4, 87–125.
— (1991b) 'Modelli di politica per la popolazione: il caso Ungherese', in *Famiglia, figli e societa in Europa*, op. cit., pp. 101–36.
Andorka, R., Z.L. Antal, J. Hegedüs, D.T. Horváth, I. Tosics and I.Gv. Tóth (1992) 'The Hungarian welfare state in transition: structure, developments and options for reform', Paper prepared for the meeting of the Hungarian Blue Ribbon Commission.
Calot, G. (1991) 'Legittimita ed efficacia delle politiche demografiche', in *Famiglia, figli e societa in Europa*, op. cit., pp. 333–41.
Chesnais, J-C. (1986) 'La transition demographique', Paris: I.N.E.D. Travaux et Documents No. 113.
Demény, P. (1986a) 'Population and the invisible hand', *Demography* **23**, 473–87.
— (1986b) 'Rethinking fertility behavior and economic security in old age: toward a pronatalist institutional reform', Population Council, Population Notes No. 4.
Famiglia, figli e societa in Europa. Crisi della natalita e politiche per la popolazione (1991), Torino: Fondazione Giovanni Agnelli.
Hoem, J.M. (1990) 'Remarkable recent fertility in Sweden: an interpretation', Stockholm Reports in Demography No. 61.
Kopits, G. (1992) 'Social security', in V. Tanzi (ed.), *Fiscal policies in economies in transition*, Washington, DC: IMF, pp. 291–311.

Kopits, G., R. Holzmann, G. Schieber and E. Sidgwick (1990) *Social security reform in Hungary*, Washington, DC: IMF, Fiscal Affairs Department.

Lesthaeghe, R. (1988) 'Are immigrants substitutes for births?', paper prepared for the Sympoisum on Population Change and European Society, Firenze.

McNeill, W. (1984) 'Human migration in historical perspective', *Population and Development Review* **10**, 1–18.

Näsman, E. (1991) 'Modelli di politica per la popolazione: il caso Svedese', in *Famiglia, figli e societa in Europa*, op. cit., pp. 169–208.

Preston, S. (1984) 'Children and the elderly: divergent paths for America's dependents', *Demography* **21**, 44–9.

Smeeding, T.M. and B.B. Torrey (1988) 'Poor children in rich countries', The Luxembourg Income Study, Working Paper No. 16.

3 Ageing and employment trends: a comparative analysis for OECD countries

MARTIN REIN and KLAUS JACOBS

This essay concerns the decline of employment of men aged 55–64. This phenomenon represents one of the most dramatic economic transformations of labour markets in modern industrial economies. The decline in the employment of older men is widely believed to have signaled a new phenomenon, 'early retirement'. In an effort to understand this development, we examine past trends, disaggregate these trends to maximize international comparability, and identify the main national patterns of employment at the end of the work career and the implications of these patterns for the future of early retirement. The quantitative significance of early exit trends will grow in the future as the proportional size of the 55–64 age group relative to the rest of the working-age population increases.

1 A conceptual framework of early retirement

Early retirement can be understood as a social invention by firms to use the available social and public infrastructure to induce older workers to leave work in order that firms can restructure their work force. Sometimes the firm supplements the resources of the state, and sometimes it substitutes private for public resources. In this view, the firm becomes a new actor in understanding the history of the evolution of the welfare state. To our knowledge no history of the welfare state has systematically examined the interrelationship between the state and the firm from this perspective. There is, of course, considerable interest among historians in welfare capitalism.

Conceptualizing early retirement in this way picks up the theoretical framework developed in the 1940s which tried to show a complementary rather than an antagonistic relationship between social policy and labour markets.[1]

The starting point was criticism of the theory that the labour market generates an original distribution of income and social protection serves only as a mechanism for redistribution. Instead the theory of a social wage was developed to show that social policy had entered into the market wage through a system of transfers which supplemented wages in the form of fringe benefits and reduced expenditures in the form of price subsidies. A meaningful wage must include earnings combined with transfers and price subsidies. According to this framework, the conventional theory of redistribution as comprising original income, transfer income in the form of social protection, and a redistribution of original market income is misleading. Social policy not only redistributes original income, but is an essential component of it.

This insight is especially important if we want to understand the evolution of early retirement. Social policy is an essential component in industrial restructuring and the firm's relationship to the state as the main provider of social protection. Will the firm acquiesce in state initiatives to reduce early retirement or will the firm develop its own autonomous social policy and continue the trend? In this view the future size and structure of the welfare state itself depends on how the interplay between firm and state works itself out. The interaction of social policy of the state and the firm shapes the national patterns of early retirement we will discuss later in this paper.

2   Trends and patterns of labour force participation of older men: the significance of early exit

In this section we examine recent trends and patterns of early exit from the labour force by men from a comparative perspective across time and space. We focus on the labour market experience of men rather than women despite the fact that there is evidence that a similar decline in the female labour force is also occurring. In the case of women, however, there are different overlapping trends of both early exit from work at the end of the life course and growing entry in the prime years. The number of married women in the labour force has continued to rise in most countries. Whereas most men work for most of their lives, the labour force participation of women varies quite sharply across countries, from a low of about one-third in the Netherlands to over 80 per cent in Sweden. In addition, the meaning of early retirement for men who, more or less, work continuously over their life course is different from women, many of whom leave work after child-bearing and re-enter later in the life course. From cross-sectional data it is often difficult to isolate those women who have remained outside of work in the years immediately preceding retirement and the low labour force participation of older women. It is

Table 3.1. *Labour force participation rates of older men below the*
'normal' retirement age of 65, 1970–90 in seven OECD countries (%)

Country	Age	1970	1980	1985	1990	% change			
						70–90	70–80	80–85	85–90
Japan	60–64	81.5	77.8	72.5	72.9	− 10.6	− 4.5	− 6.8	0.6
	55–59	91.2	91.2	90.3	92.1	1.0	0.0	− 1.0	2.0
Sweden	60–64	79.5	69.0	65.1	63.2	− 20.5	− 13.2	− 5.7	− 2.9
	55–59	90.8	87.7	87.6	87.7	− 3.4	− 3.4	− 0.1	0.1
USA	60–64	71.7	59.8	55.1	54.9	− 23.4	− 16.6	− 7.9	− 0.4
	55–59	88.3	80.9	78.9	79.1	− 10.4	− 8.4	− 2.5	0.3
UK	60–64	86.7	71.2	55.4	54.4	− 37.3	− 17.9	− 22.2	− 1.8
	55–59	95.3	90.1	82.2	81.0	− 15.0	− 5.5	− 8.8	− 1.5
Germany[a]	60–64	69.5	44.2	32.9	35.1	− 49.5	− 36.4	− 25.6	6.7
	55–59	87.8	82.3	79.1	81.1	− 7.6	− 6.3	− 3.9	2.5
France	60–64	68.0	47.6	30.8	22.7	− 66.6	− 30.0	− 35.5	− 26.3
	55–59	82.9	80.9	67.8	67.7	− 18.3	− 2.4	− 16.2	− 0.1
Netherlands	60–64	73.7[b]	48.8	27.8	22.7	− 69.2	− 33.8	− 43.0	− 18.3
	55–59	86.6[b]	74.8	64.8	66.3	− 23.4	− 13.6	− 13.4	2.3

Notes:
[a] West Germany (for 1990: the former West Germany).
[b] 1971.

Sources: OECD *Labour Force Statistics*, Paris 1991; for Germany: Statistisches
Bundesamt (Mikrozensus).

also the case that women hold a different position in the labour market. In
virtually all countries they are segmented in a limited number of occupations, and in some countries, such as Japan, are actively excluded from
core lifetime jobs. There are, therefore, both technical and substantive
reasons for treating women separately.[2]

Table 3.1 using OECD labour force statistics shows the following
pattern for older men:

(1) there is a decline between 1970 and 1990 in labour force participation for the age group 60–64 in all countries;
(2) a decline is also found for men aged 55 to 59 with the exception of
Japan;
(3) despite this overall similarity there are considerable differences in the
rate of decline for the whole period: for men in their early 60s from
almost 11 per cent in Japan to about 37 per cent in the UK to almost 70
per cent in the Netherlands; and less sharp for men in their late 50s,
from over 3 per cent in Sweden to 23 per cent in the Netherlands;

(4)   between 1985 and 1990, the pattern of labour force participation of older men changed. With the exceptions of the Netherlands and France, the decline in the labour force of men 60 to 64 either slowed down, stopped, or was even slightly reversed;[3][4]

(5)   grouping the countries in terms of their level of labour force participation of men 60 to 64 in 1990 shows that Japan is an outlier with high labour force participation (73 per cent), Sweden, US and the UK form an intermediate pattern (54–63 per cent), and the continental European countries France, Germany and the Netherlands have the lowest participation levels (23–34 per cent);

(6)   grouping the countries by the labour force participation levels of men aged 55 to 59 suggest a somewhat different pattern: Sweden and Japan; US, the UK and Germany; France and the Netherlands.

3   Disaggregating labour force participation

Since the range of labour force participation levels of older men is so wide between 'high early exit countries' and 'low early exit countries', one might think that the pattern of exit (voluntary or involuntary) of older workers does not appear to be a general phenomenon in most industrial societies. This conclusion is, however, premature. We believe that an aggregate labour force measure is a misleading unit of analysis if we wish to understand the dynamics underlying the pattern of male early exit from employment.

We want to show that early exit of men from employment is indeed a general phenomenon in mature industrial economies. The difficulty in detecting a more convergent pattern for wage and salary workers as the hard core of the labour force arises from the fact that the labour force data also include the unemployed and self-employed. In some countries these statuses include a large proportion of older workers, which helps to explain the relatively high labour force participation rates.

We believe that these statuses should be treated separately if we wish to isolate the strategic role that changes in industrial reorganization play in determining early retirement, because they are driven by rather different processes. Isolating the wage and salary workers is the key to conceptual clarity and disaggregation.

We start by examining the rationale for excluding the role of unemployment among older men.

3.1   Unemployment

The role of unemployment of older workers varies across countries. In many European countries unemployment is a step in a well-defined pathway to early retirement. This is very clear in countries like Germany, where a period of unemployment of at least one year is a necessary pre-condition for early entry into the pension system at age 60, while most men continue to enter the pensions system at the 'flexible retirement age' of 63. In France the normal retirement age for men has been lowered from 65 to 60. In these two countries those people registered as unemployed are clearly on a pathway to final exit from work, moving from unemployment directly into the pension system. In the UK and the Netherlands, the 'unemployment pathway' can also contain an interim period between unemployment and entry into the pension system, where the individual receives payments from a means-tested welfare programme called 'long-term rate of income support' in the UK and 'social assistance' in the Netherlands. In all these countries re-entry into work is extremely unlikely. The 'unemployment' of older workers is not really unemployment interpreted as a period of transition from the loss of one job while searching for another.[5]

That the unemployment rate of older workers is not really a true measure of unemployment is also revealed by the variety of rule changes introduced to treat older workers as a special group. In some countries the maximum period for receiving unemployment insurance benefits has been extended several times. Older unemployed people now can receive unemployment insurance benefits for more than two-and-a-half years in Germany, and up to five years in France. Moreover, it is no longer necessary for them to be actively seeking work. In fact, very often they are no longer counted in the official unemployment statistics. Entry into the unemployment pathway leads to final exit from work at an even younger age. Aside from disability, unemployment is the only public programme available for men below age 60. These institutional rules help to make understandable the data presented in Table 3.2, Column 2, which shows that in these countries unemployment rates are consistently higher for men in their 50s as compared to those in their early 60s.

By contrast, the meaning of unemployment in countries like the US and Japan is different from that in Europe, where the probability of re-entry is small. In these countries, the unemployment of an older worker does not necessarily imply that the worker is unlikely to return to work. In Japan, a worker reaching the mandatory retirement age of 60 is entitled to a 'period of rest' after a lifetime of employment. He can receive unemployment insurance benefits for 300 days and afterwards he may or may not continue to work. Hence in Japan, the pattern is opposite to that found in the four European countries – here unemployment rates are substantially higher for men aged 60 to 64 than for those 55 to 59. In the US there is virtually no difference in unemployment rates by age, while in Sweden

Table 3.2. *Disaggregating the labour force participation rates of older men; rates for 1989 in seven OECD countries*

Country	Age	Labour force participation rate (% of population)	Unemployment rate (% of labour force)	Self-employment rate (% of all employed)	Part-time work-rate (% of wage and salary workers)
Japan	60–64	71.4	5.9	37.8	4.3
	55–59	92.6	2.6	26.3	1.3
Sweden	60–64	62.7	1.7	20.6	30.7[a]
	55–59	87.1	0.8	16.2	6.5[a]
USA	60–64	54.2	3.3	19.3	18.8[b]
	55–59	78.8	3.5	15.7	10.7[b]
UK	60–64	53.5	4.3	19.8	8.1
	55–59	77.4	12.1	20.1	2.9
Germany	60–64	34.2	6.4[c]	30.9	3.9
	55–59	78.6	9.0[c]	17.6	1.4
France	60–64	24.1	3.7	48.3	9.8
	55–59	68.0	8.1	33.8	5.8
Netherlands	60–64	24.5	3.8	36.9	25.9
	55–59	65.3	5.6	17.5	15.2

Notes:
[a] % of all employed men (including self-employed).
[b] % of persons at work in nonagricultural industries.
[c] 1987.

Sources: Labour force participation rates and unemployment rates: OECD *Labour Force Statistics*, Paris 1991; for Germany: own calculations based on data from the Mikrozensus; Self-employment and part-time rates: own calculations based on Labour Force Surveys (Japan, Sweden), Current Population Survey (US), EUROSTAT (France, Germany, Netherlands, UK).

unemployment hardly exists among older workers. (Data presented in Table 3.3, Panel A, examining the labour force status of the total population of older men also confirm these general conclusions.)

3.2   Self-employment

Self-employment of older workers is governed by a different and more dynamic process than employment of older workers in wage and salary positions. In particular, employment and hours decisions in wage and salary positions require agreement by two people with different interests, rather than one person. In addition, access and entitlement to social

Table 3.3. *Labour force status of the population of older men in 1989 in seven OECD countries*

Panel A Disaggregated labour force status

Country	Age	Wage/salary workers Full-time	Part-time	Self-employed	Unemployed	Not in labour force	Total
		% of population					
Japan	60–64	40.0	1.8	25.4	4.2	28.6	100
	55–59	64.8	0.9	23.5	2.4	8.4	100
Sweden	60–64	33.9	15.0	12.7	1.1	37.3	100
	55–59	67.7	4.7	14.0	0.7	12.9	100
USA	60–64	34.2	8.0	10.1	1.8	45.8	100
	55–59	57.2	6.9	11.9	2.8	21.2	100
UK	60–64	37.8	3.3	10.1	2.3	46.5	100
	55–59	52.7	1.6	13.7	9.4	22.6	100
Germany	60–64	21.2	0.9	9.9	2.2	65.8	100
	55–59	58.1	0.8	12.6	7.1	21.4	100
France	60–64	10.8	1.2	11.2	0.9	75.9	100
	55–59	39.0	2.4	21.1	5.5	32.0	100
Netherlands	60–64	11.0	3.9	8.7	0.9	75.5	100
	55–59	43.1	7.7	10.8	3.7	34.7	100

Panel B Aggregated labour force status

Country	Age	Labour force participation rate	Employment activity rate	Employment rate of wage/salary workers
		% of population		
Japan	60–64	71.4	67.2	41.8
	55–59	91.6	89.2	65.7
Sweden	60–64	62.7	61.6	48.9[a]
	55–59	87.1	86.4	72.4[a]
USA	60–64	54.2	52.3	42.2
	55–59	78.8	76.0	64.1
UK	60–64	53.5	51.2	41.1
	55–59	77.4	68.0	54.3
Germany	60–64	34.2	32.0	22.1
	55–59	78.6	71.5	58.9
France	60–64	24.1	23.2	12.0
	55–59	68.0	62.5	41.4
Netherlands	60–64	24.5	23.6	14.9
	55–59	65.3	61.6	50.8

Note:
[a] Assuming that the part-time rate for all employed (including the self-employed) is also valid for wage and salary workers.

Source: Authors' calculations based on rates in Table 3.2.

security programmes is substantially harder, and often not possible, for the self-employed. In other words, they are not subject to mandatory retirement; there is no employer with an interest in expelling them from work; and moreover the economic necessity of continuing work is high for many of the self-employed who lack access to public programmes. Hence we would expect high rates of self-employment among older workers.

Table 3.2, column 3, confirms this expectation. Self-employment rates by age vary from about one-fifth of total male employment for men aged 60 to 64 in the US, the UK and Sweden to almost one-half in France. In all countries except the UK self-employment rates are higher for men in their early 60s than for men in their late 50s.

Other data from EUROSTAT for EC countries show that the share of self-employment among older workers is much higher than their share in relation to total male employment; the proportion of the self-employed increases substantially with age; and this increase by and large continues over time.[6]

We need to exercise more than a fair measure of caution in interpreting the higher self-employment rates of older men. One reason for caution is that the number of all persons employed, i.e., the denominator of the self-employment rate, varies considerably across countries. The highest self-employment rates of older men aged 60 to 64 are found in France, Japan, the Netherlands and Germany, where self-employment rates vary from about 48 to 31 per cent.

If we relate the number of self-employed to the total population in the age group rather than to the employed population, we get a deeper understanding of the underlying processes. In Table 3.3, Panel A, we find that only in Japan does self-employment account for as much as one-quarter of the total population of men aged 60 to 64. In all the other countries, regardless of the differences in the rates, the share of self-employed men in the population is strikingly similar, moving within a very narrow range of 9 to 13 per cent and considerably lower in Japan.

How can we interpret why self-employment is so high for older males? Quinn *et al.* (1990) suggest several possible answers. One interpretation is the so-called cohort effect where older men began their careers when self-employment was much more common than it is today. This was clearly the case when the agricultural sector played a greater role for the total labour market. At least in some countries self-employment was – and still is – the main employment status in agriculture. For instance it represents 64 per cent of male agricultural workers in the Netherlands and 86 per cent in the UK. In the mid-1980s agriculture accounted for only a small proportion of the total male labour force – between 3 per cent in the UK and 9 per cent in France. In some countries agriculture still contributed a much higher proportion of the labour force of men aged 60 to 64 – 14 per cent in Germany, 18 per cent in the Netherlands, 26 per cent in Japan, and 34 per cent in France. These countries also have the highest self-employment rates for older men (Quinn *et al.*, 1990, p. 33).

This example of the overlap between age-concentration and self-employment in agriculture is not conclusive in demonstrating the cohort effect. The same cross-sectional data could be interpreted as an age effect caused by large transfers of marginally employed workers into the agricultural sector as they become older. However, such a large movement of older workers into the agricultural sector seems implausible to us. Of course, an analysis of the experience of successive cohorts might enable this issue to be sorted out.

A second interpretation is that older workers stay longer in self-employment for a number of institutional reasons. Whereas wage and salary workers enter into a contract with an employer which specifies, among other things, the duration of their employment, in many European countries there is a mandatory retirement age. For example, professors are expected to retire at age 65. Anti-age discrimination legislation is in effect only in the United States. A self-employed person is not bound by such contracts and can continue to work as long as he chooses. This is clearly an important factor accounting for the difference in the exit rates of the self-employed compared to wage and salary workers.

The third interpretation is that there are many institutional mechanisms which provide exit routes from employment for wage and salary workers which are not customarily available for the self-employed. The self-employed in many countries are not automatically blanketed in by the basic public pension system. The rules governing access and benefit levels for unemployment, disability, and retirement are different. These measures affect the process of early retirement. With fewer pathways for early exit open to them, they tend to remain self-employed.

Finally, and most interesting for our purposes, is that self-employment may be seen as a way of continuing work after leaving a wage and salary position. Sometimes this transition is made in combination with receipt of a private or public pension. For example, severance pay in Japan is used by older workers to start a small business. Self-employment becomes one way of making a bridge between work and retirement. This argument, like the others, certainly seems plausible. Unfortunately, cross-sectional data do not provide evidence for work transitions in the last stage of the working life. Comparative longitudinal data are in short supply.

3.3   Wage and salary workers

We can now turn to the wage and salary earners as the hard core of the labour market. As we stated above, this is the group toward which most theories about the declining labour force participation of older workers are usually directed. At the micro level, the literature identifies two major kinds of incentives for firms to shed older wage and salary workers: adjustments in size and structure of the labour force and adjustments in labour costs due to the age-wage profiles.[7] The labour force adjustments are relatively straightforward. They include incentives for the firm to reduce the overall size of its labour force due to fluctuations in the demand for its products. Second, the firm has an interest in shedding older workers in order to provide promotion opportunities for the young. And finally, in an effort to introduce new technology firms want to reorganize the age mix of their personnel, because it is widely assumed that older workers lack the ability to adjust to new technology or it is too costly to retrain them. The interest for firms to make adjustments in labour costs is based on the assumption that older workers are overpaid relative to their productivity. Hence the incentive to shed the older, more costly, workers in the absence of an institutional practice which would make it possible to reduce the wages of older workers.

At the macro level, most theories point to high rates of unemployment in the early 1970s forcing national government politically to respond by a range of measures which facilitated early exit from the labour market as a socially acceptable way of dealing with the overall surplus of labour.

The relevant data on the employment of older wage and salary workers are presented in Table 3.3, Panel B. When we isolate male wage and salary workers from the total labour force of older men as presented in Table 3.1 we get a different picture of the relative standing of our countries. For men aged 60 to 64 we see that Japan is no longer an outlier. Instead those countries already identified as 'low early exit countries' become much more homogeneous, with employment rates of wage and salary workers varying only slightly. Therefore we discern two clear patterns of early exit: France, Germany, and the Netherlands with 'high early exit' signaled by employment activity rates of wage and salary workers ranging only from 12 to 22 per cent; and Japan, Sweden, the UK and the US with 'low early exit' and rates between 41 and 49 per cent.

Turning to the 55–59 age group a more continuous pattern is observed. Nevertheless Sweden, Japan, and the US clearly remain the countries with the highest employment rates of wage and salary workers, France and the Netherlands remain at the other extreme, while Germany and the UK appear to reverse their relative positions and are therefore more difficult to classify.

4   Patterns of early exit

In this section we try to identify the institutional processes underlying the patterns of early exit as discussed above. In the 'high early exit countries', France, Germany and the Netherlands, the very low employment rates signal that older men, by and large, move from full-time work to full-time retirement. They have increasingly used a combination of different public and/or private programmes, such as disability, unemployment, company pensions, or pre-retirement, in well-defined pathways of early exit that are usually directed to entry into the public pension system and very often begin well below the 'normal' retirement age.[8] We also know that income replacement rates in the programmes combined with pathways of early exit are relatively high and, therefore, there is only a limited economic incentive to seek employment. Abrupt transition from the major working career job to complete retirement is overwhelmingly the dominant pattern of exit.

Gradual exit with any combination of part-time work and the receipt of a public or private pension is not a relevant exit route for men. Table 3.3, Panel A, shows that only a very small proportion of older men work part-time in these countries. At first sight, the Netherlands appear to be an exception, but there is good reason to believe that the relatively high share of part-time male employment in all age groups reflects a general redefinition of the boundaries between full-time and part-time employment rather than the emergence of a true pattern of part-time work as a route to early exit. We call this pattern 'exit is exit' because it graphically illustrates that once a man leaves work, his probability of re-entering work is virtually non-existent.

What about the remaining countries where there is a significant employment rate of wage and salary workers? What Sweden, the US and Japan share in common is that at least a substantial minority of older men combine work and retirement, or have their work redefined so that the job itself signals the beginning of a retirement process. While the exit outcomes are similar in these countries, the processes creating these results are quite varied. Different processes are producing similar outcomes. We can distinguish three different patterns, each based on a different logic. To describe these patterns we draw on information from sources other than the statistical series reported earlier. We do not look at the UK separately because we do not believe that it treats older wage and salary workers in any uniquely institutionalized way which could serve as a model for redefining the process of early retirement in other countries.

4.1   Sweden: partial retirement

In Sweden, the relatively high proportion of employment of older workers in wage and salary positions is created by different ways of combining work and the receipt of a public pension. The most prominent system of partial pension arrangements introduced in July 1976 permits a worker aged 60 to 64 to get 65 per cent of his income loss as a result of working part-time. To be eligible individuals must agree to reduce their working time by at least 5 hours with a remaining working time of at least 17 hours a week. In most cases the worker receives 80 to 90 per cent of his past income. This system is both ambitious and costly. We can see from a review of the evolution of its history how the development of a reduction in the level of benefits in 1981 to only 50 instead of 65 per cent had an immediate impact on take-up rates, reducing the number of male partial pensioners by more than half. When the higher benefit level was restored in 1987, the take-up rate increased again but not quite to its former level. In the meantime, however, other partial pension programmes had continued to grow. The part-time employment rate of all men aged 60 to 64 declined from 28 per cent in 1981 to only 14 per cent in 1985, but rose again to 30 per cent in 1990.

Sweden is, of course, unique among other countries which have also tried to implement the Swedish system of partial retirement. The system apparently seems to work only in Sweden, where one finds a very strong commitment to the right to work which extends also to groups that are usually defined as marginal in other countries such as older men and those who are partially disabled. But obviously more than an abstract commitment to principles is at stake here. It is clear from the Swedish experience during the 1980s that take-up rates of partial pensions were only high when the average replacement rate was between 80 and 90 per cent. When benefit levels dropped, participation in the programme declined dramatically. By its nature such a programme is very costly, which may be the reason why the new Conservative government in Sweden tried to eliminate the partial pension system in 1992. However, this first effort failed to pass in parliament. It will be interesting to see whether there will be further efforts to retrench this programme, as the closing down of partial disability pensions in 1991 might increase the utilization and cost of the partial pension programme.

A distinctive element of the Swedish system of partial pensions is that workers can stay in the same job with the same employer and gradually reconstitute their work from full- to part-time employment. In this scheme there is an institutional commitment on the part of the employer to continue hiring the older worker and on the part of the state to create a special programme to buffer the loss of income from a reduction in hours worked and earnings.

4.2 Japan: work after lifetime employment

What distinguishes the Japanese pattern? Whereas the Swedish system emphasizes a change in the hours of work but a continuity of type of work and employer, the Japanese system emphasizes a change in the status of work, a decline in earnings level, and sometimes a change from a parent to a subsidiary employer. At a given age of mandatory termination of employment called the 'teinen age', virtually all wage and salary workers are expected to end their contracts with the firm. In the 1970s most firms had a 'teinen age' of 55. In the 1980s, this was gradually raised to age 60, when workers can also receive a public pension. 'Teinen' marks the end of 'lifetime employment'. It signals the end of the first major stage of the working life, which is characterized by job security and seniority wages. Table 3.4, Panel A, shows that since the 1986 pension reform legislation, the 'teinen' age arrangements have increasingly spread to small as well as large firms. Most workers are now covered by 'teinen' rules. In the past, however, a large number of small firms employed older workers without following 'teinen' rules because of a shortage of young workers.

After 'teinen' some workers accept a year of unemployment insurance and then leave the labour force with a combination of public and private pension. Most, however, do not follow this pattern and re-enter work, with a decline in wages being partially offset by the receipt of a lump-sum payment and a combined public and private pension subject to an earnings test.

What are the ways of re-entering employment after the 'lifetime employment' comes to an end? The first distinction is whether the firms play an active role in the prolongation of work after age 60. They can do this in three different ways: by extending the former work contract; by re-employing the worker in his former company in a lower position and with lower payment; or by transferring the worker to an affiliated firm of the parent company. If the firm does not play an active role in facilitating the continuation of work, then the individual has to rely on his own initiative in finding work. In this case, self-employment may also play a role in supplementing the pension by work income.

This national pattern is by no means static. Many changes are observable within the framework of this system. The most important institutional change was the closing of the five year-gap between 'teinen' and the receipt of a public pension. During this period of time the individual received only a company pension which was not sufficient to live on. The

Table 3.4. *Japan: the impact of 'teinen' rules (termination of 'lifetime employment')*

Panel A *'Teinen' by firm size and age*

Age of 'teinen' (retirement) in Japanese companies

	Firms with 'teinen' (%)	Age of 'teinen' (uniform age) (%)		
		55	56–59	60+
All firm sizes				
1974	67	52	12	35
1980	82	27	17	55
1987	89	23	18	59
Large firms (5,000+ employees)				
1974	100	38	51	11
1980	100	35	37	28
1987	100	3	12	85
Small firms (30–99 employees)				
1974	55	52	6	41
1980	77	37	18	44
1987	86	23	17	60

Source: Rebeck (1990, p. 34) derived from Japan Productivity Center (1988, p. 133).

Panel B *Post-'teinen' experience*

Conditions for workers who experienced 'teinen', 1972–82 (males over 55)

Year	Employment extension or reemployment (%)	Transfer (%)	Displaced (%)
1972	25	28	47
1975	29	25	46
1977	37	25	38
1978	31	23	46
1982	32	13	55
Median wage change (%)			
1972–78	−26	−36	−42
1977–82	−22	−38	−45
Job content (%)			
Identical	70–77		20–30
Related	13–20		37–43
Unrelated	10		40
Hours of work (%)			
Fewer	3		20–25
Same	94		40
More	3		40
Status (%)			
Permanent	25		50
Temporary	75		50

Sources: White paper on Teinen for 1980, 1985. Distribution within fields is assumed to be uniform for grouped data. Taken from Rebick (1990).

firms, therefore, felt a strong obligation to actively assist workers to re-enter employment. With the increase in the 'teinen age' and substantial improvements in public and private pension arrangements this obligation seems to have declined, although both the preference for and the economic necessity of work remain high. Table 3.4, Panel B, provides empirical evidence for this change as the proportion of displaced workers after 'teinen' has increased. However, the table has to be interpreted with some caution because the age effect of raising 'teinen age' has not been isolated.

The system of obligation is evolving. It is useful to keep in mind three related but different issues. First, it is a norm among large firms to continue to employ their regular workers until 'teinen' age. The state and the unions have demanded, however, that the 'teinen' age be raised, and the firms have reluctantly accepted this demand as a social obligation. Finally, the state is pressing firms to extend their social obligations even further by employing workers over 60 (i.e., raising the 'teinen' age again) or enforcing re-employment schemes. Some firms have complied. According to one Japanese specialist, 'we can not yet say that the re-employment scheme is today a social norm'.[9]

In some aspects, the process of gradual transition from work to retirement in Japan and Sweden is similar, because both countries have institutionally established a principle of 'shared responsibility' of the state and the firms and not merely an ad hoc arrangement through which the consequences of early exit from work fall on the individual alone. Of course, both systems differ in numerous ways: job reassignment; hours worked; and the rate of decline of wages.

4.3 The United States: multiple options

The distinguishing characteristic of the American system is that there is no unified institutionalized form of exit from the labour market, as in the other countries. Instead, individuals find themselves in a variety of situations which constrain the course of action that they have to pursue on their own. There are at least four institutional arrangements that reinforce reliance on multiple options.

First, private pension arrangements covering about 60 per cent of male workers aged 25 to 64 play an important role in the retirement decision of older men. These plans are not harmonized with public retirement programmes. In fact most plans incorporate strong economic incentives to leave work at a given age that is clearly below age 62, the earliest age an individual can claim a public pension.

Second, those older workers without private pension coverage, who tend to be concentrated among unskilled workers, usually find themselves in situations where they lack employment security and can easily be dismissed by their employer.

Third, the public pension system is designed to provide only a floor of social protection to prevent poverty and hardship. Unlike the European systems, it is not intended as a main source of income designed to promote the continuity of lifestyles achieved before retirement. By and large, income replacement rates compared to Europe are low, except for low-wage workers. Therefore many pensioners need to supplement their public pension income from other sources.

Fourth, legislation eliminates a mandatory retirement age and seeks to implement anti-age discrimination practice in firms. Of course, the legislation does not end age-linked hiring and firing, but it certainly is likely to reduce the extent to which age plays a role in this process. The point we want to stress here is that the existence of anti-age discrimination legislation works institutionally to support the range of individually chosen options.

Clearly, then, the different options depend on the individual circumstances. We identify some of the major options:

(a) In the case where the older worker has neither a private nor a public pension he is forced to take whatever job is available or to be supported by his family. Such jobs are usually characterized by easy entry, easy exit and less pay.

(b) Men can gradually retire from their career job and accept a part-time position which may be in their own field or in a different industry or occupation. Such part-time employment can supplement private pensions which are seldom protected against inflation.

(c) Men can also re-enter work after a period of retirement because the public and private pensions they receive turn out to be inadequate to support the lifestyle they seek to maintain, or perhaps because the lack of work undermines a meaningful life, or some combination of both financial and personal reasons.

(d) Of course, men can also leave work permanently and rely on an income package of private and public pensions, savings and from other sources.

The relative importance of these different options and the evolving trends are difficult to disentangle. The cross-sectional data we present in Tables 3.2 and 3.3 can only highlight the considerable importance of part-time employment of older workers in the United States. The other options described above require longitudinal data which traces the individual work career over time.

'Using data from the Retirement History Survey, Quinn, Burkhauser and Myers followed men from 1969, when they were 58 to 63, until 1979. The data are, therefore, not recent, but they do show that 58.7 per cent of persons working full-time at age 55 retire abruptly and remain retired. . . . at least 18 per cent partially retire at some point in time and at least 20 per cent reverse partial retirement or retirement status after initially entering it. . . . Moreover, among persons retiring or partially retiring at young ages (by 55) continuous retirement is the exception rather than the rule.'

Ruhm, Quinn and Burkhauser have made extensive use of the idea of a bridging job in their research on the gradual transition from full-time 'career jobs', which they define as jobs held for a minimum period of 10 years, to complete retirement. Bridging jobs signal a 'job-stopping' process by older workers after they leave their career jobs. At least one-quarter of wage and salary workers did not leave the labour market when they left their career jobs (Quinn *et al.*, 1990).

One important difficulty with this concept is that a substantial proportion of the bridging jobs reflect upward mobility, which is clearly not an exit pattern. The concept of a bridging job, therefore, masks two very different processes: job advancement at the last stages of a career and the beginning of the retirement process through re-entry to a job with lower wages and/or fewer hours of work. Only the second concept is relevant to our present study and the broader measure of bridging jobs may overstate the extent to which changes in the work situation signal the process of gradual exit from the labour market.

In his description of the American system, Wise stresses the importance of an abrupt transition between work and retirement. He says that

> the vast majority . . . go from full-time work to retirement overnight. Although some recent research has emphasized work after retirement, it is limited to a small proportion of retirees, is almost never at the same firm from which the employee retired, and is usually part-time and of short duration. Current institutional arrangements make gradual withdrawal from the labour force extremely difficult.' (Wise, 1992, p. 83)

If Wise is correct, then most individuals in the United States follow the European pattern of 'exit is exit'. At some landmark point individuals exit from the labour market and do not return. Many individuals supplement the minimum public pension with private pensions and savings so they are able to maintain their previous life styles by packaging pension arrangements and personal assets.

As we can see from the above discussion, characterizing the American system of exit is very difficult. We believe that the empirical evidence does not permit us to take a clear position on the relative importance of gradual retirement and the significance of bridging jobs in this process. While the new Retirement History Survey will provide more recent data, it will not resolve the conceptual question about the changing nature of work at the end of the working career. What is important in our context is, aside from the empirical and conceptual issues, that the institutional arrangements in the United States seem to reinforce a variety of alternative ways of organizing the combination of work and retirement. As a result, no single dominant national pattern can easily be identified, such as those found in Sweden or Japan.

4.4   A combination of redefined work and the receipt of pension income

Sweden, Japan and the US were classified as 'low early exit countries' because of their relatively higher employment rates of older wage and salary workers. The deeper institutional analysis of early exit patterns in these countries shows one distinctive finding that may become the key aspect in understanding the future of early retirement. Despite all differences in these three countries, we can identify a redefinition of work for many individuals at the end of their working career. Like in 'exit is exit countries', many older male wage and salary workers have left their full-time career job but, contrary to the common practice in those countries, many of them have not completely left the labour force. Instead, they continue to work in a second career which is characterized by a different kind of work in terms of less income, less working hours, a minor job status, or any combination of these factors and a simultaneous receipt of income from other sources, such as private and public pension arrangements.

Therefore a substantial proportion of the relatively higher employment rates for older male wage and salary workers in the 'low early exit countries' does not reflect that more older workers just stay longer on their jobs before they retire completely. Instead, in these countries, as compared to the 'high early exit' or 'exit is exit countries', many older workers find themselves in an interim period between their major career job and full-time retirement. In Japan, this is clearly the case for all workers after 'teinen age' who are either re-employed or transferred to new employment with active support from their former employer or have to re-enter employment on their own initiative. In Sweden, the interim period consists of a combination of part-time work and the receipt of a partial pension. And in the United States, aside from the relatively high share of part-time employment among older workers, there seems to be at least some empirical evidence based on longitudinal data for the practice of re-entry into the labour force after the termination of the major career job. Moreover in the US, the institutional arrangements of private and public pensions are not linked together and, therefore, strongly promote 'work after retirement'.

5 The future of early retirement: extending the concept of pathways of early exit from the labour force

The processes of social and labour market policy that have led to a sharp decline and sometimes to a redefinition of labour force participation of older men have been very dynamic in the past. But this is not the only reason why it seems important to address the question of the future evolution of early retirement. At least in some countries, the state, as one key actor in creating the social infrastructure in which early exit from the labour force takes place, has already taken some action to stop or even reverse the reported trends. Similar objectives on the side of the state can also be observed in other countries where first attempts at legislative changes have failed. The strong interest of the state in stopping or reversing the trend to early retirement is widely based on the belief that society 'cannot afford' the mounting costs of early retirement.

In the United States, the 1983 amendments to the Social Security Act, among other measures, stipulated a gradual increase in the age of entitlement to full public pension benefits from age 65 to age 66 by 2009, and to age 67 by 2027, and will gradually increase the reduction from full benefits for pensions drawn before this age. Germany followed this American example in its Pension Reform Act of 1992. Commencing in 2001, the age limits for all public pensions, such as pension after long-term unemployment at age 60 or 'flexible retirement' at age 63, will be gradually increased to age 65. For each year that a pension is drawn prior to this age, there will be a reduction in the benefit level.

In Japan, the first attempt to raise the retirement age from age 60 to age 65 has failed to pass parliament. The same has occurred in Sweden, where in 1992 the new Conservative government unsuccessfully tried to abolish the costly system of partial pensions. However in 1990, the state has closed off the disability programme for economic reasons, making it harder for unemployed workers to exit via this route. At the same time, there has been an expansion of private exit programmes, especially in the form of severance pay. This would suggest a substitution of public schemes by private arrangements for early exit, as has already taken place in the Netherlands during the 1980s when private VUT (pre-retirement) schemes more and more replaced public programmes, without altering the overall trend to early exit from the labour force.

These examples clearly show that in most countries, the state is aggressively seeking to reverse the trend to early retirement. From the state's perspective the changes in demography, due largely to declining fertility and increased life expectancy, have created a situation where the ratio of contributors to beneficiaries of pension schemes has declined perceptibly, putting pressure on the pay-as-you-go public social security system to raise contributions and lower benefits if it is to maintain fiscal viability. Seen from this perspective, raising the age of retirement and altering the incentives for older persons to work seem like the only available alternatives. The 'can't afford' arguments advanced by the state seem to point to a future characterized by the gradual reversal of the early retirement trends of older men by the reform of the social security system. But the review of labour market trends suggests that despite these reforms the trend to early exit continues, although the rate of decline in the retirement age has slowed down.

Our review of early exit in an international perspective suggests that in order to identify an effective scope for public policy action we need a new conceptualization of the link between patterns found in 'high and low early exit countries' and long-term employment trends of older workers. A useful point of departure is to reconceptualize the concept of 'pathways of early exit'.

Exit does not necessarily mean a dichotomous choice of working or not working. It is not only public and private social policy programmes which mark the period before definite retirement, but also the redefinition of work itself may be seen as an important component of the pathway of early exit. Thus early retirement becomes a process which begins not only with a direct and final exit from work, but by the gradual redefinition of work at the end of the working career. An extended concept of pathways needs to cover – at the least – the following three dimensions:

(1) A change in the nature of work itself which might take the form of lower wages, a reduction in normal working hours, alteration in work status, new job assignments, or any combination of the above.
(2) A change in the income package to include income from earnings combined with income from public and private pension schemes. The repackaging of income can act as an offset to the decline in earnings.
(3) The cooperation of firms in the redefinition of work and the repackaging of income. Of course, firms can pursue an antagonistic policy to that of the state, as in the case of the United States. In this situation the cost of redefining work and repackaging income falls on the individual worker and his family.

What are the implications of this reconceptualization of early exit pathways on the future of early retirement? We address this question by concretely exploring how this new approach affects the individual's view of retirement; the policy perspective of both the state and the firm; and the researcher trying to understand the retirement process.

We start with implications for research. This paper began with an argument about the need to disaggregate labour force participation rates by isolating the wage and salary workers. Our analysis of country patterns makes it evident that we need to further disaggregate the employment of wage and salary workers to include changes in hours worked, wage levels and total compensation, and especially in the combination of earned income and public and private pensions. If retirement is a gradual process, then it should be reflected in the various forms that comprise the organization of work. The research question becomes redefined as the changing nature of work at the end of the working career. Cross-sectional data are only of limited value in such an enquiry.

The implications for public policy are more difficult to pin down since a broader concept of pathways points to the importance of the intersection of social policy, labour markets and industrial relations. Perhaps early retirement has in the past been linked to the growth of productivity and societal decisions to distribute the benefits of growth in the form of a shorter working life. The lowering of the retirement age in Sweden from age 67 to 65 and the introduction of 'flexible' retirement in Germany at age 63 instead of 65 are examples of this trend. But since the mid-1970s the growth of early retirement has been much more closely intertwined with developments in labour markets and the growth of unemployment. Historically, the fields of labour markets and social policy have been treated independently both in scholarly work and in legislation, although early theorists, as noted in section 1, tried to show that social policy income is itself a component of wages. And it is to this tradition that we need to return if we are to make sense of the phenomenon of early retirement and how it can be reformed.

The experience of 'low early exit countries' seems to suggest that the key to the reorganization of work at the end of the working career implies lower wages for older workers. This is necessary in order to adjust for changes in the age-wage profile. To achieve this adjustment in a 'bloodless' way, it is necessary to combine public and private social protection to offset the wage decline. Such a formulation of the reorganization of work implies for many countries a change in conventionally accepted social norms. These norms may be the main constraint to policy change. But social norms within a country are changing. In this essay we have focused on different national patterns across countries, but often similar differences exist within countries. In Sweden and the United States only a significant minority of older men have partial pensions or bridging jobs which combine work and the receipt of public and private pension income. This means that a variety of patterns exist simultaneously within a country. The norms underlying these patterns are being reshaped by many factors, including the experience of those who retire early. And this points to the meaning of gradual retirement for the individual.

A redefined concept of early exit from the labour force which combines work and retirement as a simultaneous process has broad implications for the tri-partition of the life course of the individual as defined as preparation for work, the working career, and retirement from work. If changes in work itself define the beginning of retirement, and retirement benefits are increasingly combined with work, then the last stage of the life course is blurred. Such blurring involves a change of norms about how individuals organize meaningful lives. We know that a significant minority of individuals in the United States have a blurred life course. However, we know little about how they feel about this, especially when the blurring occurs in combination with early retirement. Perhaps individuals believe that they have a moral right to retire after a lifetime of work, reinforced by a sense of obligation to make room for the young in a tight labour market. Perhaps individuals take a different view. If they are in good health, and if the repackaged income from wages and pensions is adequate, then a fuzzy boundary separating work and retirement may be quite acceptable. Of course, much depends on what is happening in the economy. The situation in Japan with respect to this question is interesting. There has in the past been labour shortage, and in this situation the individual feels an obligation to continue working to fill the job vacancies needed by the economy. This argument assumes labour substitution, i.e., the old can substitute for the young where the scarcity of labour in some industries is serious. But in economies with high unemployment the overlap between work and retirement for the individual may have a different meaning.

In conclusion, we have tried to emphasize the peculiarity of national patterns and their dependence on public and private institutions. This approach differs from rationalistic economic models that explain labour force participation largely in terms of an individual work-leisure trade-off. Public policy has been guided by the rationalistic approach and has focused on individual incentives to retire. In our approach institutions play a critical role and the most important of these is the behaviour of firms and the relationship between the firm and the state. Understanding the future of early retirement depends on embracing such a broader framework.

NOTES

This paper is part of a larger comparative study of early retirement at the level of the firm directed by Frieder Naschold at the Wissenschaftszentrum in Berlin.

1 For a discussion of this debate see Rein and Rainwater (1987).
2 For a detailed analysis of the labour force participation of older men and women see Jacobs *et al.* (1991).
3 Using labour force data for the United States by single years of age and examining long-run trends since 1968, Quinn (1991) concludes 'that the trend toward earlier retirement may have stopped or perhaps even reversed. . . . for 8 of 10 ages (he tested) over age 61, participation rates are higher now than they were 5 years ago.' This finding may be related to the decline in private pension plan coverage, which for men decreased from 70 per cent in 1979 to 61 per cent in 1988. See Bloom and Freeman (1992).
4 The interpretation of the German data which show an increase in the rates of older men between 1985 and 1990 requires some caution because of demographic distortions in the age composition of the population of both age groups. For instance in 1990, mainly due to demographic effects of World War II, men aged 55 are relatively overrepresented in the age group 55–59, as are men aged 60 and 61 in the age group 60–64. Thus for both age groups, the reported increase in the labour force participation rates reflects, at least partly, demographic shifts rather than 'real' changes in labour force participation of older men. However, when looking at participation rates of single years of age instead of the 5-year-age groups, a slight increase can also be observed.
5 For details of the institutional mechanisms see the specific country reports in Kohli, Rein *et al.* (1991).
6 Own calculations based on unpublished data from EUROSTAT for 1983 and 1989 not reported here.
7 See for example Wise (1992).
8 For a discussion of the concept of early exit pathways and a description of the major pathways in the 'high early exit countries' see Kohli, Rein *et al.* (1991).
9 Correspondence with Takeshi Kimura, Professor of Public Finance at Yamagata University, 1991.

REFERENCES

Bloom, D. E. and R. B. Freeman (1992) 'The Fall in Private Pension Coverage in the United States', *American Economic Review* **82**, 539–45.
Jacobs, K., M. Kohli and M. Rein (1991) 'The Evolution of Early Exit: A Comparative Analysis of Labor Force Participation Patterns', in Kohli *et al.*, pp. 36–66.
Japan Productivity Center (1988). *Handbook of Labor Statistics.*
Kohli, M., M. Rein, A.-M. Guillemard and H. van Gunsteren (eds.) (1991) *Time for Retirement*, Cambridge, New York: Cambridge University Press.
Quinn, J. P. (1991) 'The Transition from Work to Retirement in the United States', mimeo.
Quinn, J. P., R. V. Burkhauser and D. A. Myers (1990) *Passing the Torch: The Influence of Economic Incentives on Work and Retirement*, Michigan: W.E. Upjohn Institute for Employment Research.
Rebick, M. E. (1990) 'After Lifetime Employment in Japan', paper prepared for the Japan Economic Seminar, Brookings Institute, Washington D.C., mimeo.
Rein, M. and L. Rainwater (1987) *The Public-Private Interplay in Social Protection: A Comparative Study*, Armonk, New York: M.E. Sharpe, Inc.

Ruhm, C. J. (1991) 'Bridge Employment and Retirement Transition', mimeo, University of North Carolina at Greensboro.
Wise, D. A. (1992) 'Firm Pension Policy and Early Retirement', in: A.B. Atkinson and M. Rein (eds.), *Work, Age and Social Security*, London: Macmillan.

Discussion

HEATHER JOSHI

The phenomenon of earlier retirement in industrial economies, documented in this chapter, may be one means to forestall ageing among the labour force, but it seems a perverse reaction to the ageing of the population. Longer life expectancy and relatively smaller cohorts of working age are now leading some governments, as the authors point out, to call for later retirement. Raising the age (or perhaps ages) at which pension contributors become pension recipients is seen as one way to ease the problems of paying for pensions. It certainly seems preferable to the 'solution' described by Prof Andorka in Hungary of allowing inflation to erode the value of pensions once awarded.

Retaining older workers, or drawing them back into employment has also been advocated as one source of labour to substitute for shortages of young workers. Before the current recession, the drop in labour force entrants anticipated for the 1990s in the UK was dubbed a 'Demographic Time Bomb' (NEDO, 1989). Note the irony that demographic changes often attract this image of a menace slowly ticking away, whether they refer to the prospects of population growth for Planet Earth or of its decline in industrial countries. As concerns the latter, are trends in early retirement worsening trouble or achieving adjustment?

The evidence in this chapter about the process of men's exit from employment over the recent past in a number of industrial countries is of variety around convergence. The question of why women's retirement is not covered arose in discussion as well as in the paper. As the authors rightly say, women's employment flows in this part of the life course merit a study of their own. The picture would be even more complex. One reason they give is that women, on the whole, are not employed in the 'core' labour market of secure employment contracts from which men's exit patterns are being traced. The experience of combining employment and other roles, which the authors detect is 'blurring the lifecourse' for a 'significant minority of individuals' (sic), has already been followed by more than a minority of women in most countries. Another reason for focusing on men's early retirement is that the pension costs per year of pension are likely to be significantly greater than women's.

The story about exit patterns is largely inferred from cross-sectional surveys, illuminated, in the US and Japanese cases, by longitudinal data. It was felt that it might have been possible to tell a little more about the experience of cohorts from the survey material, and that, at least in due course, there may be more evidence around on direct longitudinal experience of individual routes out of the labour force.

Participants at the workshop shared the authors' regret that internationally comparable longitudinal data is not available. As they acknowledge, such material could confirm how far the over-representation of the self-employed among men aged 60–64 is a result of a cohort effect, slower retirement from self-employment or movements from wage labour into self-employment as an exit route. There was also speculation that in some countries men might move (back) into agriculture in semi-retirement, but no-one at the meeting had any evidence either way.

Richer survey data could also help to fill in some other aspects of these not-quite-senior citizens' lifestyles. What is their state of health? What are their sources of income? Is health certification for invalidity benefits becoming less stringent? How is exit behaviour affected, for example, by other people in the household? An 'empty nest' may mean the need for income has dropped. The presence of someone requiring care may increase the need to stay at home. Another piece of the jig-saw puzzle is how far men in this age group are active in voluntary work, and whether those with or without paid work are more likely to be involved.

Another direction into which the paper could lead, is the issue of labour market structure – indeed Didier Blanchet's discussion of wages by seniority is just such a development. It is necessary to look back at conditions of employment contracts before age 55 as well as after it. It may be useful to think of the process described within a very stylized two-sector model of a segmented structure, 'core' and 'periphery', with permanent and temporary contracts respectively, the former being held by (some) men, the latter by women and other men, including those in 'bridging jobs' between a career in the core and complete inactivity and those working on their own account. The very inflexibility of employment obligations in the core has led to 'restructuring' – offering generous early retirement benefits to 'get rid of' older workers rather than, say, re-train or redeploy them. Perhaps if labour market structures continue to evolve towards more devolved and 'flexible' forms of organization (sometimes labelled 'post-Fordism') the tendency to generate 'exit is exit' forms of early retirement will weaken. The retirement process could become more diffuse, occurring at a range of ages and across a range of pathways.

The distinctive Swedish option of moving into part-time employment is, as explained, the result of institutional arrangements whereby a partial pension is provided and reductions of hours often arranged in existing jobs. Note that this provision has its counterpart in another piece of Swedish legislation which gives the parents of young children the right to hold jobs which were originally full-time at reduced hours. Otherwise it is unusual for hours to be downwardly flexible in 'core' jobs or for the combination of roles to be facilitated in core-type jobs.

An important feature of the age-range considered in this paper, 55–64, is that these are the ages where mortality rates begin to rise substantially. Most of those who die before they ever collect a pension do so over these ages. Furthermore the risk of premature death varies markedly with occupational class. The early retirement on health grounds of the least privileged workers with the lowest life expectancy seems a valuable, equitable, feature of the present, otherwise less defensible, 'system' of early retirement. If it does not prove possible to tighten up the health certification system (currently under discussion in the Netherlands, we were told), there may be a fairer solution in linking pension entitlement to years since entering the labour force, rather than age.

It is hard to predict whether early retirement trends should be expected to continue or to reverse. What can be concluded more safely is that, as discussed by Rein and Jacobs, they will become increasingly difficult to define. The prospects for greater flexibility seem more certain than those for greater fairness.

REFERENCE

NEDO (1989) *Defusing the Demographic Timebomb*, London: National Economic Development Office.

4 Ageing and the labour market in Poland and Eastern Europe

STANISLAWA GOLINOWSKA

1 Introduction

The process of ageing now taking place in the rich countries of Western and Northern Europe has not yet affected Central and Eastern Europe or the countries of the former Soviet Union, Hungary being the sole exception. This process is influenced by, on the one hand, a lower average number of children in families of each succeeding generation and, on the other hand, longer average life spans. In Hungary there is a degree of similarity with demographic trends in the post-industrial societies, but only in the area of birth rates.

In most of Central and Eastern Europe the trend towards lower fertility first emerged in the 1970s, which was a decade of rising consumer aspirations in the wake of improved GNP growth, although in Poland the decline in birth rates began somewhat later. It should be noted that in these former socialist countries the state pursued active pro-birth policies using the whole gamut of social policy instruments available for this purpose: extended maternity and child-rearing leave; child-rearing allowances; guaranteed jobs for mothers returning from child-rearing leave; an extensive network of state-sponsored child-care institutions – nurseries, kindergartens, day-care centres in schools; subsidies for young couples (in some of these countries contingent on having children); family allowances; and heavily subsidized prices of children's clothing, school books, toys and sports equipment.

High birth rates continuing over many years in Central and Eastern European countries and in the Soviet Union have in consequence resulted in rapidly growing productive-age populations. By the turn of the century these populations will start to age. The increase of older labour resources in the countries of Central and Eastern Europe after the year 2000 will be the highest in Europe. Will the transforming and modernizing economies of these countries have the capacity to employ the available labour

79

resources? The ageing of the labour force in Central and Eastern Europe is a major challenge, both for the countries directly involved and for Europe as a whole.

The next section of this paper contrasts the population projections for Central and Eastern Europe with those for Western Europe, and the following section examines further the demographic trends in Poland. Section 4 considers the interaction of demographic and economic developments in Poland since the 1970s, and the final section evaluates the implications for Polish economic and labour market policies of future population pressures.

2   The position of Central and Eastern Europe in the process of European demographic change

The UN (1991) population forecast for the years 1990–2010 points to three characteristic population trends in Central and Eastern Europe (excluding the former Soviet Union), which distinguish this region from other European countries. First, Central and Eastern Europe will have the highest growth of total population, around 7.1% (on the basis of medium variant projections). This is more than twice the growth rate for Europe as a whole (3.5%), and five times the rate for Western Europe (1.3%). In a number of West European countries such as Germany, Austria and Switzerland there will be an absolute decline in the size of the population over this twenty-year period.

Central and Eastern Europe will also experience the highest rate of growth of the productive-age population, which will grow by 9.1% (and in the territories of the former Soviet Union by 16.5%). In Western Europe, meanwhile, the productive-age population is projected to decline by 2%, and rise by a minimal 1% to 3% in Southern and Northern Europe. The declining trend in the size of the productive-age population in the EC countries will already be well-established by the mid-1990s.

Within these overall trends, clear differences can be seen for distinct age groups. If the productive age population is divided into a younger, more mobile group (ages 15 through 44) and an older, non-mobile group (ages 45 through 59 for women [pensionable age 60] and through 64 for men [pensionable age 65]), then the projections reported in Table 4.1 indicate that in Central and Eastern Europe the size of the younger age group will remain stable while in the twelve EC member states it will shrink by over 11%. For the older age group the increase in Eastern Europe (28.2%) is more marked than in Western Europe (25.2%). A particularly large increase in this older labour force will take place in countries of the former Soviet Union during the first decade of the next century. This

Table 4.1. *Growth of mobile (15–44) and non-mobile (45–59/64) working-age population in Western and Eastern Europe, 1990–2010*

Year	Europe total		EC		Eastern and Central		Poland		The countries of the former Soviet Union	
	mobile	non-mobile	mobile	non-mobile	mobile	non-mobile	mobile	non-mobile	mobile	non-mobile
2000 Population growth from 1990 (%)	– 2.2	10.7	– 3.5	8.7	1.7	15.4	2.8	24.7	7.6	4.2
2010 Population growth from 1990 (%)	– 8.3	25.2	– 11.4	23.5	0.7	28.2	1.7	49.1	8.7	35.4

Source: United Nations (1991).

reflects the time spread in peak 'baby booms' after the Second World War. The 'baby boom' in Eastern Europe was more pronounced and lasted longer (in Poland, for instance, until the mid-1950s) than in Western Europe. The population of 'baby boomers' will be responsible for a particularly rapid increase of older labour resources throughout Eastern Europe after the year 2000.

3   Poland's position in the process of European population change through the year 2010

In population terms Poland is a country with exceptionally intensive growth. The end of this trend is already in sight, but for the next twenty years the consequences of Poland's population growth will present a problem of economic and social policy both internally and for other European countries.

Poland's population represents some 7.7% of the European total and by the year 2010 its share will have grown to some 8.2%. This relative increase in Poland's share of the total European population will occur despite a reduction in the rate of national population growth. In 1990 the index of net population change amounted to 4.1 per thousand, compared with 9.6 per thousand as late as 1980. The main reason for the declining rate of net change in Poland's population is the reduction in the average number of children born per fertile-age woman, which in 1990 was 2.04 compared with 2.28 in 1980. This fall in the birth rate has led some demographic experts to sound warning bells about a long-term decline in the size of the Polish population (Holzer, 1991). It should be noted, however, that the Polish fertility rate is still among the highest in Europe; only Romania, Albania, Ireland and countries of the former Soviet Union have rates of similar magnitude. All these countries are marked by traditional social and economic structures due to their late start on industrialization and, in consequence, a delayed process of modernization.

The main demographic indicator that sets Poland apart from most other European countries is the increase in labour resources. The increase of these resources in Poland through the year 2010 is estimated at 3.5 million people, equivalent to 54% of the total increase in European labour resources, even though Poland's share in the total European productive-age population will come to only 8.2%. The characteristic trait of the structural dynamics of this growth is the high share of young people (in the 15–24 age bracket) in the first five years of the period analysed (until 1995). In the following years there will be an increase in older labour resources, to such an extent that in the first decade of the next century the increase in the older group (aged 45–59/64) in Poland will be among the highest in Europe.

Despite the decline in Poland's overall rate of population growth, the country will continue to have a relatively high share of children in its population structure. In this respect Poland will fall behind only Albania and Ireland. Children under 14 currently make up a quarter of the country's total population, and even though by the year 2010 they will represent no more than one-fifth of the total, the population age structure in Poland will continue to be more favourable than in other countries. As in Poland, a relatively young demographic structure is also characteristic of the countries of the former Soviet Union. In most other European countries, however, the share of children in total population will be below 20% and in several countries (Germany, Sweden and Switzerland) below 15%.

As a corollary of this young population age structure, Poland is and will continue to be one of the European countries with the lowest proportion of elderly people (above 60/65). This is a consequence not only of the positive element of high birth rates, but also the very negative position of Poland in statistics of average length of life. In Poland as well as in the other countries of Central and Eastern Europe, the average life span is over 5 years shorter than in the affluent countries of the West. The average life expectancy of a male infant in Poland in 1990 amounted to 66.5 years, while the corresponding life expectancy in Western Europe was around 72 years.

Male life expectancy in Poland has been falling since the mid-1960s, and this has been due mainly to a rise in the number of deaths from circulatory tract diseases and, more recently, because of a rise in deaths from accidents and toxins. Similar trends are now beginning to be seen in the female population. The average life span for females over 15 is shortening, and demographic specialists claim (Okolski, 1988) that the same increase in morbidity first noted for males in the mid-1960s had started to affect the female population by the mid-1980s.

The demographic structure of Poland has also been heavily affected by mass migration abroad which has continued for four centuries. Ever since the Second World War there has been a net loss of population through foreign migration, even though two large waves of Poles have resettled home from the Soviet Union in the second half of the 1940s and in the second half of the 1950s (see Table 4.2). During the 1980s there was a considerable increase in the number of people leaving the country for political, economic and family reasons. The large global diaspora of Poles (some 15 million people with Polish roots) is a major motivating factor for additional migration.

Table 4.2. *International migration from Poland during 1946–90 (in thousands)*

| | CSO data | | GCP data |
Time period	immigration	emigration*	emigration**
1946–50	4,499.9	2,543.6	—
1951–55	16.6	17.9	—
1956–60	261.1	359.5	—
1961–65	13.9	119.5	—
1966–70	10.4	104.3	—
1971–75	8.1	83.7	—
1976–80	8.1	142.0	—
1981	1.4	23.8	79.1
1982	0.9	32.1	27.3
1983	1.2	26.2	45.5
1984	1.6	17.4	41.4
1985	1.6	20.5	55.8
1986	1.9	29.0	67.4
1987	1.8	36.4	108.3
1988	2.1	36.3	228.0
1989	2.2	26.6	—
1990	2.6	18.4	—

Sources: Central Statistical Office (1991) and Government Commission on Population (1989).

Notes:
* CSO emigration data deal only with changes of domicile.
** GCP emigration data also include temporary movements to work.

Even with the removal of the political factor motivating people to migrate, another wave of migration to the West can be expected in the near future. The main motivations to leave the country will be the prolonged economic crisis at home and the explosive growth of unemployment. It is likely that, in contrast to the earlier waves, these will not be permanent migration, but rather temporary moves in search of work. The first target of this wave of emigrants will be Germany.

4   Ageing and the labour market in Poland

Demographic factors are far from being the only determinant of overall labour resources in Poland. Attempts over the last twenty years to stimulate industrial development through central planning and state-directed

Table 4.3. *Labour force participation rates in Poland by sex and age,*
1960–88

	Age				
	45–49	50–54	50–59	60–64	over 65
Total					
1960	81.1	79.4	74.8	64.0	42.3
1970	86.5	84.2	78.3	42.1	42.1
1978	85.2	78.8	68.6	25.4	25.4
1988	85.3	76.6	60.7	25.8	25.8
Men					
1960	96.2	94.9	91.7	59.7	59.7
1970	95.1	94.0	90.9	56.4	56.4
1978	92.1	87.1	81.5	36.2	36.2
1988	89.6	82.4	72.0	33.8	33.8
Women					
1960	68.4	65.7	60.5	31.7	31.7
1970	79.2	75.9	68.1	33.0	33.0
1978	78.5	71.6	57.9	19.4	19.4
1988	81.2	71.1	50.6	20.7	20.7
Changes in labour force participation rates (%)					
1978–88	+ 0.1	− 2.2	− 7.9	− 0.4	− 0.4
1970–88	− 1.2	− 7.6	− 17.6	− 16.3	− 16.3

Source: Own calculations on the basis of the CSO's general census data for 1960,
1970, 1978 and 1988.

resource allocation have also been of fundamental importance in determining the size of the work force and the performance of the labour
market. Seven key factors in the development of the Polish labour market
since 1970 can be identified.

First, until the end of the 1970s labour force participation was growing
steadily. During the 1970s the third stage of the industrialization plan was
implemented, and this resulted in a 20% increase in employment over the
level of the 1960s, which had also been a decade of very rapid job creation.
The industrialization plan was pursued in parallel with an extension of
social benefits; social security was extended to cover farmers and their
families, child-rearing leave was introduced for women with small children, expenditure on health care and education rose, and living conditions, especially the housing stock, were vastly improved.

However, by 1978 the economic boom had levelled off and a long-lasting

Table 4.4. *Educational structure of the Polish population aged 25–29 and over 60, 1960–88*

Education and age	1960	1970	1978	1988	Differences in percentage points 1988–1960
Higher					
25–59	2.8	4.2	6.8	9.2	+ 6.4
over 60	1.3	1.6	2.0	3.5	+ 2.2
Secondary					
25–59	10.8	14.2	22.2	29.6	+ 18.8
over 60	5.6	6.4	8.6	12.1	+ 6.5
Basic vocational					
25–59	3.8	8.8	16.9	27.6	+ 23.8
over 60	1.0	2.5	3.5	5.9	+ 4.9
Primary					
25–59	34.9	49.7	45.6	31.2	− 3.7
over 60	22.3	34.8	46.7	56.4	+ 34.0
Without basic education and primary school not completed					
25–59	47.7	23.1	8.1	2.4	+ 45.3
over 60	69.8	54.7	39.1	22.1	− 47.7
Total in age of:					
25–59	100.0	100.0	100.0	100.0	
over 60	100.0	100.0	100.0	100.0	

Sources: Level of education of Polish population, CSO (1991); Statistical data and Reports, General Census (1988).

depression set in. The rate of participation in the labour market declined; as Table 4.3 shows, by the end of the 1980s participation rates for men were lower than during the 1960s, even though work was made mandatory for productive-age males in 1982.

Second, the labour resources of the female population were tapped for the industrialization effort. The rate of growth in labour market participation by women was particularly high during the 1950s and 1960s. During the 1970s it declined more sharply than similar rates for men, particularly for the older age groups. At present the share of women participating in the labour market is declining steadily, even though it is still relatively high by West European standards.

Third, the industrialization process resulted in a sustained outflow of

Table 4.5. *Wage differences by age, sex and type of labour*

Age	Age group with the highest wage = 100	Wage differences by sex: women's wages where men's wages = 100	Intellectual type labour where wages in blue collar jobs = 100
19 and under	66.5	93.6	94.3
20–29	80.9	79.2	90.5
30–39	93.8	77.2	100.5
40–49	100.0	79.7	112.6
50–59	98.9	80.9	123.3
60 and over	98.0	83.2	143.3
Total	93.6	79.1	107.9

Source: From household surveys of CSO, in Work 1990; CSO *Statistical Year-book 1991*, Warsaw.

younger workers from agriculture, with the result that older workers have increasingly become concentrated in agriculture. Despite the national system of central planning, Polish agriculture has been firmly rooted in a system of private family farms which offer few opportunities to farmers to increase the size of their farm land. At present the typical Polish farmer is an owner of a small farm (about 7 hectares) and is well advanced in age.

Fourth, along with industrialization, a major effort was launched in Poland to upgrade the level of education and the stock of skills (Table 4.4). Educational structures were adjusted to meet the needs of the economy, resulting in a large increase in the number of people with basic vocational training qualifying them to hold skilled jobs. Simultaneously, extended secondary education became more common, so that nearly one-third of the entire adult population of Poland now holds secondary school graduation certificates.

Fifth, a characteristic trait of pay structures for people working in the state-owned sector has been the relatively small age-related differentials in pay compared with other variables, such as type of job (blue or white collar), gender and education (Table 4.5). Among blue-collar workers the highest average pay is still earned in the 40–49 age bracket, but older workers receive pay that is only slightly (2–3 percentage points) lower. By contrast, in white collar occupations the highest pay is earned by the oldest employees, those above 60, and the spread between these and the group of 20–29 year olds can amount to 40–45 percentage points. The pay of women is markedly lower than the pay of men, although the differences

Table 4.6. *Disabled people per 1,000 in various age groups*

	1978		1988	
Age	Total	Disabled from the III group*	Total	Disabled from the III group*
Total	71	21	99	36
below 20 years old	7	2	6	0
20–29	15	6	17	6
30–39	31	13	36	12
40–44	60	28	72	23
45–49	98	49	129	41
50–54	154	76	214	71
55–59	200	85	300	113
60–64	227	64	317	145
65–69	227	44	316	153
70–74	247	31	346	145
75–79	287	24	368	121
over 80	337	18	414	88

Note:
* The III group is persons who are partially able to work, in spite of recognised disability.

Source: Disabled People in Poland. *Statistical Data and Reports*, General Census (1988).

are less acute when the women are very young (under 20). During the last two years a growing pay differential has emerged between the state-owned and private sectors, although the small size of the private sector means that there has been little overall effect so far on national age-wage profiles.

Sixth, the process of accelerated national industrialization, given the relatively low standard of living, has resulted in many negative consequences for the health standard of the population. The increasing incidence of job-related accidents and occupational diseases has led to higher numbers of handicapped people and a reversal of the improving mortality trends evident until the mid-1960s. Data in Table 4.6 show that recorded disability rises with age, and has increased significantly over the decade since 1978. Among those over 50, one-third of the population has been certified as suffering from some disability. This results in withdrawal from active labour and the award of a disability pension. In Poland disability pensions represent approximately 35–37% of the cost of all

Table 4.7. *Structure of unemployment in Poland by age (%)*

Age	1991	1992
up to 24 years	35.1	33.2
25–34	29.9	30.6
35–44	24.6	25.3
45–54	8.6	9.1
55 years and over	1.8	1.8
Total	100.0	100.0

Source: Unemployment in Poland. Statistical information, CSO, Warsaw, 2nd quarter, 1992.

social security pensions. In the years 1989–91, the rate of disability rulings increased still further, and in 1991, the number of disability pensions was 10% higher than in 1988 (data from *Materialy Informacyjne ZUS* [*Information Bulletin of the Social Security Administration*], 1992).

Seventh, the period of unbroken economic growth associated with the successive stages of industrialization came to an end in Poland towards the close of the 1970s. The following decade was a time of prolonged political and economic crisis, with some slight improvement of economic growth trends in the years 1983–5. The transformation of the political and economic system in 1989 took place against a background of a long-standing economic crisis which developed into a deep recession. Mass unemployment for the general population was a consequence of these processes; in two years unemployment grew from zero to 12%. A characteristic trait of the unemployed population is the exceptionally high share in it of young people (Table 4.7). The older, immobile groups have been effective in averting the threat of unemployment, mainly by opting for early retirement schemes and by pressing for disability rulings (with corresponding disability pensions).

The possibility of early retirement was first offered by law in Poland in 1981, a year in which the output of the Polish economy suffered its first major decline since the Second World War. It was hoped that the economic reforms launched at that time would make redundant large numbers of superfluous employees from state enterprises, and early retirement was seen as the preferred means for addressing labour market problems. Nonetheless, disability pensions continued to serve as the main form of securing 'early retirement'. It was not until the 1989–91 period that the increase in regular early retirement pensions overtook the increase in the number of disability pensions. Early retirement became the

Table 4.8. *Main indicators of economic and social development in selected Eastern and Central European countries, 1989–91*

Indicators		Economic activity GDP at constant prices 1989 = 100	Unemployment rate (%) (registered)	Consumer price inflation (%)
Poland	1989	100.0	—	251.1
	1990	88.4	6.1	585.8
	1991	93.0	11.5	70.0
Hungary	1989	100.0	0.5	17.0
	1990	96.0	1.5	28.9
	1991	91.0	7.7	33.0
Czechoslovakia	1989	100.0	—	1.0
	1990	98.9	1.0	10.0
	1991	84.0	6.6	56.0
Romania	1989	100.0	—	—
	1990	92.6	—	100.0
	1991	87.0	3.0	294.9
Bulgaria	1989	100.0	—	5.6
	1990	90.9	1.5	23.8
	1991	83.3	12.0	380.0

Source: Employment Observatory, Central and Eastern Europe, *Employment Trends and Developments*, No. 29, (1992). Commission of the EC.

main instrument applied on a mass scale to ward off unemployment among employees with long work records. In consequence, the increase of retirement benefit payments in the last 2–3 years has been substantially higher than the increase in the cost of disability pensions.

Nonetheless, the economic crisis and price inflation, with its consequences for the level of real incomes, has led both disability pensioners and retired people to seek work without forfeiting their pension rights. Currently discussions are under way about a new regulation which would limit the possibility of earning extra income without suspension of pension rights. These discussions are fraught with emotion, and the proposed regulation has been referred to the Constitutional Tribunal on appeal.

In effect the population aged 45–59/64, which at the turn of the century will weigh so heavily on the character of Polish labour resources, shows a marked tendency to formal withdrawal from the labour force. This trend could be tempered by the introduction of more strict eligibility rules for social security pension benefits. Nevertheless, two objective facts, namely the high level of unemployment and the poor state of health of the Polish people, will be conducive to swelling the ranks of the social services' clientele, recruited from the occupationally immobile population groups.

5   Population pressures and labour market trends in Poland and Eastern Europe, 1990–2010

The main population problem to be faced by the countries of Eastern and Central Europe, and above all by Poland, in the next twenty years will be to find ways of absorbing the growing labour resources, of younger people through the year 2000, and of older people through the year 2010. The significant increase in the productive-age population coincides with the process, inaugurated two years ago, of economic restructuring along market-oriented lines, a process which has created an acute economic and employment crisis in all the countries of Eastern and Central Europe (Table 4.8). The Polish economy, in effect, faces the problem of absorbing some 1.7 million additional productive-age people on the one hand, and of reducing employment in the state sector by 2 to 4 million people, in keeping with the need for effective restructuring of that sector, on the other. In the context of demographic and social challenges it is possible to identify several areas of action which only with the greatest difficulty manage to gain recognition as economic policy priorities, but which are vital from the point of view of addressing the problems presented by the growth of labour resources.

Development of the private sector through formation of new businesses. Economic policy emphasizes the creation of a market economy more through privatizing state-owned enterprises than through the establishment of private firms. Privatization of state-owned enterprises results initially in negative consequences for employment, while the formation of private businesses generates new employment. Several studies devoted to private enterprise (Bednarski, 1991) indicate the continued existence of regulatory and psychological barriers which hamper private company development.

Selective development of the state sector in industry. Shortage of capital in Poland and a very modest level of foreign investment (on a much smaller scale than in Hungary and, until recently, in Czechoslovakia) offer little real chance for quick privatization of Polish industry. For many years to come, state-owned industry will continue to be the main provider of employment. Modernization and the efficiency of that industry will determine employment opportunities for the growing pool of Polish labour resources.

Educational expansion geared to labour market needs. Poland still lacks a non-school based system of vocational training, and the formal school system has only now started to prepare for reform. While the number of independently offered courses has grown immensely, these are addressed mainly to prospective business people and are available only in the large cities. There is a marked shortage of training initiatives in regions of high unemployment and those threatened by unemployment. Studies concerning the schooling and retraining of the unemployed and those in danger of redundancy point to inertia of local authorities and labour exchanges, but also to a shortage of funds which would make such initiatives possible. There is also a lack of interest on the part of those who should potentially be interested in retraining, though in recent months attitudes here have noticeably altered, in a positive direction (Janowska *et al.*, 1992).

Exercise of control over international migration by active labour market policies. The East to West migrations of people motivated by economic differences, differences in demographic dynamics and in social security standards leads to heavy social costs for the migrants and gives rise to new social problems in their countries of settlement. Poland, traditionally, has been a country from which people went abroad in search of a better life, but has now become a target country for mass economically-motivated migration by people from the countries of the former Soviet Union. They offer their labour cheaply, on terms very attractive to employers; as a rule they work illegally. They represent very serious competition for the Polish jobless. At the same time, Polish labourers travel for work to Western Europe, and ever more often this takes place under formal bilateral accords setting quotas for the number of Polish labourers legally accepted for employment in a given country (Marek, 1992). Such bilateral arrangements, although representing the first positive step in grappling with the problem of East to West labour migration, are not an approach capable of addressing the scale of the problem which has now developed in Eastern Europe. With continuing recessionary economic trends in Eastern Europe, the pressures to go abroad in search of better work opportunities will continue to mount, leading to mass-scale migrations from East to West. Countering such pressures, though with all due respect of the right of people to move freely, will be possible by policies leading to employment creation in countries from which the potential migrants originate. This calls for more than just the transfer of know-how to such regions. This will require additional capital injections, or at least checking the process of capital outflow. The post-socialist countries have considerable external debts; the need to service these presents a major obstacle to

using resources to invest for development. Development through investment in the regions which are potential sources of migrating labour
should be further supported by policies conducive to the development of
markets for the products originating from such regions. In particular, a
policy of free trade in Europe would give access to Western European
markets for Eastern European products (including farm produce).
Organization of social security pension schemes. Reforms of social security
systems in the post-socialist countries aim in the direction of replacing the
budget-linked systems with retirement insurance-based schemes. Discussions are also underway about organization of pension schemes based on
capitalizing the premiums paid, in contrast to the 'pay-as-you-go'
approach. Inflationary processes which have been severely affecting the
Polish economy for several years now, limit the opportunities for radically switching the pension system to a capitalized model. Still the
effective capacity of the present pension system to cope with the needs is
steadily weakening. This is due to employment deactivation of the people
caused by crisis trends in the economy, and also to changing forms of
ownership in the economy, since the amounts paid as social security dues
by the private sector in Poland are very low. The same is true also of the
private farmers. The demographic processes affecting Poland at the turn
of the century do not represent a threat to the retirement pension system
in the same way that an increasing pensioner population may threaten the
financial stability of the German or Italian pension system. On the
contrary, the largest population increases in Poland will be seen among
productive-age people. Threats to the pension system are presented by
economic processes and employment deactivation of the population.
Deactivation takes three forms: disability pension, unemployment or
early retirement. A third of the entire productive-age population of
Poland has been deactivated from employment in one of these three ways.
Many of these people are active in the unofficial economy: unregistered
trade, seasonal work in the private sector, unregistered household services, etc. This type of activity by productive-age people alleviates their
income problems, but exacerbates the problems of strained capacity of
the pension system (and also of the newly introduced personal income tax
system). In effect, the changes which are being made in the system of
social security boil down to applying more stringent rules of eligibility for
benefits, and reducing the value of benefits. The maximum amount of
possible pension benefits was capped in 1991 at 250% of the average pay.
The younger pensioners with higher skills, and hence receiving better pay,
have started returning to their jobs. A recent Central Statistical Office
study confirms the trend to the employment reactivation of 'young'
retirees (Witkowski, 1992). The constant change and adjustments in the

rules governing the pension system in Poland serve as expedient measures to alleviate any short-term problems which may emerge. However, the state of the Polish economy is the real key to a stable pension system. The economy has to regain its capacity to save, enabling it to create enough jobs for the growing labour resources with which Poland will be so amply endowed at the turn of the century.

6   Summary and conclusions

The late onset of the fertility decline in Central and Eastern Europe means that the working age population of these countries will continue to grow well into the second decade of the twenty-first century, while in Western Europe this labour resource will be shrinking. The labour market consequences of population ageing are, therefore, very different in East and West. The social security problems are also very different – whereas the proportion of pensioners in the population of Western Europe will rise from 17 per cent to almost 21 per cent between 1990 and 2010, in Eastern Europe the increase will be much more modest, from just under 14 per cent to just under 16 per cent. Since a shrinking workforce and the escalating cost of public pension schemes have been identified as the primary problems associated with population ageing in the West, at first glance it appears that ageing will have little adverse impact on the economies of Central and Eastern Europe.

This paper has shown that such an optimistic outlook is unwarranted. The interaction of demographic change and economic transformation in Central and Eastern Europe poses real labour market and public policy problems. The labour market problems are both quantitative and qualitative. The continued growth through the 1990s in the number of younger, more mobile workers at a time of high unemployment increases pressure for publicly-funded job creation at a time when governments are trying to scale down economic intervention and give greater rein to free-market forces. This pressure can create internal political problems or, if these younger workers choose to migrate, external political and labour management problems in the destination countries. Recent (August 1992) anti-immigrant riots in Germany have given an unpalatable foretaste of reactions to large-scale European labour migration.

Even if the challenge posed by the growing size of the labour force in the countries of Central and Eastern Europe, especially Poland, could be met, a second demographic circumstance has to be faced after the year 2000 – the rapid ageing of the workforce. Although the East European workforce will continue to grow in the first decade of the next century, almost all this growth will be of workers aged between their mid-40s and mid-60s.

Unless considerable efforts are made to improve and update the skills of these workers (which in many cases are already below those of their counterparts in Western Europe), the ageing workforce of the East will be unable to compete effectively in a more competitive and integrated European economy.

The most common means of dealing with a surplus of older workers in the past has been to offer pensions, either formally through giving easier access to early retirement arrangements, or informally, through disability pensions. These are both options for the future, but they necessarily involve large public transfer payments and increased taxes on those still in employment. Although politically attractive in the short run, more extensive early retirement arrangements run the risk of prematurely imposing on East European countries the problems of public pension financing now being faced in most of Western Europe.

REFERENCES

Bednarski, M. (1992) 'Hamulce rozwoju sektora prywatnego w Polsce' ('Restraints on Development of the Private Sector in Poland'), *Gospodarka Narodowa* No. 4, Warszawa.

Government Commission on Population (1991) *'Sytuacja demograficzna Polski. Raport Rzadowej Komisji Ludn osciowej'* (*Demographic Situation in Poland* [1991]. *Report of the Government Commission on Population*), Warszawa: CUP.

Holzer, J.Z. (1990) 'Perspektywy demograficzne Polski do roku 2030' (Demographic Predictions for Poland by 2030), *Monografie i Opracowania SGPiSS* No. 6/300, Warszawa.

Janowska, Z., J. Martini-Fiwek and Z. Goral (1992) 'Bezrobocie kobiet w Polsce' ('Unemployment Among Women in Poland'), *Polityka Ekonomiczna i Spoeczna*, Z. 18, Warszawa Fundacja im. Friedericha Eberta.

Marek, E. (1992) *Auswanderung aus Polen*, Warschau: Friedrich-Ebert-Stiftung, IPiSS.

Okolski, M. (1988) *Reprodukcja ludnosci a modernizacja spoleczenst wa. Polski syndrom* (*Reproduction of Population versus Modernization of the Society. Polish Syndrome*), Warszawa: KiW. Poland (1991).

United Nations FPA (1991) 'The Sex and Age Distributions of Population. The 1990 Revision of the United Nations Global Population Estimates and Projections', *UN Population Studies* No. 122, New York.

Witkowski, J. (1992) *Bezrobocie w swietle badania aktywnosci ekonomicznej ludnosci* (*Unemployment in the Light of Survey of Economic Activity of the Population*), Warszawa: GUS.

Discussion

WALTER KRÄMER

This is a mostly descriptive paper, with heavy emphasis on the data and their trends. Its main concerns are (i) a comparison of the actual and future growth of the labour force in Western and Eastern Europe, particularly in Poland and to a lesser extent (ii) the policy implications of any growth differentials.

As to (i), it is certainly of interest to learn that of the total increase of labour force in all of Europe through 2010, 54% will take place in one country (Poland) – a forecast which might very well come true. Other trends which are cited in the paper, for instance the UN population forecasts for the years 1990–2010, appear obsolete, however, in view of the fall of the iron curtain which took place after these projections were made. In particular, forecasts of total population for countries like Germany or Austria based on internal demographics are almost worthless nowadays in view of mass migration which dwarfs all other demographic developments.

Other data in the paper invite criticism as well. For instance, the disability figures in Table 4.6, and the marked increase in recorded disabilities from 1978 to 1988, might well be caused, not by an increase in disability as such, but by ever wider definition of the term (which is not given in the paper). It is quite striking, for instance, that the largest percentage increase in disability occurs for the age brackets 50–65 where the associated benefits – i.e. early retirement with disability pensions – are largest. In such matters of intertemporal comparisons of health and illness, much more caution should be exercised.

As to the policy implications of the population and labour force projections, the pessimistic outlook given in the summary section of the paper appears more based on personal sentiment than on an unbiased analysis of the facts. There is no reason for instance why the Polish labour market should not be able to absorb the projected inflow of younger workers, or why mass migration of labour should by necessity lead to anti-immigration riots in the receiver countries. As many societies have shown in the past (for instance Germany after World War II), much higher numbers of migrants can easily be integrated if only the institutional framework is right, and it is this latter problem – creating an environment that encourages competition and productivity – and not demographic change that seems to plague the Eastern European economies the most.

A final comment concerns the alleged 'reversal of the improving mortality trends evident until the mid-1960s'. Like the deteriorating health indicated by the disability figures in Table 4.6, this might well be a statistical artifact. It has long been known among demographers that period life tables do not provide optimal approximations for the true life expectancy of the cohorts alive in the respective period. The discrepancies are usually quite small, but can become large and seriously distorting after traumatic events such as a major war. A similar disappointing development of male life expectancy at birth was for instance also reported in Germany, where the reasons given in the paper – bad health and low standard of living – do not apply.

Like Poland, however, and also like the former Soviet Union, which likewise experienced a decline in male life expectancy during the 1960s (and therefore ceased publication of the figures), Germany lost high percentages of many male age cohorts in the war. To the extent that these losses were heavier among good risks (healthy young men drafted into service) than among bad risks (e.g. men not fit for service), empirical survival probabilities in subsequent decades will be biased downwards, and wrongly indicate a fall in cohort life expectancy (Dinkel, 1985). Or to put this differently: had all 20–30 year olds, say, who died in World War II, survived into the 1960s and contributed to period life tables then, there would probably have been no decline at all.

This is not to deny that bad health, alcoholism or environmental damage might lower the life expectancy of cohorts. This cannot be inferred from period life tables, however, which measure a quite different entity.

REFERENCE

Dinkel, R.H. (1985) 'The Seeming Paradox of Increasing Mortality in Highly Industrialized Nations: The Example of the Soviet Union', *Population Studies* **39**, 87–97.

5 The implications of cohort size for human capital investment

CHRISTOPHER J. FLINN

1 Introduction

As the labour force ages in many of the most highly industrialized countries of the world, it is natural to consider the effects of these shifts in the age distribution of the labour force on aggregate productivity and the intergenerational distribution of wealth. In this paper and a companion paper (Flinn, 1991), we attempt to more precisely characterize the manner in which the age distribution of an economy determines the level of investment in human capital and the wealth distribution. In Flinn (1991), our focus of interest was cohort-specific investment in formal schooling. In this paper, we turn our attention to the issue of investment in general human capital on the job.

There is a large, primarily theoretical literature on human capital investment on the job;[1] modern general statements of the theory and some empirical implications which follow from restricted versions of it can be found in Becker (1975) and Mincer (1974), for example. Human capital investment in our model will take place within an overlapping generations economy in which the process generating the cohort size sequence is unrestricted. Our focus on the effect of the cohort size sequence on human capital investment patterns was also the focus of Dooley and Gottschalk (1984), though our analysis is at the same time more ambitious in the sense of being cast in a partial equilibrium framework and less ambitious in the sense that our empirical analysis is extremely limited and makes no attempt to account for within (birth) cohort variance in human capital investment or earnings. Other examples of empirical and theoretical analysis of the effect of the cohort size sequence on human capital investment and earnings outcomes, often in non-equilibrium settings or in partial equilibrium models with tight restrictions on the cohort size process, are Berger (1983, 1984), Connelly (1986), Freeman (1979), van Imhoff (1989), Nothaft (1985), Tan and Ward (1985) Wachter and Kim

(1982), and Welch (1979). Perhaps the most ambitious attempt to date to perform empirical analysis of the cohort size-human capital investment relationship is to be found in Stapleton and Young (1984), in which Current Population Survey data are used on the schooling choices and earnings of large numbers of individuals to estimate a rational expectations model of educational choice (not on-the-job human capital investment). Their model makes heavy use of stationarity assumptions on the cohort size process and precludes human capital investment on the job.

The potential effects of the cohort size sequence on human capital investment and wealth are many. For example, changes in the number of individuals investing in the acquisition a particular skill can affect the incremental productivity of each individual possessing the skill; such direct production externalities are the focus of recent work in the area of economic development. Another example concerns the possibility of factor substitution; fluctuations in the size of the labour force may affect the development and usage rate of other factors of production, thereby indirectly affecting the return to human capital investment. In this paper, all these other factors are subsumed within an exogenous process which shifts the demand for human capital each period in a relatively unrestricted manner. The only effect of the cohort size process on the human capital investment process occurs through the intergenerational substitutability of human capital. Given the sequence of exogenous productivity shifters, the rental rate on human capital in each period will be a decreasing function of the amount of human capital in the economy in the particular period. Because members of different cohorts are assumed to be perfect substitutes in production, the rental rates on human capital a member of cohort t faces throughout his lifetime will be a function of the cohort sizes and investment choices of all cohorts alive at any point during this period. In this paper we provide necessary conditions for the existence of an unique equilibrium in rental rates and human capital investment levels under two very different informational assumptions. Besides characterizing the qualitative features of the equilibria derived, we use historical population and earnings data from the US in conjunction with the partial equilibrium models to quantitatively assess the impact of changes in the population process on investment and wealth levels of selected birth cohorts.

The plan of the paper is as follows. In section 2 we lay out the assumptions from which we build the perfect foresight equilibrium model and what we term the static expectations equilibrium model. We then present a brief discussion of the manner in which perturbations in the cohort size sequence affect cohort investment profiles and the intercohort wealth distribution in equilibrium. In section 3 we discuss the data and method used to determine the parameters of the equilibrium models and then present the parameter values. Section 4 contains some tabular and graphical depictions of the implications of the computed equilibrium models, as well as simulated investment and wealth outcomes for alternative cohort size sequences. A brief conclusion can be found in section 5.

2   Model structure and the characterization of equilibrium

In this section, we will examine two equilibrium models of the human capital investment process. The first model will be the focus of our attention, and is the only one of the two fully consistent with rational behaviour on the part of labour market participants. The second model is presented by way of contrast, and its empirical implications provide a useful benchmark with which to compare the empirical results from the perfect foresight equilibrium model. The section concludes with a discussion of the relationship between human capital investment, wealth, and cohort size in equilibrium.

2.1   Perfect foresight equilibrium

In the economy, there exists a sequence of m cohorts, $1 \leq m < \infty$, each of which contains members who live for $l + 1$ periods, where $1 \leq l < \infty$; thus the economy is in existence for a total of $m + l$ periods, where $2 \leq m + l < \infty$. Cohort members are assumed to be expected wealth maximizers. Within each period of his life, each population member is endowed with one unit of time. In the first period of his labour market life, a cohort member spends some portion of his time investing in on-the-job training. This training is completely general in the sense that its productive value is the same across all firms in the economy at any given point in time. As pointed out by Becker (1975) and others, the cost of such training will be paid by the worker and all the returns to the investment will accrue to him. Due to the wealth maximization hypothesis, each worker's stock of human capital will be inelastically supplied to the labour market in periods 2 through $l + 1$ of his life. The rest of his time endowment in the first period of his life is spent in the labour market.

It is undoubtedly somewhat restrictive to require all human capital investment to take place in the first period of labour market life. In defence of this assumption, we can appeal to the common theoretical prediction that investment will take place in the initial stages of labour market participation so that the returns to the investment will be realized over a longer horizon. While such predictions typically are produced within models in which economic environments are assumed constant (e.g., human capital rental rates are time-invariant) which is not the case in the framework utilized below, our empirical results suggest that a relatively small proportion of the individual's first period of life is spent investing in human capital for all cohorts present in our data. This result is largely attributable to our using a very long definition of a period (ten years); if we defined periods to be of shorter duration, the model would have to be generalized in a straightforward (but tedious) manner to allow for corner solutions within periods and intermittent investment activity.

All individuals are initially endowed with one unit of human capital. The amount of human capital they possess in the second through $l + 1^{st}$ periods of their life is only a function of the time spent investing in their first period of labour market participation. If an agent spends no time investing in the first period, he will continue to possess one unit of human capital for the remaining l periods of his life.[2] The maximum amount of human capital which can be produced by the agent for use after his first period of life is $\bar{h}$ ($< \infty$). Following the first period of life, there is no further depreciation of the human capital stock until death. The assumption that human capital in periods 2 through $l + 1$ belongs to the interval $[1, \bar{h}]$ is important in establishing uniqueness of the equilibrium rental rate sequence; it is not essential for proving existence. Since our main interest is in the empirical ramifications of full-rationality in the choice of investment level and the returns to human capital investment, the uniqueness property of the equilibrium described below is highly desirable.

In each period, there exists an inverse demand function for human capital. This function is essentially constant over time, except for an allowance for exogenous time-dependent multiplicative shifts.[3] These shifts are explicitly assumed *not* to be a function of the cohort size process. One rationalization for such an assumption could be that labour services are a non-mobile factor to indigenous firms producing for a world market. If each country has an independent cohort size process, then there may be no shifts in world-wide demand for the product; in this case the demand shifters may be thought of as reflecting productivity variability over time which is not related to the population size process. The constant portion of the inverse demand function will be assumed to be strictly decreasing over the positive real line. We now lay out the assumptions of the model in more specificity.

Assumption 1 The cohort size sequence $(n_1, \ldots, n_m)$ and the sequence of demand shifters $(\lambda_1, \ldots, \lambda_{m+l})$ are known by all members of all cohorts. The sequences will be denoted by the vectors $n \equiv (n_1, \ldots n_m)'$ and $\lambda = (\lambda_1, \ldots, \lambda_{m+l})'$, where $n \in \mathbb{R}^m_+$ and $\lambda \in \mathbb{R}^{m+l}_+$.

The perfect foresight assumption is crucial in establishing the existence and uniqueness of competitive equilibrium in the labour market in the method of proof used below. Given perfect certainty and the finiteness of life, we are able to prove uniqueness for *any* cohort size sequence, no matter what the nature of the process generating it. The very generality of this result may make it difficult to argue that the decision rules generated under a perfect foresight assumption are good approximations to those used by agents living in a world of uncertain future cohort sizes. The quality of such an approximation will often hinge on whether or not the future is sufficiently predictable with respect to the past. Obviously there will be a continuum of processes which could generate a legitimate cohort size sequence (from the point of view of establishing uniqueness) for which this will not be the case (e.g. those for which the expected value of certain functions of future values of the process with respect to its history are not even defined). The empirical results reported below were found not to be sensitive to whether the equilibrium computed was based on the perfect foresight assumption or on the assumption of a (particular) 'non-rational' expectational mechanism.

In terms of the assumption that the economy is of finite duration, it is made to simplify the handling of the end-point conditions. The finiteness of the economy may not actually necessitate its extinction in a literal sense; rather it may be taken to apply to a given production technology for which agents in cohorts 1 through m are trained. Say that a new technology for which the particular type of human capital investment modelled here is unproductive comes into existence in period $m + 1$ of the economy. Then cohort m is the last cohort which acquires training for the old production technology; beginning in period $m + 1$ and until the time of the next change of technologies all cohorts acquire the 'new' form of human capital.[4] There can then be an infinite succession of these finite economies, each defined by its unique production technology.

Assumption 2 Each agent in each cohort takes the human capital rental rate vector $r = (r_1, \ldots, r_{m+l})' \in \mathbb{R}_+^{m+l}$ as given when making his human capital investment decision.

Given the large size of a cohort, each agent's investment decision has an infinitesimal effect on the price of human capital over the agent's lifetime. Furthermore, workers are not able to collude effectively so as to withhold human capital from the market, thus increasing aggregate earnings.[5] The perfect foresight assumption regarding cohort sizes (A1) along with (A3–A5) below allow each member of each cohort to solve for the competitive equilibrium rental rates that they and all other population members will face.

Assumption 3 Each cohort member is endowed with one unit of human capital in his first period of labour market participation. There exists a human capital production function h which maps time spent investing during his first period of participation into his human capital stock when he is of labour market age $2, \ldots, l + 1$. This function has the following properties:

$$H: [0,1] \rightarrow [1, \bar{h}], \quad 1 < \bar{h} < \infty \tag{1}$$

h is continuously differentiable through the second order, with
$h'(s) > 0, h''(s) < 0, s \in [0, 1]$
and $\quad h'(0) = \infty$ and $h'(1) = 0$

Human capital stock in ages 2 through $l + 1$ is a concave function of the proportion of the first period of participation spent investing. The limiting conditions on the first partial derivatives of the human capital production function will ensure the existence of an interior solution to the human capital investment function for any cohort facing a future rental rate process which is bounded.

Assumption 4 Each member of cohort j has the following value of his human capital investment problem

$$V(r_j, \ldots, r_{j+l}) = \max_i E_{\mathcal{H}_j}\{r_j(1 - i) + Q_{j+1} h(i)\} \tag{2}$$

where $Q_{j+1} \equiv \beta r_{j+1} + \beta^2 r_{j+2} + \ldots + \beta^l r_{j+l}$
$\beta \in (0, 1]$

and $E_{\mathcal{H}_j}$ denotes the expectational mechanism used by members of cohort j given their common information set $\mathcal{H}_j$.

The objective of the agent is simply the maximization of the expected present value of income over his lifetime. All cohort size effects are reflected solely in the rental rate sequence he faces, which in general is determined by the cohort size and human capital investment decisions made by the members of all of the cohorts which will participate in the economy.[6] Under the perfect foresight assumption A1 and assuming rational expectations of the members of all cohorts, expected and *ex post* rental rates will coincide in (2).

Assumption 5 There exists an inverse demand function for human capital in period t which is of the form

$$r_t = \lambda(t) R(H_t), \quad t = 1, \ldots, m + l \tag{3}$$

where $\quad R: \mathbb{R}_+ \rightarrow \mathbb{R}_+$

R is first-order continuously differentiable with $R'(x) < 0$, $x \in \mathbb{R}_+$, and $\lim_{x \to 0} R'(x) = \infty$

H_t denotes the supply of human capital to the market in period t; and $\;\; < \lambda(1), \lambda(2), \ldots, \lambda(m + l) > \,\in \mathbb{R}_+^{m+l}$

With this basic set of assumptions, we are ready to analyse the perfect foresight model. First, we must characterize the decision rule utilized by all cohort members, which is a straightforward task. Under A1–A5, the optimal human capital investment of a member of cohort j is the solution to

$$0 = - r_j + Q_{j+1} h'(i_j^*) \tag{4}$$

$$\Rightarrow \quad i_j^* = i^*(r_j, Q_{j+1}) = g(r_j/Q_{j+1})$$
where $\;\; g \equiv (h')^{-1}$.

By A3, g has the following properties:

$$g: \mathbb{R}_+ \to [0, 1) \tag{5}$$

g is first-order continuously with $g'(x) < 0$, $x \in \mathbb{R}_+$

Now consider the determination of the equilibrium rental rate sequence. First, some formal definitions are required. Because human capital is inelastically supplied by all cohorts alive in period t other than the one born in period t (which supplies $(1 - g_t)n_t$ of human capital to the market), the total amount of human capital supplied in period t is $H_t = (1 - g_t)n_t + h_{t-1}n_{t-1} + \ldots + h_{t-l}n_{t-l}$, where $h_s n_s \equiv 0$ for $s < 1$. This quantity can be written in terms of the rental rate sequence as follows.

Definition 1 The total amount of human capital supplied to the market at time t is

$$H_t = \begin{cases} (1 - i^*(r_1, Q_2))n_1 \equiv \zeta_1((r_1, \ldots, r_{l+1})'), & t = 1 \\ \quad \vdots \\ (1 - i^*(r_l, Q_{l+1}))n_l + h(i^*(r_{l-1}, Q_l))n_{l-1} + \ldots \\ \qquad + h(i^*(r_1, Q_2))n_1 \equiv \zeta_l((r_1, \ldots, r_{2l})'), & t = l \\ (1 - i^*(r_t, Q_{t+1}))n_t + h(i^*(r_{t-1}, Q_t))n_{t-1} + \ldots \\ \qquad + h(i^*(r_{t-l}, Q_{t-l+1}))n_{t-l} \equiv \pi((r_{t-l}, \ldots, r_{t+l})'), & \\ \qquad\qquad\qquad\qquad\qquad\qquad t = l+1, \ldots, m & (6) \\ h(i^*(r_m, Q_{m+1}))n_m + h(i^*(r_{m-1}, Q_m))n_{m-1} + \ldots \\ \qquad + h(i^*(r_{m-l+1}, Q_{m-l+2}))n_{m-l+1} \equiv \chi_l((r_{m-l+1}, \ldots, r_{m+l})'), & \\ \qquad\qquad\qquad\qquad\qquad\qquad t = m+1 & \\ \quad \vdots \\ h(i^*(r_m, Q_{m+1}))n_m \equiv \chi_1((r_m, \ldots, r_{m+l})'), & t = m + l \end{cases}$$

The functions $\zeta_1, \ldots, \zeta_l, \pi, \chi_l \ldots, \chi_1$ are also functions of the cohort sizes $\{n_1\}, \ldots, \{n_1, \ldots, n_l\}, \{n_{l-l}, \ldots, n_l\}, \{n_{m-l+1}, \ldots, n_m\}, \ldots, \{n_m\}$, respectively, but we have omitted these arguments for notational simplicity.

Now, given the total amount of human capital supplied in period t, from A5 we have that

$$r_t = \lambda(t)R(H_t) \tag{7}$$

$$= \lambda(t) \times \begin{cases} R(\zeta_1((r_1, \ldots, r_{l+1})')), & t = 1 \\ \quad \vdots & \\ R(\zeta_l((r_1, \ldots, r_{2l})')), & t = l \\ R(\pi((r_{t-l}, \ldots, r_{t+l})')), & t = l+1, \ldots, m \\ R(\chi_l((r_{m-l+1}, \ldots, r_{m+l})')), & t = m+1 \\ \quad \vdots & \\ R(\chi_1((r_m, \ldots, r_{m+l})')), & t = m+l \end{cases}$$

Thus in equilibrium each period's rental rate on human capital is an implicit function of itself and the rental rates in l adjacent periods in either direction, or up to the beginning or ending date of the economy if either is within l periods of the reference date.

Definition 2 The operator $T(r)$, where $r = (r_1, r_2 \ldots r_{m+l})'$, is given by

$$T(r) = \begin{bmatrix} \lambda(1)R(\zeta_1((r_1, \ldots, r_{l+1})')), \\ \quad \vdots \\ \lambda(l)R(\zeta_l((r_1, \ldots, r_{2l})')), \\ \lambda(l+1)R(\pi((r_1, \ldots, r_{2l+1})')), \\ \quad \vdots \\ \lambda(m)R(\pi((r_{m-l}, \ldots, r_{m+l})')) \\ \lambda(m+1)R(\chi_l((r_{m-l+1}, \ldots, r_{m+l})')), \\ \quad \vdots \\ \lambda(m+l)R(\chi_1((r_m, \ldots, r_{m+l})')) \end{bmatrix} \tag{8}$$

The following theorem which states that this model possesses an unique perfect foresight equilibrium is proved in Flinn (1991).

Theorem 1 For every cohort size vector $n \in \mathbb{R}_+^m$ there exists an unique $r^* \in \mathbb{R}_+^{m+l}$ for which $r^* = T(r^*)$.

Given the lack of structure on the classes of cohort size and demand shifter sequences allowed, it is very difficult to derive comparative statics results for the model. We can however examine the local properties of the model given a functional form assumption on h and for particular realizations of the $\{n_t\}$ and $\{\lambda(t)\}$ sequences, and will do so in section 4.

2.2 Static expectations equilibrium

The perfect foresight assumption A1 is undoubtedly strong. A more realistic specification of the information set of cohort j might be $\mathcal{H}_j \subseteq \{r_1, \ldots, r_j, n_1, \ldots, n_j, \lambda(1), \ldots, \lambda(j)\}$. In addition, members of cohort j may well be uncertain as to the length of life of the market for human capital in which they are investing, which we have denoted by m. For these reasons, it may be of interest to explore the empirical implications of the relaxation of assumption A1.

Assumption 1' Each member of cohort j is uncertain as to future values of the sequences n, λ, and r at the time of his human capital investment decision.

In addition to A1', we will require an assumption about the manner in which expectations are formed. We will assume the following:

Assumption 4' The objective function of each member of cohort j is as is implied by (2), where the expectations operator is of the form

$$E_{\mathcal{H}_j}(r_k) = \kappa_j(\mathcal{H}_j) < \infty \quad \text{for all } k \geq j \tag{9}$$

While (9) restricts expectations of future rental rates to be constant no matter what the information set, it does not impose any restrictions on the value of the constant other than it be finite.[7]

Under A4', the solution to a member of cohort j's investment problem is given by

$$\begin{aligned}
0 &= -E_{\mathcal{H}_j}(r_j) + E_{\mathcal{H}_j}(Q_{j+1})h'(i_j^*) \tag{4'}\\
&= -\kappa_j(\mathcal{H}_j) + \kappa_j(\mathcal{H}_j)(\beta + \ldots + \beta')h'(i_j^*)\\
\Rightarrow \quad i_j^* &= g(1/(\beta + \ldots + \beta')) \forall j
\end{aligned}$$

The most significant features of the static expectations equilibrium are summarized in the following theorem.

Theorem 2 Under A1', A2, A3, A4', and A5, human capital investment by each cohort is a constant which is independent of the cohort size and demand shifter sequences, with $\hat{i} = g(1/(\beta + \ldots + \beta'))$. There exists an unique equilibrium rental rate sequence $(\hat{r}_t)$, where $\hat{r}_t = \lambda(t)R((1 - \hat{i})n_t + h(\hat{i})(n_{t-1} + \ldots + n_{t-l}))$ and where $n_s \equiv 0$ for $s < 1$.

This result follows immediately from (9). We claim this equilibrium is an interesting case for comparative purposes because of the lack of dependence of the human capital investment process on the cohort size sequence. Due to the absence of rational behaviour on the part of investors in the model, we do not pursue further analysis of its comparative statics properties.[8]

2.3 The relationship between cohort size, human capital investment and wealth in equilibrium

Within the perfect foresight equilibrium model (hereafter PFE), it is clear from inspection of the operator T specified in (8) that the rental rates, and therefore the human capital investment decisions, made in *all* periods are simultaneously determined. As in Flinn (1991), we will be interested in partitioning the effects of perturbations in the cohort size sequence into 'direct' and 'indirect' effects. The former are those changes in the cohort wealth distribution which are produced holding the human capital investment levels of all cohorts fixed, while the latter are those changes attributable to adjustments in the equilibrium human capital investment levels across the cohorts. In performing these exercises, in all cases we will be holding demand conditions constant, i.e., the $\{\lambda(t)\}$ sequence will be fixed.

We begin by defining the effect of an infinitesimal change in the size of one cohort $s \in \{1, \ldots, m\}$ on the lifetime welfare of cohort t, $t \in \{1, \ldots, m\}$. The lifetime welfare of cohort t is given by

$$
\begin{aligned}
U_t = {} & \lambda(t)R((1 - g_t)n_t + h_{t-1}n_{t-1} + \ldots + h_{t-l}n_{t-l})(1 - g_t) \quad (10) \\
& + \beta\lambda(t+1)R((1 - g_{t+1})n_{t+1} + h_t n_t + \ldots + h_{t-l+1}n_{t-l+1})h_t \\
& + \ldots \\
& + \beta^l\lambda(t+l)R((1 - g_{t+l})n_{t+l} + h_{t+l-1}n_{t+l-1} + \ldots + h_t n_t)h_t
\end{aligned}
$$

From (10), we immediately note that when the investment decisions of all cohorts are held fixed (i.e., the $\{g_t\}$ sequence and its one-to-one mapping $\{h_t\}$), direct effects on the welfare of cohort t members will only be observed if one of the cohort sizes in the subsequence $(n_{t-l}, \ldots, n_{t+l})$ changes. By contrast, changes in *any* of the cohort sizes $(n_1, \ldots, n_m)$ will generally have indirect effects on the welfare of cohort t members.

These 'effects' are reported in the form of elasticities evaluated at the computed model parameters and observed cohort size sequence. Consider the partial derivative of (10) with respect to the size of cohort s, or

$$
\frac{\partial U_t}{\partial n_s} = \frac{\partial U_t}{\partial n_s}\bigg|_{\{i_k^*\}} + \sum_{k=\max(1, t-l)}^{\min(m, t+l)} \frac{\partial U_t}{\partial i_k^*} \frac{\partial i_k^*}{\partial n_s} \quad (11)
$$

where all derivatives are partial in the sense that all cohort sizes except that of cohort s are held fixed; for the partial derivatives $\partial U_t/\partial i_k^*$, n_s is also held fixed. The first term on the right-hand side of (11) corresponds to the direct effect of the cohort size change, and the second term to the indirect effect of the change. To define elasticities, we multiply both sides of (11) by n_s/U_t. We also have computed elasticities to measure the responsiveness of human capital investment to changes in the cohort size measure; the elasticity of time spent investing in human capital by cohort k with respect to an infinitesimal increase in the size of cohort s is given by

$$\frac{\partial i_k^*}{\partial n_s} \frac{n_s}{i_k^*} \tag{12}$$

In section 4 we present some computed values of these elasticities for selected values of k and s under fixed functional form assumptions. Note that in the PFE, the equilibrium rental rates and investment levels are implicitly determined. To compute the elasticities in this case, we made use of numerical methods to compute approximate (partial) derivatives. Also note that from Theorem 2, the investment levels in the static expectations equilibrium (hereafter SEE) are independent of the cohort size sequence. It follows that in this model the indirect effects of perturbations in the cohort size sequence are identically zero for all values of s and t in (11).

3   Empirical analysis

We will be interested in using the PFE and SEE models to empirically attempt to account for changes in the human capital investment patterns and inter-cohort wealth distribution of white males in the US labour market from the 1920s through the 1990s. To fit the models described in Section 2, we utilize data on cohort sizes of white males in the US between the ages of 15 and 24, inclusive, in 1880, . . ., 2010, where projected cohort sizes are utilized for 2000 and 2010. The 'dependent variable' used to compute the parametric equilibria is the aggregate average wage rates of white males in the US manufacturing sector for the years 1925, . . ., 1985. The computed parameters are then used to calculate the elasticities discussed in the previous section and to perform some simulation exercises.

In computing the parametric equilibria,[9] we first must choose functional forms for $h(\cdot)$, the human capital production function, and $R(\cdot)$, the 'systematic' part of the inverse demand function for human capital, which ideally should be characterized by as few parameters as possible (since the number of data points available to us is so small) and which satisfy all relevant assumptions required in the proofs of Theorems 1 and 2. For purposes of comparison, we have utilized (essentially) the same functions for $h(\cdot)$ and $R(\cdot)$ as in Flinn (1991). For the endogenous portion of the inverse demand function we have simply used the inverse of the human capital stock, or

$$R(H_t) = H_t^{-1} \tag{13}$$

To determine h, we first select a function g which maps the positive real line into the unit interval, which is monotone decreasing, and which is everywhere differentiable. One class of functions which fits these requirements is that of survivor functions for continuously distributed random variables with support equal to $\mathbb{R}_+$. We have selected a survivor function for an exponentially-distributed random variable,

$$g(x) = \exp(-ax), \quad a > 0 \tag{14}$$

The human capital production function which generates g is found as follows:

$$i = g(x) = (h')^{-1} = \exp(-ax) \tag{15}$$

$$\Rightarrow \quad h'(i) = -\frac{1}{a} \ln(i) = x$$

Then

$$h(i) = -\frac{1}{a} \int_0^i \ln(y)\mathrm{d}y + h(0) \tag{16}$$

$$= -\frac{1}{a} i(\ln(i) - 1) + 1, \quad i \in [0, 1]$$

since $h(0) = 1$. For this choice of g, we see that the upper bound on the amount of human capital possessed by the member of any cohort when they are two periods of labour market age or older is $h(1) = a^{-1} + 1$.[10]

The $\{\lambda_t\}$ is determined in a different manner here than in Flinn (1991). We posit that the demand shifter sequence is a smooth function of a quadratic in the period number, or

$$\lambda(t) = \exp(\xi_0 + \xi_1 t/10 + \xi_2 t^2/100), \quad t = 1, \ldots, m + l. \tag{17}$$

This parameterized version of the model is characterized by the five-element vector $\vartheta \equiv (a, \beta, \xi_0, \xi_1, \xi_2)'$.

The data used in this exercise pertain to cohorts of white males residing in the US. For each of the years 1880, 1890, ..., 2010, we have ascertained the number of white males between 15 and 24 years of age (inclusive). For all years except 2000 and 2010 actual numbers were used; for these two years US government forecasts were employed. A detailed description of data sources and the manner in which the various series utilized in the model-fitting exercise were constructed can be found in the Appendix.

In terms of our model, we interpret a 'period' as lasting 10 years. Cohorts are defined in terms of groups of white males of the age 15–24 in the years 1880, 1890, ..., 2010. It is useful to think of the representative member of each of these cohorts as being of age 19.5 in the reference year. This representative cohort member's first period of labour market participation begins at age 19.5 and ends at age 29.5. During this period, the agent spends a proportion i of the ten years investing in general human capital. While working during this period, the agent has a human capital stock of 1 unit. In this exercise, we will assume that agents from all cohorts spend a total of four periods in the labour market (i.e., $l = 3$).[11] For each of the three periods in the labour market following his first, the agent's stock of human capital is $h(i)$.

To fit the model parameters, we utilize data on average wages for white males in manufacturing industries for the years 1925, ..., 1985, which occur approximately at the mid-point of each of our ten-year periods.[12] Since the 1920 decade constitutes the fifth period in our model, we denote these average wage levels by $w_5, \ldots, w_{11}$. Implied values of these wages from either the PFE or SSE model are given by:

$$\tilde{w}_t(\vartheta) = \tilde{r}_t(\vartheta) N_t^{-1} \left\{ \sum_{j=1}^{3} n_{t-j} h(\tilde{i}_{t-j}(\vartheta)) + n_t(1 - \tilde{i}_t(\vartheta)) \right\} \tag{18}$$

where the total population size in period t is given by

$$N_t = \sum_{j=0}^{3} n_{t-j}$$

$\tilde{i}_t(\vartheta))$ denotes the equilibrium human capital investment of cohort t given the cohort size sequence and given the vector of values of the parameters ϑ, and $\tilde{r}_t(\vartheta)$ makes explicit the dependence of the equilibrium rent rate at time t on the vector of parameters ϑ. The generic equilibrium quantities '$\tilde{x}$' should be replaced by 'x^*' when considering the PFE model and '$\hat{x}$' when considering the SEE model.

We determined ϑ by selecting that value which minimized the sum of squared errors, or

$$\vartheta = \min_{\vartheta} \sum_{s=5}^{11} (w_s - \tilde{w}_s(\vartheta))^2 \tag{19}$$

for the PFE and SEE models. Due to the notorious difficulty of obtaining well-behaved estimates of the discount factor in structural dynamic optimization models, we fixed a value of β from the outset. Using a real interest rate of 4.5% per year, the ten-year per period discount factor was set at 0.644. The dimensionality of ϑ was therefore reduced to four.

There are few attempts at estimating structural models of human capital accumulation in the literature (but see, e.g., Haley, 1973; Rosen, 1973; Heckman, 1976b). As discussed by all of these authors, determining conditions for global and local identification of structural parameters is a difficult task, even within the non-equilibrium contexts in which they work. The main reason for the existence of identification problems in on-the-job human capital investment models is the lack of observability of the 'true' dependent variable of the model, time spent investing. In the absence of information on investment levels, all properties of the parametric functions characterizing the model must be imputed from the time series on average wage levels. We can expect identification to be even more treacherous when working within a partial equilibrium context. In our model, while we could not show analytically that the human capital production function parameter a was *not* identified, at least for our sample realizations a was very poorly determined. As a consequence, we decided to essentially normalize a at the value 1. While this choice was completely arbitrary, it seemed to make little difference with respect to the computed elasticities which are the focus of the following section.

The computed and pre-set values of the parameters determined within the PFE model are given in Table 5.1, along with an indication of the fit of this model to these wage data. The values of the deterministic process of demand shifters implies that the maximum of the process occurs approximately in the year 2000. The assumptions of the model are that no human capital of the type acquired by labour market participants in 1992 will be acquired by individuals born after 2019 or before 1880. This is consistent with positive $\lambda(t)$ outside of our sample period (1880 through 2040) as long as the value of acquiring the different types of human capital exceeds the value of acquiring the current form. Alternatively, the $\{\lambda(t)\}$ process which has been computed can be viewed as a polynomial approximation to the true process over the period 1880–2040, implying that any out-of-sample extrapolation is invalid. The value of a implies that the maximum amount of human capital which can be acquired by any cohort member is two units (see (16)).

From Panel B of Table 5.1, we see that the PFE model fits the seven wage observations reasonably well, with the largest residuals corresponding to the period of the Great Depression and World War II. We decided not to estimate a higher-order polynomial approximation to the $\{\lambda(t)\}$ sequence to avoid 'over-fitting' the model and due to numerical problems in the determination of ξ parameters.

The identification problems discussed in the last few paragraphs set the stage for a discussion of the problem of empirically distinguishing between the PFE and SEE models. Given that the exogenous demand shifter sequence $\{\lambda(t)\}$ seems to be driving the model, it is not too surprising that starting from our final estimates of the PFE model the estimator of the SEE model converged to essentially the same point. For purposes of enhancing comparisons between the implications of the two

Table 5.1. *Computed model parameters and observed and implied values of wages, 1925–85*

Panel A		
Parameter	Definition	Value
a	Parameter in human capital production function	1.000
β	Discount factor [not estimated]	0.644
$\lambda(t)$	Period-specific demand shock $= \exp(\xi_0 + \xi_1 t/10 + \xi_2 t^2/100)$ where:	
	ξ_0	-2.700
	ξ_1	6.150
	ξ_2	-2.350

Panel B			
	Average wage†		
Period	Observed	Predicted	Difference
1925	0.28	0.287	-0.007
1935	0.28	0.356	-0.076
1945	0.48	0.429	0.051
1955	0.55	0.542	0.008
1965	0.67	0.633	0.037
1975	0.65	0.661	-0.011
1985	0.64	0.651	-0.011

Notes:
† Wages are weekly average wages of white males in 100's of 1925 dollars.

models for the inter-cohort wealth distribution, we decided to use the parameter values in Table 5.1 to compute elasticities and perform simulations within both models. It is probably the case that in order to empirically distinguish between the two models, it is necessary to have some investment data. When no investment data are available, tests which could potentially sharply distinguish between the two models would of necessity rely on unrealistically tight functional form restrictions.

4   Computed elasticities and simulation exercises

We now turn to a discussion of the wealth and investment elasticities which are computed using parameter values from Table 5.1 and the actual

Table 5.2. *Elasticity of human capital investment with respect to cohort size (perfect foresight equilibrium), 1920–70*

| Cohort size | Cohort on-the-job investment | | | | | |
	1920	1930	1940	1950	1960	1970
1920	− 0.069	0.123	0.184	0.363	0.016	0.018
1930	− 0.336	− 0.091	0.105	0.232	0.469	0.017
1940	− 0.191	− 0.139	− 0.110	0.120	0.267	0.485
1950	− 0.065	− 0.158	− 0.276	− 0.076	0.119	0.219
1960	− 0.008	− 0.071	− 0.166	− 0.336	− 0.052	0.133
1970	− 0.005	− 0.009	− 0.089	− 0.238	− 0.501	− 0.047

cohort size sequence for white males in the US. We have presented elasticities for cohorts born in 1920, . . ., 1970 because the equilibrium values determined for these cohorts are less likely to be sensitive to the arbitrary endpoint conditions which were imposed for purposes of computation.

Table 5.2 contain the PFE human capital investment elasticities. While none of the values in the table is large in terms of absolute magnitude, several interesting patterns are clear. The 'own cohort size' elasticities which lie along the diagonal of the matrix are all negative and small in magnitude. While being in a large cohort decreases the opportunity costs of investment in the first period of participation, it also reduces the expected return in the future. These effects appear to approximately offset one another. Some of the largest effects in absolute value are those associated with the size of cohorts born three periods earlier. For example, a one per cent increase in the size of the cohort entering the market in 1940 increases the investment time of the representative member of the 1970 cohort by 0.485 per cent. This effect is of course due to the decrease in the opportunity cost of human capital investment to the 1970s cohort engendered by the larger stock of human capital they face in their first period of labour market participation. Conversely, increases in the size of future cohorts decrease investment levels as shown by the negative elasticity values in the lower diagonal of Table 5.2. The size of the previous cohort in general has the largest depressive effect on investment levels. Obviously, this effect operates through the reduction in the return to investment due to the larger stocks of human capital to be faced in the future.

In terms of the SEE model, all investment elasticities are zero, as has been pointed out above. Given our parameter values, in the SEE all

Table 5.3. *Elasticity of cohort wealth with respect to cohort size (perfect foresight equilibrium), 1920–70*

Cohort size	Cohort wealth					
	1920	1930	1940	1950	1960	1970
1920	− 0.231	− 0.198	− 0.141	− 0.078	− 0.011	− 0.007
1930	− 0.187	− 0.253	− 0.225	− 0.171	− 0.098	− 0.012
1940	− 0.108	− 0.184	− 0.251	− 0.232	− 0.178	− 0.103
1950	− 0.037	− 0.087	− 0.145	− 0.196	− 0.183	− 0.139
1960	− 0.004	− 0.040	− 0.089	− 0.146	− 0.206	− 0.190
1970	− 0.003	− 0.005	− 0.049	− 0.105	− 0.180	− 0.270

cohorts invest $0.470 = \exp(-1/(0.644 + 0.644^2 + 0.644^3))$ of their first period of participation acquiring human capital, and therefore possess $1.825 \ [= -0.470(ln(0.470) - 1) + 1]$ units of human capital in their remaining periods of participation. Fluctuations in the aggregate stock of human capital over time are purely attributable to the cohort size sequence itself within the SEE.

Table 5.3 presents the 'total wealth elasticities in the PFE, which correspond to the left-hand side of (11) after multiplication by n_s/U_t. A change in the size of any cohort for which the elasticities were computed decreases the welfare of any other cohort, including (especially) its own. It is interesting to note that the largest magnitude is associated with the own-size elasticity for the 1970 cohort, the members of which were born at the beginning of the 'baby boom'. The magnitudes of the elasticities tend to decrease in a systematic way as we move away from the diagonal. The effects of an increase in the size of a cohort born j periods in the future are generally less strong than are the effects of an increase in the size of a cohort born j periods earlier. These elasticities are neither huge nor are they negligible, and they conform more or less to those found by Welch (1979) using very different methods and data.

In Table 5.4 we present the 'direct effect' elasticities in the PFE model; recall that these measures the effect of cohort size increases holding constant human capital investment levels. The striking feature of this table is its similarity to Table 5.3, thereby implying the significance of indirect effects of cohort size changes on the inter-cohort distribution of wealth which operate via changes in investment levels. In fact, none of the indirect effect elasticities is larger than 2 per cent in absolute value.

Given the small magnitudes of the indirect effects in the PFE model, and given that the same parameter values are used in computing elasticities in

Table 5.4. *Elasticity of cohort wealth with respect to cohort size, holding human capital investment constant (perfect foresight equilibrium), 1920–70*

| Cohort size | Cohort wealth | | | | | |
	1920	1930	1940	1950	1960	1970
1920	− 0.252	− 0.221	− 0.111	− 0.031	− 0.001	0.000
1930	− 0.194	− 0.263	− 0.152	− 0.053	− 0.010	0.000
1940	− 0.102	− 0.159	− 0.205	− 0.100	− 0.037	− 0.029
1950	− 0.047	− 0.091	− 0.164	− 0.195	− 0.089	− 0.082
1960	− 0.002	− 0.046	− 0.160	− 0.235	− 0.242	− 0.238
1970	0.000	− 0.001	− 0.135	− 0.236	− 0.258	− 0.270

the PFE and SEE models, it is perhaps not surprising that the total wealth elasticities computed for the two models are very similar. Table 5.5 contains the wealth elasticities computed using the SEE model. Within the SEE model, own cohort size effects are slightly more pronounced than within the PFE model. In terms of off-diagonal elements, it appears that cohort size effects for those cohorts born closer in time to the reference cohort are larger in magnitude in the SEE model, while more distant cohorts have relatively stronger effects on welfare in the PFE model. These differences, for the most part slight, indicate that radically different assumptions on the information sets of agents and expectation mechanisms used are of little consequence empirically in behavioural models in which identification is so fragile. On the positive side, the imputed elasticities are not sensitive to arbitrary or 'unrealistic' assumptions concerning the forecasting and computing abilities of labour market participants.

We now turn to a consideration of the implications for investment and wealth of a discrete shift in the *entire* cohort size sequence rather than an infinitesimal change in the size of a particular cohort. In performing these simulations, we have utilized the parameter values in Table 5.1. In particular, we have always conditioned on the sequence $\{\lambda(t)\}$. While our analysis has proceeded under the assumption that this sequence is exogenous, radical shifts in the cohort size sequence are not in fact likely to leave this sequence constant under any reasonable interpretation of what drives it. Without delving further into the origins of the demand shifter sequence, we have decided to leave it untouched in what follows.

We have computed optimal investment levels and the inter-cohort distribution of wealth under three assumptions on the cohort size sequence, all

Table 5.5. *Elasticity of cohort wealth with respect to cohort size (static expectations equilibrium), 1920–70*

Cohort size	Cohort wealth					
	1920	1930	1940	1950	1960	1970
1920	− 0.256	− 0.215	− 0.138	− 0.050	0.000	0.000
1930	− 0.203	− 0.281	− 0.247	− 0.169	− 0.065	0.000
1940	− 0.107	− 0.202	− 0.283	− 0.259	− 0.183	− 0.072
1950	− 0.024	− 0.086	− 0.161	− 0.224	− 0.209	− 0.145
1960	0.000	− 0.026	− 0.089	− 0.165	− 0.232	− 0.217
1970	0.000	0.000	− 0.033	− 0.106	− 0.200	− 0.294

of which hold the total number of agents in the labour market over its period of existence fixed. They are (1) the actual cohort size sequence; (2) a constant cohort size sequence (i.e., $n_s = 1.059 \, \forall s$); and (3) a sequence which is the mirror image of that which is observed.

In Figure 5.1, we have plotted the amount of time spent in human capital acquisition by the members of all cohorts under the three cohort size sequences. Not much should be made of the investment decisions of the cohorts born close to the beginning or end of the market because of the dominant effects of the arbitrary endpoint conditions. We see that throughout the duration of the labour market, the human capital investment levels of cohorts in (3) are much higher than those in (1), which is to be expected given increased value of human capital investment due to the smaller human capital stocks individuals in (3) faced in comparison to individuals in (1). Cohorts in (2) by and large make investments intermediate between those in (1) and (3). Also note that the human capital investment of cohort members are decreasing over the period 1930 through 1970 for (1), (2), and (3). This is primarily due to the behaviour of the $\{\lambda(t)\}$ process.

It is interesting to note that the implied human capital investment levels under the actual cohort size sequence lie between 0.12 and 0.24 except for the cohorts born near the beginning and end of the labour market. Since periods last ten years, this implies that between 1.2 and 2.4 years are spent in human capital investment on the job. Heckman (1976b) reports estimates from a life-cycle model of human capital investment and labour supply decisions under several different assumptions regarding the human capital production function. His total imputed time investments in human capital over the life cycle are quite similar to ours (assuming that a work year is comprised of about 2,000 hours), though the intertemporal distribution of investment is slightly different.[13]

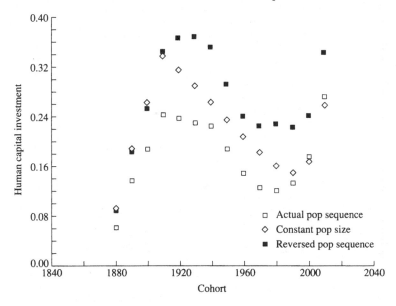

Figure 5.1 Cohort size and human capital investment

The inter-cohort wealth distribution is plotted in Figure 5.2 for the PFE model. Because of the rapid increase in the $\{\lambda(t)\}$ process over most of the life of the labour market, the wealth sequence is increasing over time within (1), (2) and (3). Under (1), the actual cohort size sequence, the wealth of white males entering the labour market in 1880 was less than 1/3 of the wealth level of white males entering the labour market in 2010. Wealth is slightly declining for baby boomers, whose members were mainly entering the labour market in the 1970 and 1980 cohorts. One measure of the 'price' baby boomers paid is to compare their wealth levels with those which would have been realized under optimal investment policies and the computed demand conditions if they would have faced (2). Their wealth was about 20–30% less under (1) than under the constant population size regime (2), and of course was far less than if they had belonged to an unusually small cohort (3) rather than an unusually large one.

Figure 5.3 contains inter-cohort wealth distributions determined within the SEE model. As is to be expected, when cohort members are making suboptimal investment decisions with respect to those made by their counterparts living in the PFE, average welfare levels are reduced.[14] The general pattern of the inter-cohort wealth distribution is approximately the same in the two models.

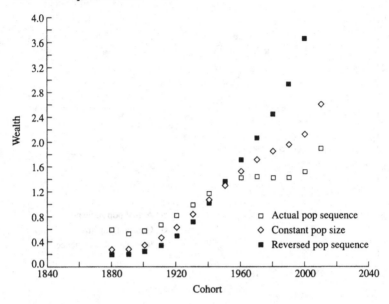

Figure 5.2 Cohort size and wealth (perfect foresight equilibrium)

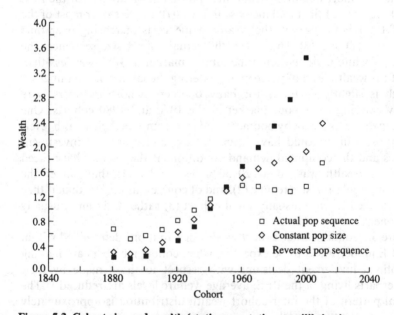

Figure 5.3 Cohort size and wealth (static expectations equilibrium)

5   Conclusions

In this paper we have investigated the effects of changes in the size of cohorts entering the labour market on the pattern of investment in human capital and the inter-cohort distribution of wealth. Using two different definitions of equilibrium in the labour market and a number of functional form assumptions regarding the human capital production technology and the inverse demand function for human capital, we found that while investment levels were somewhat sensitive to changes in the cohort size sequence, the inter-cohort wealth distribution was mainly explained by an 'exogenous' sequence of demand shifters and by the 'direct effects' of fluctuations in the total amount of human capital in the market which were computed at fixed human capital investment levels. We feel that we have estimated a lower bound on the contribution of fluctuations in human capital investment on wealth because the sequence of demand shifters should not properly be considered exogenous. Our current research in this area seeks to edge this partial equilibrium model closer to a general equilibrium one by including physical capital. This will serve to diminish the role of the $\{\lambda(t)\}$ sequence in driving the empirical results and introduce other potentially measurable variables into the analysis (such as capital investment levels or stocks), thereby enhancing the identifiability of structural parameters.

Appendix: Data sources and construction

Population Size: The number of white males between the ages of 5 and 14 inclusive was ascertained for each of the years 1880, 1890, . . ., 1990. The source for the cohort sizes from 1880 through 1970 is *Historical Statistics of the United States, Colonial Times to 1970* (Series A119–A134). The figure for 1980 is from the *Statistical Abstract of the U.S., 1991* (No. 22). The 1990 cohort size was obtained from the US Department of Commerce's CENDATA data base. Projected cohort sizes for 2000 and 2010 are the 'middle' values appearing in *Current Population Report*, Series P–25, No. 1018, Table 4. The value for the cohort size sequence (expressed in tens of millions of individuals) is [0.5239, 0.6321, 0.7382, 0.8292, 0.9834, 1.1077, 1.0004, 1.0860, 1.5659, 1.7667, 1.4092, 1.445, 1.5172, 1.3916].

Wages: All figures are taken from the *Statistical Abstract of the United States* for various years, and refer to the average weekly wages of white males in manufacturing industries at the midpoint of each of our periods, i.e., 1925, 1935, . . ., 1975. The relevant editions and tables are *S.A. 1930*, No. 368 (for 1925), *S.A. 1940*, No. 386 (for 1935), *S.A. 1970*, No. 342 (for

1945 and 1955), and *S.A. 1980*, No. 700 (for 1965 and 1975). The figures were expressed in terms of 1925 dollars and were divided by 100, yielding the sequence [0.28, 0.28, 0.48, 0.55, 0.67, 0.65].

NOTES

This research was partially supported by the National Institute of Child Health and Human Development grant R01–HD28409 and by the C.V. Starr Center for Applied Economics at New York University. I am grateful to Ken Burdett and Klaus F. Zimmermann for helpful discussions and comments. Francis Gupta provided excellent research assistance. All errors and omissions are my responsibility.

1 A nice survey of this literature and some of the main results to be found within it is contained in Weiss (1986). Good examples of the models frequently employed in investigating life cycle patterns of human capital investment are Ben-Porath (1967), Blinder and Weiss (1976), Heckman (1976a), Rosen (1973), and Ryder *et al.* (1976). In many of these models, the objective of the agent is taken to be the maximization of expected discounted sum [or integral] of a time-separable lifetime welfare function, where the arguments of the agent's contemporaneous utility function include consumption of a good purchased in the market and leisure. We abstract from all labour supply considerations in what follows, and assume our agents are expected wealth maximizers.

2 This assumption can be relaxed easily to allow for standard forms of multiplicative depreciation or appreciation of human capital over the lifetime at the cost of the introduction of an additional parameter and further notational complexity.

3 An interesting extension of the model would be to explicitly incorporate vintage effects – so that the quantity or quality of human capital acquired by workers depends partially on their investment effort and partially on the date at which it is acquired. Allowance for effects such as this would probably necessitate dropping the perfect substitutability assumption.

4 It must also be the case that all cohorts stay with the production technology for which they were originally trained throughout their lifetimes (i.e. retraining costs are prohibitive) to support this interpretation of the assumption.

5 Ignoring this externality will produce some divergence between the human capital investment levels in this equilibrium and the solution to the social planner's problem in which wealth maximization is the objective.

6 Or at least all cohorts which will participate in the phase of an infinitely-lived economy characterized by the current production technology, under the interpretation of the finite duration assumption given following A1.

7 Note that (9) covers the cases in which r_j is known to cohort j at the time of their investment decision and when it is not. When r_j is known at the time of the investment decision, (9) implies that this cohort expects this rental rate to persist over the following l periods.

8 It may be possible to 'rationalize' static expectations by restricting the information sets of agents in particular ways, but it is not obvious what form the restrictions should take.

9 We cannot entertain the possibility of nonparametric estimation of the h and R functions given the small number of data points available.

10 We would have preferred to have been able to index the human capital production function by the formal schooling level of the representative member of each cohort so as to [very imperfectly] take into account the effect of large increases in formal schooling levels observed over the period 1880–2010 on human capital quality. Unfortunately, data on completed schooling levels by cohort are not available prior to 1920 so that we could not pursue this idea. To some extent, changes in the quality of human capital not accounted for solely by on-the-job investment will be empirically captured by the $\{\lambda(t)\}$ sequence. This sequence may also pick up changes in the labour market [partially] exogenous to the behaviour of white males which affect their decisions [e.g., the increased number of female participants in the last half of the twentieth century].

11 While life expectancy for white males has increased over the last 110 years, life expectancy conditional on survival to age 10 may not have changed quite so markedly over this period for white males. According to official statistics (National Center for Health Statistics, 1988), in 1900 a ten-year-old white male could expect to survive an additional 50.6 years, while in 1988 the corresponding figure was 63.2, a difference of 12.6 years. (By contrast, life expectancy for white males born in 1900 and 1988 was 48.2 and 72.3, a difference of 24.1 years.) Although it would be possible to prove Theorems 1 and 2 under the weaker condition that cohort lifetimes $l + 1$ were cohort-specific (with each cohort-specific l greater than or equal to 1), we believe the differences in life expectancy are not sufficiently great to warrant such an extension for purposes of conducting this exercise.

12 To the extent that manufacturing wages are differentially representative of the earnings of average cohort members across cohorts (due to shifts in the industrial composition of the labour force), the model is certainly misspecified. This source of econometric misspecification highlights the limitation of our one-sector view of the economy.

13 See especially Figures 4 and 7 in Heckman (1976b).

14 While average welfare measures are reduced, this does not imply that the welfare of *all* cohorts is smaller in the SEE than in the PFE. Any given cohort's optimization errors may be more than offset by those of other cohorts and result in a net increase in its welfare level.

REFERENCES

Becker, G. (1975) *Human Capital: A Theoretical and Empirical Analysis, with Special Reference to Education* (Second Edition), Chicago: University of Chicago Press (for NBER).

Ben-Porath, Y. (1967) 'The Production of Human Capital and the Life Cycle of Earnings', *Journal of Political Economy* **75**, 352–65.

Berger, M. (1983) 'Changes in Labor Force Composition and Male Earnings: A Production Approach', *Journal of Human Resources* **17**, 177–96.

(1984) 'Cohort Size and the Earnings Growth of Young Workers', *Industrial Labor Relations Review* **37**, 582–91.

Blinder, A. and Y. Weiss (1976) 'Human Capital and Labor Supply: A Synthesis', *Journal of Political Economy* **84**, 449–72.

Connelly, R. (1986) 'A Framework for Analyzing the Impact of Cohort Size on Education and Labor Earnings', *Journal of Human Resources* **21**, 543–62.

Dooley, M. and Gottschalk, P. (1984) 'Earnings Inequality among Males in the United States: Trends and the Effect of Labor Force Growth', *Journal of Political Economy* **92**, 59–89.

Flinn, C. (1991), 'Cohort Size and Schooling Choice', C.V. Starr Center Working Paper, New York University. Forthcoming in *Journal of Population Economics* (1992).

Freeman, R. (1979) 'The Effect of Demographic Factors on Age-Earnings Profiles', *Journal of Human Resources* **14**, 289–318.

Haley, W. (1973) 'Human Capital: The Choice Between Investment and Income', *American Economic Review* **63**, 929–44.

Heckman, J. (1976a), 'A Life Cycle Model of Earnings, Learning, and Consumption', *Journal of Political Economy* **84**, 511–44.

(1976b) 'Estimates of a Human Capital Production Function Embedded in a Life-Cycle Model of Labor Supply', in N. Terlekyj (ed.), *Household Production and Consumption*, New York: NBER.

van Imhoff, E. (1989) *Optimal Economic Growth and Non-Stable Population*, Berlin: Springer-Verlag.

Mincer, J. (1974) *Schooling, Experience, and Earnings*, New York: NBER.

Nothaft, F. (1985) 'The Effect of Cohort Size on Human Capital Investments and Earnings Growth', Working Paper No. 42, Board of Governors of the Federal Reserve Board, Washington DC.

Rosen, S. (1973) 'Income Generating Function and Capital Accumulation', Discussion Paper No. 306, Harvard Institute of Economic Research.

Ryder, H., F. Stafford and P. Stephan (1976) 'Labor, Leisure, and Training over the Life Cycle', *International Economic Review* **17**, 651–74.

Stapleton, D. and D. Young (1984) 'The Effects of Demographic Change on the Distribution of Wages, 1967–1990', *Journal of Human Resources* **19**, 175–201.

Tan, H. and M. Ward (1985) 'Forecasting the Wages of Young Men: The Effects of Cohort Size', Rand Corporation Report R–3115–ARMY, Los Angeles CA.

US Bureau of the Census (1990), *Current Population Report Series P–25* [No. 1018]. Washington DC: US Government Printing Office.

(Various years), *Statistical Abstract of the United States*, Washington DC: US Government Printing Office.

(1975), *Historical Statistics of the United States, Colonial Times to 1970; Bicentennial Edition, Part I*, Washington DC: US Government Printing Office.

US National Center for Health Statistics (1988), *Vital Statistics of the United States (1988), Volume 2 (Mortality)*, Washington DC: US Government Printing Office.

Wachter, M. and C. Kim (1982) 'Time Series Changes in Youth Joblessness', in R. Freeman and D. Wise (eds.), *The Youth Labor Market Problem*, Chicago: University of Chicago Press (for NBER).

Weiss, Y. (1986) 'The Determinants of Life Cycle Earnings: A Survey', in O. Ashenfelter and R. Layard (eds.), *The Handbook of Labor Economics*, Amsterdam: North-Holland.

Welch, F. (1979) 'Effects of Cohort Size on Earnings: The Baby Boom Babies Financial Bust', *Journal of Political Economy* **87**, S65–97.

Discussion

KENNETH BURDETT

Chris Flinn's study is useful in that it stimulates the reader to think again about the human capital investment decision. Since the pioneering and innovative contributions of Mincer (1974) and Becker (1964), there had been precious few theoretical innovations in this area. The literature on this topic has been dominated by empirical work that has focused on the decision problem and not on the resulting equilibrium problem. To illustrate, being informed the rate of return on higher education is (say) 10 per cent, what conclusions should the reader draw from an equilibrium point of view; especially if this return is different from other assets? Suppose, for example, the rate of return is greater than the return on other physical assets. Will this lead to an increase in human capital accumulation that will lower the future return to education?

The Flinn study presents a framework in which many interesting questions about human capital accumulation can be posed and answered within the context of a market equilibrium. The particular focus in the Flinn study is on the relationship between the numbers born in each future period and the amount of human capital purchased by each generation. To illustrate, suppose n indicates both the number who are born and number who die in each period. Each generation is endowed with the same amount of human capital but can purchase more of it in the first period of their lives (but only in this period). Given the demand function for human capital remains constant through time, it can be shown (with a few added technical restrictions) that there exists an equilibrium where each generation purchases the same amount of human capital and the rate of return on human capital is a constant. At this equilibrium the rate of return in each future period is correctly forecast by individuals. Suppose now the numbers born in some period t is halved. At the new equilibrium (given one exists) will individuals born in any particular period t purchase more or less education? It is questions such as this that Flinn addresses. In my comments I shall concentrate on demonstrating how fruitful this framework can be. The careful, if somewhat heroic, empirical work provided by Flinn I will mainly ignore – due mainly to my ignorance.

To illustrate the framework considered by Flinn a special stripped-down version is presented to highlight the issues under consideration. As will be apparent, no attempt is made at realism.

The basic idea is simple. At the start of any period t, n_t individuals are born. Each member of this generation must immediately decide how much human capital to purchase. Once this decision has been made it cannot be changed in the future. These individuals then work for two periods, $t + 1$ and $t + 2$. Some further detail is now provided.

Each individual is born with one unit of human capital. However, at cost $h(x)$, x units of human capital can be purchased, where $h(\cdot)$ is a strictly increasing convex function of x. The individual then supplies $z = x + 1$ units of human capital per period until he or she leaves the market. The objective of each individual is to maximize expected discounted lifetime income.

Given this objective function the human capital investment choice made will clearly depend on what an individual knows when making his or her education choice and what is exected to be the case. Assume any individual born in t knows (a) z_{t-1}: the current human capital of all born in $t - 1$, and (b) n_t and n_{t-1}: the numbers born in periods t and $t - 1$ respectively. Using this knowledge, an individual born in period t can calculate the supply of human capital in period $t + 1$, H_{t+1}, as $H_{t+1} = z_{t-1}n_{t+1} + (x + 1)n_t$, where x is the amount of human capital purchased by those born in period t. To an individual born in period t the total supply of human capital in period $t + 2$ cannot be known with certainty as the numbers born in period $t + 1$ as well as the amount of human capital they will purchase is not known. Let $H^e_{t+2} = (x + 1)n_t + z^e_{t+1}n^e_{t+1}$ denote the expected total supply of human capital in period $t + 2$.

Keeping things as simple as possible, assume the demand function for human capital is a constant each period. Hence, the rental rate of human capital in any period t depends on the total supply of human capital in period t and the number of participating workers. Let $r(H)$ indicate the rental rate of human capital in a period given the total supply is H. Assume $r'(H) > 0$ and $\lim_{H \to 0} r'(H) = \infty$.

The amount of human capital purchased by an individual born in period t will depend on the number born in period $t + 1$ as well as the amount of human capital they purchase. Hence, an individual's decision to purchase human capital in period t depends indirectly on the number born at each period in the future as well as the amount of human capital they purchase.

To get round this modeling difficulty Flinn assumes the world ends at the end of some period T in the future. He then demonstrates that a perfect foresight equilibrium in the framework considered (which is more general than the one presented here) exists given a few technical restrictions are imposed. Although the proof of this claim is not provided, the basic nature of it is fairly obvious.

It should be noted that Flinn's claim is very general as it imposes few restrictions on the underlying process that generates the numbers born in each generation. Although I have not checked the details, it is reasonable to conjecture the restriction that there exists a final period T can be dropped. By assuming instead the number born each period birth is driven by some stationary stochastic process it may be possible to establish the existence of a rational expectations equilibrium.

Given the existence of a unique equilibrium, the consequences of a change in any of the market parameters can be considered. In particular, Flinn considers the changes induced by a change in the number born in a particular future period. In future work I would like to see more structure placed on the birth process. For example, suppose the numbers born in each period is a constant. In such a framework it should be possible to answer the many interesting questions. For example, what are the equilibrium consequences of a decrease in those born in every period after some period? What are the equilibrium consequences of an increase in the longevity of individuals? What are the equilibrium consequences of a systematic demand shock?

In all the framework developed by Flinn should provide a more than useful basis in which to supply answers to important questions relating to the economics of education. I look forward to it.

REFERENCES

Becker, G. (1964) *Human Capital: A Theoretical and Empirical Analysis*, New York: Columbia University Press for the National Bureau of Economic Research.

Mincer, J. (1974) *Schooling, Experience, and Earnings*, New York: Columbia University Press for the National Bureau of Economic Research.

6 Does an ageing labour force call for large adjustments in training or wage policies?

DIDIER BLANCHET

Population ageing is often viewed as a source of major economic problems after the turn of the next century, calling for strong policy responses if we wish to avoid growing disequilibrium in a large number of fields (Clark *et al.*, 1978; Bös and von Weizsäcker, 1989). In fact, close inspection of predictable effects of population change shows that they are not uniformly important. At one extreme, there is little doubt that it will be hard to maintain current performances of pension systems with age structures like those expected for the next century: large adaptations will be necessary either in the relative level of pensions, in contribution rates by workers, or in retirement age. On the other hand, the impact of ageing on a wide range of economic phenomenona is surprisingly low. This is for instance the case with consumption patterns, even for goods and services whose demand is strongly related to age at the individual level (e.g. health expenditures).

This paper will try to examine where labour force problems fall between these two extreme situations, between high or almost nonexistent sensitivity to ageing. We shall do so by considering two basic aspects of labour force problems and labour force management:

● The age-productivity relationship and the question of optimal human capital accumulation and on-the-job training in an ageing population. We shall first examine how changing age distributions may affect average productivity, relying both on simulations and simple analytical relations. This impact will appear to be rather weak and its sign may be positive or negative. This does not exclude that changes in the age-productivity profiles could be profitable in an ageing population: we shall examine how educational policies could be used for that purpose (section 1).
● The relationship of wages to age. This relationship is only a problem in so far as wage growth and productivity growth over the life cycle are

126

disconnected. In particular, if wages grow faster than productivity over the life cycle, global ageing may now have a significant relative impact on economic variables such as the profit rate (section 2). Yet this potentially high impact can be avoided by slight reductions in the steepness of career profiles.

This will finally lead us to a few considerations concerning changes in the retirement age (section 3). Such changes are often considered from the point of view of pension systems; we shall approach them from the point of view of labour force management, recalling that some discrepancies may appear between the two points of view. Specifically, if there exists an excess growth of wages over individual life-cycles and if this excess growth cannot be reduced, employers may react to global ageing by relying more heavily on early retirement, a policy which would clearly worsen the pension problems which are expected after the turn of the century.

All these topics will be examined by using a series of small heuristic models or crude simulations, putting more emphasis on demographic accounting than on sophisticated economic modelling: the general idea is to exhibit qualitative results and rough orders of magnitude rather than proposing detailed projections whose precision, given the long-term perspective and all related uncertainties, would be largely illusory. Each aspect of the problem will be also dealt with separately: the ultimate goal would be to construct a comprehensive model of optimal labour force management, simultaneously giving the optimal levels or age profiles for wages, training, and entry to or exit from the labour force. This model would then be used to show how these various policy instruments should be coherently fine-tuned to adjust efficiently to population ageing, but such a general model, of course, remains currently out of reach.

1   Ageing, productivity and optimal accumulation of human capital over the life cycle

1.1   Partial effects of population ageing on average productivity

Assume a given age-profile of productivity. This profile can be applied to any projected age structure of the labour force to derive figures for the average productivity per worker during the next century. The limits of such an exercise are obvious, but it provides the inescapable point of departure for our discussion.

Figures 6.1(a) and (b) give average productivities per worker depending on future fertility levels projected for the French population, with TFR (total fertility rate) ranging from 1.5 children per woman to 2.4. Some

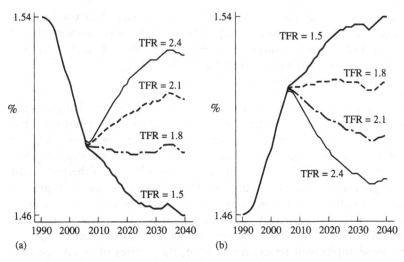

Figure 6.1 Average productivity projections; (a) average productivity with individual productivity declining from 2 to 1 between ages 20 and 60; (b) average productivity with individual productivity increasing from 1 to 2 between ages 20 and 60

very crude economic assumptions have been retained: working people are all people between ages 20 and 60, and two opposite scenarios have been chosen for the relationship of productivity to age. In Figure 6.1(a), individual productivity $\pi(a)$ at age a is assumed to decline linearly from 2 to 1 between ages 20 and 60; for Figure 6.1(b), it is conversely assumed to rise linearly from 1 to 2.

As could be expected, these two scenarios lead to images which are exactly symmetrical: productivity declines over time in the first case, and increases in the second. Given that we are not sure in which exact way productivity changes with age (its most likely profile is in fact hill-shaped – Chesnais, 1978), there is an ambiguity concerning the sign of the relationship between ageing and average productivity.[1] This is the reason why we proposed our two opposite scenarios. But the important point is that, whatever the sign of the effect, its absolute importance is indeed very moderate, despite the fact that the two scenarios are strongly biased against or in favour of ageing. Long-run differences between the four very contrasted fertility scenarios only imply changes of less than 10% between average productivity levels: there are variations which would not be at all negligible over the short run, but given that changes are expected to occur over a very long time span, they will be easily overwhelmed by all other potential sources of productivity growth.

This relatively negative outcome may look surprising for a reader who is not accustomed to the simple arithmetic of age structures and average values. But the surprise comes from an *a priori* confusion between *individual* and *collective* ageing: it is one thing to observe productivity problems for ageing workers, but this is not sufficient to prove the plausible changes in the *proportion* of old workers will turn this individual problem into a significant macroeconomic one. To make sure of this, one additional proof is available, using a simple analytical result we will use systematically throughout this text. We know that, for any age-dependant variable $x(a)$, if we call $\bar{x}$ the average value of x over an age group $[a,\beta]$, then long-run changes of $\bar{x}$ for a change dn of the population growth rate can be written:

$$\frac{d\bar{x}}{\bar{x}} = (A - A_x)dn \tag{1}$$

where A is the mean age in the entire age-group and A_x the same age after weighting by $x(a)$.[2] Here A is roughly 40 years, and for $x(a) = \pi(a)$ defined as for Figures 6.1(a) or (b), A_π is around 42 or 38 years, respectively. Shifting n from $+0.5\%$ per year to -0.5% per year only results in $\pm 2\%$ for $\bar{\pi}$. This is actually the kind of estimate provided by the more complete simulations of Figures 6.1 (a) and (b).

A general formula such as expression (1) has the further advantage of allowing a series of straightforward applications. Consider for instance another problem, the problem of productivity *growth* rather than level. We can try to evaluate the impact of age structure on the rate of innovation. Assume (an extra assumption), that all good new ideas occur to workers between ages of 20 and 40, so that $A_x \approx 30$. In that case, the impact of n shifting from 0.5% to -0.5% is a decrease of the rate of innovation by one-tenth, a minor effect as compared to the supposedly crucial effects of ageing on innovative capacity.[3] In fact, the repetition of such computations will systematically lead to the same conclusion. This can be seen once for all by computing an absolute upper bound to the effect given by equation (1). If we limit labour force participation to ages $[a,\beta]$, A_x is bounded by a and β and $A - A_x$ is bounded, in absolute value, by $(\beta - a)/2$, that is half the length of the working-life span, i.e. a value comprised between 20 and 25. In other words a change of the population growth rate by 1 percentage point cannot have an aggregate impact of more than 20–25% on any age-dependent phenomenon. And this is an upper limit obtained under very extreme assumptions (concentration of the phenomenon at either of both ends of working life). Actual impacts will always be much smaller.

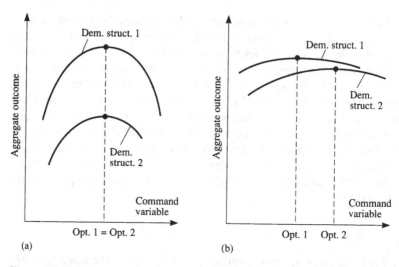

Figure 6.2 Two patterns of relationship between an aggregate variable, demographic structure, and a policy instrument

1.2   Ageing, productivity and optimal training policies

As far as the direct link between age and productivity is concerned, it seems, therefore, that internal ageing of the labour force is not a major problem. Despite this result, it is often argued that ageing of the labour force will call for a significant effort to increase productivity at later ages (Clark *et al.*, 1978). As productivity is not, by itself, a control variable, this means changes in variables influencing productivity, human capital being one of these. Since human capital is accumulated through education or on-the-job training, we shall therefore ask what could be optimal adjustment of educational policies as a response to changes in the demographic structure.

One parenthesis may be necessary here: the fact that changes in age-structure do not result in large changes in aggregate or average productivity does not necessarily imply that large changes in productivity management over the life cycle are not useful. Figures 6.2(a) and (b) give, for instance, two polar situations in terms of dependency between a given aggregate variable on the one side, and demographic structure and a given policy instrument on the other: in the case of Figure 6.2(a), shifting from demographic structure 1 to demographic structure 2 implies large changes of the aggregate outcome, but does not change the optimal value of the control variable.[4] In Figure 6.2(b), conversely, we only have minor changes of the aggregate variable from one demographic structure to the next, but demographic change induces a large shift for the optimal value of the control variable. Of course, the pattern displayed in this figure also means that failure to implement the new optimal policy in the new demographic context will not result in considerable welfare losses. It remains, however, that a natural tendency should exist toward this policy adjustment.

To see whether education or training correspond to this latter situation, we can introduce changing age structures in a model transposing, at the aggregate level, the classical problem of optimal human capital formation by individuals (see the survey in Weiss, 1986). Assume that productivity at age a is a function f of the human capital stock $k(a)$ at this age. Let us rule out any distinction between basic education and on-the-job training: both activities are time-consuming, $t(a)$ being the amount of time devoted to them at age a, with $t(a)$ constrained between 0 and 1. The evolution of human capital with age can therefore be described by the differential equation:

$$\dot{k}(a) = - \delta k(a) + g(t(a)) \tag{2}$$

with the initial condition $k(0) = 0$, δ being a rate of depreciation,[5] and $g(t)$ a production function for human capital assumed to be the same at all ages (ability to learn does not decrease at later ages).

Let us assume, at last, that all time which is not devoted to training is devoted to work, until retirement age β which is exogenously given. If $s(a)$ is the survivorship function at age a and n the population growth rate, the optimal policy for the control variable $t(a)$ may be considered as the one which maximizes output, i.e.:

$$\max_{t(a)} \int_0^\beta e^{-na} s(a)(1 - t(a)) f(k(a)) da \tag{3}$$

subject to (2). The solution to this optimal control programme is given in Appendix A2. Figures 6.3(a) and (b) give the results of three simulations both in terms of $t(a)$ and $k(a)$ under three scenarios:

- a reference scenario with $f(K) = k$, $g(t) = \sqrt{t}$, $\beta = 60$ years, $n = 0$, $\delta = 1\%$, and $s(a) = 1$ until retirement age.
- a scenario of population decline, with the same parameters as the reference scenario except a negative rate of population change of -1%.
- a scenario of delayed retirement age: n is kept to the level of 0, but it is assumed that, in order to restore equilibrium for pension systems, the retirement age is increased to 65 years.

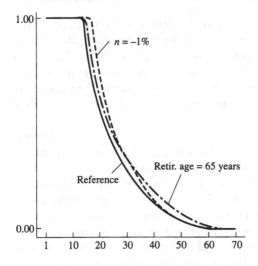

Figure 6.3(a) Optimal profiles of education and on-the-job training for three demographic scenarios

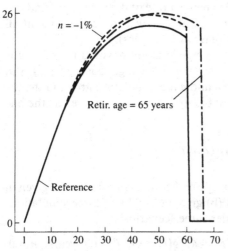

Figure 6.3(b) Optimal stock of human capital by age for three demographic scenarios

The results are coherent with those obtained, through a much deeper analysis, by Van Imhoff (1989). Ageing of the population resulting from lower population growth makes more attractive a relative increase in schooling and on-the-job training. This mainly takes the form of a longer stay in the educational system before entry to the labour market (the age

Table 6.1. *Optimal levels of training and production according to three demographic scenarios*

Demographic scenario	Time spent on training (years)	Total prod. over the life cycle (cohort index)	Average productivity (period index)
Reference	25.42	759.80	12.88
Pop. decline ($n = -1\%$)	27.75	755.95	14.46
Inc. retirement age ($\beta = 65$)	27.48	876.53	13.70

at first entry is raised by about 4 years, which is not a marginal change). This can be explained by cost considerations. Schooling is more costly from a collective point of view in an economy where young age groups are relatively important. This collective cost is reduced when population grows more slowly or even decreases, so that lengthening the initial phase of capital accumulation is possible. This argument is nothing else than a purely Malthusian one. The point is not that population decline creates economic *losses* which we try to *compensate* through larger training efforts. The point is rather that population decline *allows* more intensive training which will result in higher human capital and productivity of workers. In this respect, population decline is a positive factor rather than a problem for the productivity of the labour force. This is illustrated by Table 6.1, which gives the number of years spent in education or training and production per capita under the three scenarios: total time spent in training rises by about two years between the stationary and the declining population, so that 2 years are 'lost' for production. But total production over his life-cycle by an individual hardly changes, thanks to his higher productivity when working, and the average productivity, taking the age structure into account, is greater because, with this model, productivity is globally increasing with age.

Figure 6.3 and the third row of Table 6.1 show how the optimal time profile of education should be changed if we chose to solve pension problems by a higher retirement age. This form of ageing also leads to increased training, by a total amount which is once again equal to two years, but instead of occurring in the early years of existence, the pattern of additional training is tilted toward later ages. There is now a strong benefit in terms of total production over the life-cycle, because we cumulate the effects of higher productivity with the fact that people definitely leave the labour force later. This second effect disappears with the index of *average* productivity given on the last column, but average output remains nevertheless higher than in the reference scenario.

As a whole, it is clear that optimal management of education and training in an ageing labour force may require some changes which are not marginal: we are nearer to the situation in Figure 6.2(b) than to that in Figure 6.2(a). But it remains true that failure to implement such optimal adjustments cannot lead to productivity losses exceeding those obtained, without adjustments, in the previous section. Second, ageing, in a sense, may be seen as widening our possibilities concerning training policies, rather than constraining them: it makes initial training less expensive (if population declines), or more rewarding (if the duration of working life increases). In a sense, and within this partial equilibrium context which ignores other aspects (e.g. pensions), ageing can be seen as at least as much an opportunity as a challenge.

2   Ageing, career profiles and wages

2.1   Career profiles

Career profiles are conditioned by age structures. We shall first explore some aspects of this dependency which are of a purely demographic nature. A pioneering study by Keyfitz (1973) examined how a declining population growth rate implies an increasing median age of the labour force. Assuming that the average hierarchical position is linked to age or seniority, this means that people will enter the upper half of the hierarchical structure later than they would do in a growing population.

Following Keyfitz's approach, we can examine how the whole career profile is affected by a changing population growth rate. Assume again that the hierarchical position is monotonically linked to age. Let us call $r(a)$ the relative hierarchical position of a person aged a, starting from $r(a) = 0$ at the beginning of the career, and ending with $r(\beta) = 1$ just before retirement. For a survival schedule $s(a)$ and a population growth rate of n, $r(a)$ will be given by:

$$r(a) = \frac{\text{Number of people below age } a}{\text{Total labour force}} = \frac{\displaystyle\int_a^a e^{-na} s(a)\,da}{\displaystyle\int_a^\beta e^{-na} s(a)\,da} \qquad (4)$$

We can also define a rate of progression through the hierarchy which is the derivative $\dot{r}(a)$ of r with respect to a.[6]

The two indexes $r(a)$ and $\dot{r}(a)$, rescaled in percentages, are given in Figures 6.4(a) and (b) for three levels of the population growth rate. Figure 6.4(a) gives a result which is consistent with those given by Keyfitz: shifting the population growth rate from $+1\%$ per year to -1% per

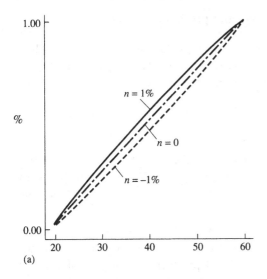

Figure 6.4(a) Position within the hierarchy as a function of age

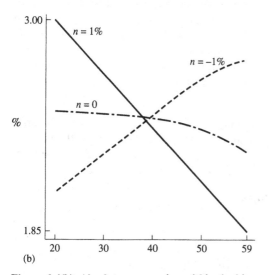

Figure 6.4(b) Absolute progression within the hierarchy as a function of age

year increases the mid-career age by 4 years. Not a minor change, but obtained, once again, under highly contrasted demographic scenarios. This does not mean, anyway, that progression is slower at all ages. In fact, since average progression over the whole life-cycle is given (it is 100% divided by the length of the career), there are some compensations between progression at the start and progression at the end of the life cycle: a declining population implies a higher rate of progression at the end of the career, with a negative concavity for the career profile, while the converse is true in an increasing population. The effects are nevertheless small, once again, so that we had better turn to another aspect of career profiles.

2.2   Wage-productivity differentials

This other aspect of career profiles is *absolute* wages, instead of *relative* status in an hypothetical hierarchical structure. Why be concerned with age-wage relationships in an ageing population? Two situations can be considered:

● Either we make the assumption that, at any age, wage is equal to productivity. In that case, analysing the evolution of average wage levels in an ageing population will produce the same results as the analysis of section 1.1. Average wage in an ageing population could, for instance, increase, but this would simply parallel the evolution of average productivity in the population: changes in average wages and average productivity would be two faces of the same phenomenon and this would not need further comments.

● Alternatively we can make the assumption that wages and productivity are not equal over the life-cycle, and this may be, this time, the source of a major problem.

Let us explain why problems may be here more significant than those raised up to now. Assume first, that the variable of interest is the ratio of average wages to average productivity (or similarly, the ratio of the total wage bill to total production). This ratio can be written as:

$$\frac{W}{\Pi} = \frac{\displaystyle\int_{a}^{\beta} e^{-na} s(a) w(a) da}{\displaystyle\int_{a}^{\beta} e^{-na} s(a) \pi(a) da} \tag{5}$$

With a simple generalization of expression (1), we get:

$$\frac{1}{W/\Pi} \frac{dW/\Pi}{dn} = -A_w + A_\pi \tag{6}$$

where A_w and A_π are now the mean ages of the labour force weighted respectively by wage and productivity functions $w(a)$ and $\pi(a)$. The difference between these two values has no new reason to be very high, given that mean values are not very sensitive to moderate variations in

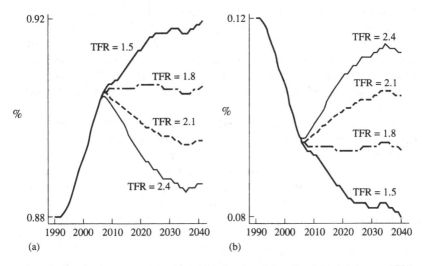

Figure 6.5 The total wage bill and total production: (a) ratio of the total wage bill to total production; (b) relative gap between the total wage bill and total production

weighting functions. Assume therefore that this difference is only of a few years: then, as earlier, we get the relatively negative result that W/Π will be only marginally changed by changes of the population growth rate.

But the point is that W/Π is not necessarily the right variable to look at. A more significant one may be the relative difference $1 - W/\Pi$, which can be interpreted as a rate of profit of the firm (assuming that labour is the only factor of production). And relatively *small* variations of W/Π may result in *large* relative variations of $1 - W/\Pi$. This kind of effect is illustrated by the simulations which are displayed in Figures 6.5(a) and (b). These figures use the same demographic scenarios as Figures 6.1(a) and (b). We assumed that productivity is now flat and equal to 1 between ages 20 and 60, while wages are increasing with seniority. This increase is linear, from 0.6 to 1.2, these two values being chosen to imply a reasonable ratio of W to Π. The variable displayed in Figure 6.5(a) is this ratio W/Π, and the variable displayed in Figure 6.5(b) is the relative difference $1 - W/\Pi$.

The shape of simulated profiles for both variables are nearly indistinguishable from the one we had in Figures 6.1(a) and (b), but the scale of variations in Figure 6.5(b) is now much more significant. From one scenario to the other, this relative difference varies by about one-third. If we interpret $1 - W/\Pi$ as a rate of profit, such large variations are of course of considerable importance, and this may be a source of major difficulties in terms of competitiveness, profitability, investment and all related variables. This raises two questions: the first one is to know whether such a wage-productivity gap exists and whether it goes in the right direction. Second, assuming that the answer to the first question is positive, what form of adjustment would be required for $w(a)$ under changing demographic structures to avoid a growing imbalance between productivity and labour costs?

The first question is an unresolved one. Seniority effects, i.e. excess of wages over productivity at later phases of the life cycle can be explained by insider power in wage determination, or by monitoring rules such as proposed by Lazear (1979, 1986, 1990): delaying part of workers' remuneration to the end of their productive lives is a convenient way to make them loyal and to prevent them from shirking (losses resulting from being discovered and fired being higher when there exists a seniority effect on wages). This can be viewed as a life-cycle version of efficiency wage theory, where work effort is not conditioned by current wage only, but by the whole structure of the wage path over the productive life. Yet the empirical evidence on this point is hard to find and contradictory (Medoff and Abraham, 1981; Hutchens, 1989; Brown, 1989).[7] Furthermore, we have alternative and convincing models explaining why the relationship between wages and productivity could be the opposite one: wages higher than productivity at the beginning of the career, and lower afterwards. For instance, assuming firm-specific on-the-job training (see again Hutchens, 1989), firms may very well offer an excess remuneration to young workers during their phase of initial formation, this excess remuneration being paid back later through excess productivity (the risk of losing workers just after their phase of formation being limited if human capital acquired on-the-job is highly firm-specific). All that shows that, although quantitative effects such as those displayed in Figure 6.5 are high, and are actually the highest of those that we shall have encountered in this paper, they rely on assumptions which remain strongly conjectural.

This does not forbid us to raise the second of the two questions we have mentioned. Assuming that these seniority effects actually exist, how should they be adjusted under a new demographic structure? Assume for simplicity that the seniority effect takes the form of an exponential function of age, i.e., at age a the full wage is:

$$w(a) = w_0 e^{\lambda(a-a)} \qquad (7)$$

where w_0 is a base wage (and the seniority effect is zero for $a = a$, i.e. at the start of their working life). Then the ratio W/Π is:

$$\frac{W}{\Pi} = \frac{\int_{a}^{\beta} e^{-na} s(a) w_0 e^{\lambda(a-a)} da}{\int_{a}^{\beta} e^{-na} s(a) \pi(a) da} \qquad (8)$$

The logarithmic derivative of this ratio with respect to n has been given by equation (6). In a similar fashion, its logarithmic derivative with respect to λ is:

$$\frac{1}{W/\Pi} \frac{dW/\Pi}{d\lambda} = A_w - a \qquad (9)$$

Using the theorem of implicit functions, we get the change in λ which is required to offset a given change of n. It is:

$$\frac{d\lambda}{dn} = -\frac{d(W/\Pi)/dn}{d(w/\Pi)/d\lambda} = \frac{A_w - A_\pi}{A_w - a} \qquad (10)$$

This coefficient is positive, as expected, if $A_\pi < A_w$: *lower* population growth rate implies *slowing down* the progression of wages with age, but this slowdown is not dramatic. Assume for instance orders of magnitude as those used for Figures 6.5(a) and (b), i.e. $A_\pi = 40$ years, $A_w = 42.5$ years and $a = 20$ years, then $d\lambda/dn \approx 0.11$: changing the population growth rate from 0 to -1% implies reducing the annual growth of wages by 0.11%. Cumulated over 40 years of working life, this amounts to reducing the final wage by about 5%. This is not considerable. The question could be asked, to follow Lazear's line of thought, whether this adjustment would not produce a decline in productivity which would, in turn, imply further adjustments of wages, but it seems likely, on the whole, that all these effects are of second-order importance as compared to other sources of variation of career profiles. We are in a situation which is polar from that of Figure 6.2(b), where large economic consequences of a changing population growth rate n (those shown by Figure 6.5(b)) can be compensated by relatively small changes of economic command variables (λ or $w(a)$).

Do we get something different if we consider the ageing of the labour force which would result from raising the retirement age? Keeping the same notation, we can compute the relative variation of the ratio W/Π for a given variation $d\beta$ of retirement age. We have (for $n = 0$):

$$\frac{1}{W/\Pi} \frac{dW/\Pi}{d\beta} = \frac{w(\beta)}{W} - \frac{\pi(\beta)}{\Pi} \qquad (11)$$

so that the compensatory change required for λ if we want to keep w/Π constant is:

$$\frac{d\lambda}{d\beta} = -\frac{1}{A_w - a}\left(\frac{w(\beta)}{W} - \frac{\pi(\beta)}{\Pi}\right) \tag{12}$$

We can evaluate once again this expression for values such as those retained for the simulations of Figure 6.5. We have, in that case, $w(\beta) = 1.2$, $W \approx 36$, $\pi(\beta) = 1$ and $\Pi = 40$ so that:

$$\frac{d\lambda}{d\beta} \approx -0.0004 = -0.04\% \tag{13}$$

In other terms, raising the retirement age by one year requires moderating the yearly seniority effect by 0.04 percentage point if we want to maintain the ratio of the total wage bill to total productivity. Raising it by 5 years (the order of magnitude generally considered for future reforms of pension systems) requires moderating the progression of wages over the life cycle by about 0.2 points of annual growth, twice the effect we had with a change of the population growth rate from 0 to -1%.

3   Retirement age

This computation immediately suggests another one, and this leads us to the last of the three points we raised in the introduction. Let us assume that there is a strong resistance to any change in career profiles so that the adjustment of $w(a)$ is not possible. In such a situation, firms may be tempted, if they can do so, to induce people to retire earlier. Let us suppose that they have complete control over the age at which people leave the labour force. What would be their desired change of the retirement age in the face of a given reduction of the population growth rate, assuming they still wish to keep the ratio W/Π constant? It is here that we shall come to a result clearly in contradiction with common wisdom concerning desirable trends of the retirement age. Given expressions (6) and (11) we can simply write:

$$\frac{d\beta}{dn} = -\frac{d\lambda}{dn}\bigg/\frac{d\lambda}{d\beta} \tag{14}$$

$$= \frac{A_w - A_\pi}{\dfrac{w(\beta)}{W} - \dfrac{\pi(\beta)}{\Pi}} \tag{15}$$

The numerical value under the same assumptions does not require additional computations. It will be simply $0.11/0.0004 = 275$, a very large number indeed. It means that a decline of the population growth rate by 1% would lead employers to choose a *drop* of the retirement age by 2.75

years, exactly the opposite of the kind of evolution which is generally expected for the retirement age for the next century.

At this point, three remarks can be made. First, the tendency toward earlier retirement is actually what we currently observe in developed countries (Schmähl, 1989), despite the fact that, in most of them, the ageing process is already well under way. This suggests that the model developed here has some relationship with reality. On the other hand, it may well be that the general tendency to earlier withdrawal from the labour force is only one aspect of the general contradiction of the labour force in a context of economic instability and of technical progress allowing a rapid substitution of capital for labour. This policy would not be specifically due to a problem of wage-productivity gap at the end of the life cycle: it would simply have provided the easiest way to curb labour force growth, with a reduced social cost, because early retirement is generally better supported than unemployment.

Second, the model is only valid if early retirement imposes no additional cost on the firm. This will be true if pension systems are organized on a wider basis than the isolated firm. This is the case in countries like France: early retirement has a cost in terms of contributions foregone and additional pensions, but this cost is diluted at a collective level (this may induce free-rider behaviour by firms: encouraging workers to leave as early as possible without facing the collective cost that this implies). Things will be more complicated if at least one part of the pension is directly paid by the firm, but the qualitative result remains: there is a motivation for firms to encourage early withdrawal from the labour force.

Last, if this tendency toward earlier retirement would certainly go against the will of pension systems, it is not necessarily in contradiction with the desires of workers. Even if demographic constraints increase the relative cost of a long period of retirement in terms of contributions during working life, people may well choose to accept this cost if technical progress allows a sufficient increase of their labour income. A simple model of income-leisure tradeoff can very well account for this kind of behaviour, which roughly corresponds to historical experience in developed countries. In that case, there would be no contradiction between global ageing, early retirement and the continuation of seniority systems. On the other hand, there will be a problem:

either if increased leisure time is not the solution people prefer, in which case there will be a strugle of old workers to remain in work, at the possible expense of their overall performance or at the expense of young workers' employment.

or if people actually choose to have more leisure, but not concentrated at the end of their lives. In that case, a full reorganization of work effort over the life cycle will be required, involving also changes in on-the-job-training intensity and schedule we have discussed in section 1.2. In that case, it is clear that seniority rules, where they exist, will be necessarily involved in such massive organisational changes.

4   Conclusions

Let us sum up briefly. We have essentially examined how changes of the population growth rate, by affecting the age structure of the labour force, could affect the average levels of a basic set of economic variables. Plausible changes are in most cases rather limited. This is also true when ageing of the labour force is due to an increase of the retirement age.[8] In fact, there is almost only one consequence of ageing which appeared to be strongly significant: it is its consequences on the balance between aggregate production and the total wage bill in the case where ageing is coupled with the maintenance of strong seniority rules. In that case, ageing may imply large financial disequilibrium for firms, and may encourage them to rely increasingly on early retirement, behaviour which may reinforce problems for pension systems. Yet, this potentially high effect heavily depends upon the actual importance of the seniority effect: does there exist a significant excess of wages over productivity at later ages, or is wage growth over the life cycle the consequence of productivity growth? This suggests the importance of research attempting to test the seniority hypothesis.

Two additional points may increase our motivation to examine this point. First, there is one element which gives more importance to ageing problems *within* the labour force as compared to other aspects of ageing, such as pension problems: it is that they will appear in a shorter run. For instance, the various projections we have displayed for France show that, with fertility returning to a level of 2.1, the age structure of the labour force will roughly stabilize around 2010, while the ratio of pensioners to workers should stabilize much later, around 2040. Relative proximity of these problems may partly compensate for their lower economic significance in our research priorities. Second, when discussing potential variations of demographic growth rates, we have considered changes of plus or minus one percentage point as rather extreme values. This was the case because we considered the growth of the *total* labour force, which roughly correspond to the growth rate for total population. But growth rates can take much more contrasted values within some specific segments of the labour force, i.e. between contracting and expanding professions and sectors. Ageing problems such as the ones discussed here will be much more marked in sectors experiencing rapid decline (either because their share in total production declines or because of a rapid substitution of capital for labour), and they will be amplified in those sectors which had irregular recruitment policies in the past. But these meso-economic problems are not demographic *stricto sensu*, even if their analysis still makes use of demographic tools: these problems are linked to general structural changes within the economy.

Appendix A: Sensitivity of an age-related phenomenon to the population growth rate

In a population growing at rate n with a survivorship function $s(a)$, the average value of a variable $x(a)$ taken between ages a_1 and a_2 is:

$$\bar{x} = \frac{\displaystyle\int_{a_1}^{a_2} x(a)s(a)e^{-na}\,da}{\displaystyle\int_{a_1}^{a_2} s(a)e^{-na}\,da} \tag{16}$$

The logarithmic derivative of the numerator with respect to n is:

$$-\frac{\displaystyle\int_{a_1}^{a_2} ax(a)s(a)e^{-na}\,da}{\displaystyle\int_{a_1}^{a_2} x(a)s(a)e^{-na}\,da} \tag{17}$$

which is minus the mean age A_x for the distribution $e^{-na}x(a)s(a)$. The logarithmic derivative of the denominator is, in the same fashion, the mean age A associated to the distribution $e^{-na}s(a)$. We have, therefore:

$$d\log\bar{x} = \frac{d\bar{x}}{\bar{x}} = (-A_x + A)dn \tag{18}$$

whence expression (1) in the text.

Appendix B: Optimal training

We must solve the following programme:

$$\max_{t(a)} \int_0^{\beta} e^{-na}s(a)(1 - t(a))f(k(a))da \tag{19}$$

subject to:

$$\dot{k}(a) = -\delta k(a) + g(t(a)) \tag{20}$$

$$k(0) = 0 \tag{21}$$

$$0 \le t(a) \le 1 \tag{22}$$

Introducing the co-state variable $p(a)$, we get the Hamiltonian:

$$H(k,t,p) = e^{-na}s(a)(1 - t(a))f(k(a))da + p(a)[g(t(a)) - \delta k(a)] \quad (23)$$

The optimal solutions for $p(a)$ and $t(a)$ must therefore satisfy the two additional conditions:

$$\dot{p}(a) = - \frac{\partial H}{\partial k} = - e^{-na}s(a)(1 - t(a))f'(k(a)) + p(a)\delta \quad (24)$$

and (maximization of H with respect to $t(a)$):

$t(a) = 0$ if $- s(a)f(k(a))e^{-na} + p(a)g'(0) < 0$

$t(a) = 1$ if $- s(a)f(k(a))e^{-na} + p(a)g'(1) > 0$ (25)

$$t(a) = g'^{-1}\left(\frac{s(a)f(k(a))e^{-na}}{p(a)}\right) \quad \text{otherwise}$$

plus the transversality condition $p(\beta) = 0$.

For practical applications, we have taken the following functional forms:

$$g(t) = t^{0.5} \quad (26)$$

and

$$f(k) = k \quad (27)$$

Mortality before retirement age has been neglected, i.e. $s(a) = 1$ for all a.

NOTES

I thank Denis Kessler for useful discussions and much advice. Any errors remain mine.

1 For instance, recall that, in their quantitative analysis of French economic growth in the post-war period, Carré *et al.* (1972) attributed a *positive* impact to ageing on the economic growth rate, not a negative one.
2 This relation is demonstrated in appendix A. It is widely used in mathematical and economic demography (Coale, 1972; Arthur and McNicoll, 1978; Lee, 1980; Preston, 1982).
3 This remark does not apply to the Kuznetsian idea that population decline would be harmful because innovation is related to population *size* (rather than structure). This is an entirely different topic. Recall however, that new growth theory warns us against confusion between the stock of human capital (which is the true determinant of technical progress) and population size (Romer, 1990).
4 One illustration of this first situation is provided by the Solow growth model with a Cobb-Douglas production function. The model predicts that changes in the population growth rate n will affect capital intensity and income per capita. But the optimal savings rate is independant of n (it is equal to the capital coefficient of the production function).

5 δ may incorporate some elements of 'relative' depreciation, or technological obsolescence, i.e. the fact that units of human capital accumulated in the past are less productive than newly acquired ones. This is expected to reinforce the need for on-the-job training in an ageing population. But correct examination of this point would need a more detailed exploration.

6 We use an absolute derivative because a logarithmic one (i.e. the growth rate of r) is not defined at $a = a$.

7 The basic problem being that it is in sectors where productivity is difficult to measure directly that such a monitoring of work effort is likely to occur. Testing the model *requires* some measure of productivity, but the model is only valid where such a measure does not exist. So that we are obliged to rely on indirect estimations, or to secondary consequences of the model, such as the existence of mandatory, retirement or pension benefits which are actuarially unfair (i.e. providing an incentive to leave work early).

8 We did not consider ageing of the labour force due to reduced mortality. A growing life expectancy is actually a major source of ageing in developed countries, but essentially at later ages.

REFERENCES

Arthur, B. and G. McNicoll (1978) 'Samuelson, population and intergenerational transfers', *International Economic Review* **19**, 241–6.

Bös, D. and R.K. von Weizsäcker (1989) 'Economic consequences of an ageing population', *European Economic Review* **33**, 345–54.

Brown, J.N. (1989) 'Why do wages increase with tenure? On the job training and life-cycle wage growth observed within firms', *American Economic Review* **79**, 972–91.

Carré, A., P. Dubois and E. Malinvaud (1972) *La croissance française*, Paris: Le Seuil.

Chesnais, J.C. (1978) 'Age, productivité et salaires', *Population* **33**, 155–89.

Clark, R., J. Kreps and J.J. Spengler (1978) 'The economics of ageing: a survey', *Journal of Economic Literature* **16**, 919–62.

Coale, A.J. (1972) *The growth and structure of human populations*, Princeton, NJ: Princeton University Press.

Hutchens, R.M. (1989) 'Seniority, wages and productivity: a turbulent decade', *Journal of Economic Perspectives* **3**, 49–64.

Keyfitz, N. (1973) 'Individual mobility in a stationary population', *Population Studies* **27**, 335–52.

Lazear, E.P. (1979) 'Why is there mandatory retirement?', *Journal of Political Economy* **87**, 1261–4.

Lazear, E.P. (1986) 'Retirement from the labour force', in O.C. Ashenfelter and R. Layard (eds.), *Handbook of labor economics*, Amsterdam: North-Holland.

(1990) 'Adjusting to an ageing labour force', in D.A. Wise (ed.), *Issues in the economics of ageing*, Chicago: University of Chicago Press (for NBER).

Lee, R.D. (1980) 'Age structure, intergenerational transfers and economic growth: an overview', *Revue Économique* **6**, 1129–56.

Medoff, J.L. and K.G. Abraham (1981) 'Are those paid more really more productive? The case of experience', *Journal of Human Resources* **16**, 186–216.

Preston, S.H. (1982) 'Relations between individual life cycles and population characteristics', *American Sociological Review* **47**, 253–63.

Romer, P. (1990) 'Endogenous technical change', *Journal of Political Economy* **98**, S71–102.

Schmähl, W., (ed.), (1989) *Redefining the process of retirement: an international perspective*, Springer-Verlag.

Van Imhoff, E. (1989) *Optimal economic growth and non-stable population*, Springer Verlag.

Weiss, Y. (1986) 'The determination of life-cycle earnings: a survey', in O.C. Ashenfelter and R. Layard (eds.), *Handbook of labor economics*, Amsterdam: North-Holland.

Discussion

PAUL G. CHAPMAN

1   Introduction

This paper provides an interesting and stimulating view of the relationship between some aspects of an ageing labour force and the implications for training and other employer decisions. Most of my comments will be concerned with the economic modelling issues which underlie this paper while the author explicitly states that he is 'putting more emphasis on demographic accounting than on sophisticated economic modelling' (p. 127). In this sense the points I want to make can be largely seen as putting the theoretical foundations of the paper into context and pointing out the dangers of putting any great weight on the specific predictions of the analysis.

The paper deals with the following main issues. First, there are explicit definitions of ageing. These include a decline in population growth and an increase in the average age of the working population through a rise in the retirement age. The paper explores several possibilities. The paper reminds us of the micro-macro distinction in understanding the ageing process. Individuals will progress through a life-cycle which reflects previous human capital accumulation decisions and which generates a lifetime pattern of earnings which will typically reach a maximum before retirement. For example, Weiss (1986) gives a typical time pattern of earnings, training and hours worked. The economy, consisting of many individuals at different phases of their own life cycle, will also display an age attribute which reflects the sum of the individual cases. Second, the paper notes that the size of any structural changes in the workforce composition and the size of optimal policy response changes may be quite poorly related. For example, the workforce may become older but the total training required could remain constant. While this cannot be dismissed as an unimportant issue it does not seem to me necessary or central to the main parts of the analysis. Third, the optimal training time per worker increases with a declining population or an increase in the retirement age. It is argued that the increases in training times are relatively small although the reported average increase of two years would seem to be of considerable importance (the author notably points out later than a reduction in the retirement of two years is of considerable importance). Fourth, the paper examines what happens in a seniority model of wage determination when ages and productivity diverge (which many labour economists would regard as the typical wage outcome for many different reasons). In this analysis a key assumption, which is discussed below, is that the objective is to maintain a constant ratio of the wage bill to profits for the economy as a whole. In the case of the ageing population or ageing working population this leads to a reduction in the optimum progression of wages with age. Fifth, the paper raises the possibility that employers faced with a decline in population growth and a reluctance or inability to reduce the growth in seniority wages, may themselves prefer to reduce the retirement age. It is argued that this is in accord with the observed trend in the retirement age in developed countries.

Before raising the more substantive issues I would like to raise one point of potential confusion arising from Figures 6.1(a) and (b). These are based on equation (1) and an assumption about individual productivity change. The latter seems to require that individual productivity rises (falls) *over time at all ages*. An alternative is that productivity rises (falls) with age for the individual. The latter would be contrary to the hill-shaped relationship described in Weiss (1986). If this is the case, why does the productivity level change before 2010? It is questionable to assume that this relation can take any form. Next we can examine the more substantive issues arising.

2   Main commentary

Several questions are raised about labour market participation. There is no mention of the labour force entry issues equivalent to retirement, nor the division of the population into the economically active and inactive and the further subdivision of the economically active into the employed and unemployed. Another important issue is the rising proportion of part-time workers and reductions in hours worked which further reduce the effective working population. Contrary to these effects is the rise in female activity rates which has swelled the labour force. The relationship between population size and the working population is more complicated than the paper suggests and the effects which are ignored could well outweigh the factors which are explored in the paper. For example, the population changes might induce changes in the participation in the labour force making the impact of changes in population cohort sizes hard to predict. Furthermore, this is complicated by other processes which influence participation rates indicated by the evidence on gender differ- ences. For example, in the OECD countries male participation has fallen from 88.1% in 1973 to 83.6% in 1988 whereas for females the percentage has risen from 48.2% to 59.1%.

In the later sections of the paper a very crucial assumption is introduced into the analysis. The analysis explores what compensatory changes are required for an ageing labour force 'if we want to maintain the ratio of the total wage bill to total productivity' (p. 140). This assumption is a kind of 'golden rule', which there is no basis to believe will hold in practice. We should be mindful of the parts of the analysis which are conditional on this assumption.

The analytical framework is plainly and openly a partial equilibrium approach. It effectively presents several slices of an n-dimensional problem. Of course partial analyses can be revealing but they should also be treated with a large degree of caution, especially in a paper with clear policy overtones. There have been many examples in economics in which as soon as a statistical regularity which has been observed is used for policy purposes then the same regularity shifts. The relation of an ageing population, participation in the labour force, productivity growth and training is clearly a complex matter and whether the particular dimen- sions which are identified in the paper are the most crucial is open to speculation. A further complicating modelling issue is the treatment of any control variables. For example, it is assumed in one part of the analysis that the employer might react by raising the retirement age. Is this realistic when retirement ages are linked to eligibility for state pensions and these are infrequently changed? Furthermore, early retirement would seem to be at least partly worker-determined, perhaps in negotiation with firms and assisted by the state. In other sections of the paper the retirement age is an exogenous factor which leads to one form of ageing. Of course it is difficult to resolve how such variables should be treated in a partial equilibrium framework.

It is always possible to question the selection of a particular measure of productivity. This paper is quite clear in the choice of labour productivity as the key variable linking wages to age. However, it is an important point to note that different measures of labour productivity may give different insights. For example, the importance of per capita output rather than labour productivity is crucial in the provision of pensions. It is easy to forget that the retired population are in effect supported by the working population and the distinction between unemployment and retirement referred to (p. 141) is in this respect potentially misleading. Perhaps more might be made in the paper of the different measures of productivity.

There is a fundamental question about what underlies the age-productivity relation. According to human capital theory, embodied in the Mincer wage equation, is the view that on-the-job training (experience) leads to higher productivity and assuming some positive wage-productivity link, higher wages. However, experience acquisition is also age-related and older workers may be less well motivated (there are arguments in favour of motivation rising with age and falling after a peak in middle age). For manual workers it is well established that age has a detrimental effect on productivity. See the review by Clark *et al.* (1978).

Finally, the paper points out that ageing may be most influential through its effect on the profitability of the firm. Two issues are of concern here. First, profitability is measured by the share of profits rather than the more conventional profit on capital. Firms may be only weakly influenced by variations in the profit share. Second, the variability of the profit share $(1 - x)$ relative to the variability of the wage share (x) will depend on $x/(1 - x)$. This relative variation approaches infinity as the wage share approaches one. Whether the firm will be heavily influenced by what is essentially an accounting feature is an empirical issue.

3   Conclusions

This paper raises a number of very important issues about the potential implications of an ageing labour force. One question is the definition of ageing itself. Although this might seem a fairly obvious question, the paper examines several different definitions. First, for the individual, age is measurable and we can make behavioural assumptions about how age might effect productivity (productivity-age assumptions). A related issue is the link between productivity and the wage (productivity-wage assumptions). Second, the labour force collectively might age through variations in population growth. There will be some form of economic interaction between the life-cycle earnings of the individual and the ageing pattern of the work force. This has always been obvious in an empirical sense. Third, the labour force will age through variations in the ages of exit and entry into employment. The paper concentrates solely on the exit side of this equation.

Models are meant to tell an interesting and empirically relevant story. While this paper satisfies this aim, I have argued that an examination of the model structure suggests that there may be some other important relationships which might merit our attention. Consideration of these factors is especially important if we were to accept, in even a qualified sense, the explanation given in the paper for the falling retirement age.

I have not referred to wider issues. The author points out that the analysis is based on economy-wide changes averaged out which can include much larger sectoral changes (p. 142). It seems inevitable that ageing will have very severe implications for particular segments of the whole population whatever the macroeconomic results. The different classes of worker might depend on personal characteristics or the particular cohort to which each worker belongs. A further issue which must be very important in understanding the ageing process is the stage of economic development. The ageing economy may be seen as a typical characteristic of a mature economy and it is arguable that the relationship between ageing and productivity will both depend on and be a consequence of the stage of economic development.

REFERENCES

Clark, R., J. Kreps and J.J. Spengler (1978) 'The economics of ageing: A survey', *Journal of Economic Literature* 16, 919–62.

Weiss, Y. (1986) 'The determination of life-cycle earnings: A survey', in O.C. Ashenfelter and R. Layard (eds.), *Handbook of Labor Economics*, Amsterdam: North-Holland.

7 On ageing and earnings

N. ANDERS KLEVMARKEN

1 Introduction

Stimulated by the work of Schultz (1961), Becker (1962, 1964) and Mincer (1958, 1962, 1970, 1974) the relation between earnings and schooling, experience, seniority and age is one of the most well researched areas in microeconomics. Complementary to the human capital approach are a number of studies which have analysed the dynamics of age-earnings profiles, i.e. how changes in the demand for and supply of labour will systematically change the location and shape of the profiles. An issue of particular interest in a society which experiences major changes in its age distribution is the (supply) effect on earnings profiles of cohort size. The mobility of earnings is another area which has also received attention in the past, but we know much less about this topic than about the properties of average earnings functions. There is thus relatively less to be said about ageing and earnings mobility.

This paper first summarizes a few important findings from the human capital literature on age-earnings profiles, which gives an interpretation of the general static pattern of wage progression as people age. The emphasis on the human capital approach does not necessarily imply that alternative interpretations of empirical findings suggested in the literature lack explanatory power, but most empirical work has been done in the human capital tradition and it is a relatively simple but yet powerful approach.

The next step is to allow age-earnings profiles to shift and change in shape as a result of general productivity increases and changes in the demand and supply of labour. Of particular interest are the effects on wages of changes in the age distribution. The literature on the supply effects on earnings of changes in cohort size is briefly reviewed, before an attempt is made to estimate these effects from Swedish panel data.

The last part of the paper extends the analysis of average wage rate profiles to an analysis of the mobility around these profiles, and in particular, it investigates how mobility depends on age.

2   The human capital approach

Human capital theory suggests that people's decisions to invest in human capital by schooling and on-the-job training activities are determined by expected future earnings of alternative job careers. People are only willing to invest if they are compensated by higher future earnings for the earnings foregone while investing. An optimal investment strategy suggests that most of the investment will be done at the beginning of a career. The theory also suggests that people with a given level (and type) of schooling have a choice when they leave school between careers which involve relatively much learning activities in the beginning and thus low pay but with high future wages, and careers which involve less learning in the beginning, relatively high initial pay but a slower wage progression in the future. The choice between these alternatives is determined by personal preferences (the personal rate of discount) and each individual's ability to go through with an 'investment programme'.

The general shape of the earnings profile suggested by this theory is the well-known reversed U-shaped curve of earnings as a function of experience. When people become older and gain in experience their wages increase relative to those of young people until a maximum is reached. The size of this maximum and how early in life they reach it depend on their choice of career. Those who choose to invest much in the beginning of their career will experience a steeper profile and reach the maximum later in life than those who invest less. The standard Mincer model explains the log of earnings as a linear function of years of schooling and a quadratic function of years of experience. In this model age does not enter explicitly. However, in empirical applications one sometimes finds the age variable included as well.[1] One reason is that the age variable might capture differences in human capital at the time of graduation from school. Students do not graduate and join the labour force at the same age even if they have the same schooling level. As suggested in Klevmarken and Quigley (1976), age differences are indicative of differences in ability and human capital. For graduate engineers they found a U-shaped relation between initial pay and age at graduation, which could be explained by the high ability of the selected group which graduated at a very young age and the investments in human capital done by those who graduated at a relatively high age. The latter group typically had a lower level engineering degree and a few years of experience before they entered a technical university.

In a study of American scientists Weiss & Lillard (1978) and Lillard & Weiss (1979) introduced into the earnings function both pre-degree experience and age at highest degree. They found a positive return to pre-degree experience which decreased with increasing post-degree experience, and also a small positive effect of the age at highest degree which rapidly decreased and turned negative with increasing post-degree experience. Those who had pre-degree experience and graduated late thus got into jobs with a relatively high initial pay, but with a slower wage progression.

Another reason to include the age variable in the specification of an earnings function is that it might capture at least part of the depreciation of human capital. Our physical as well as mental ability will eventually decrease as we get older. Part of the depreciation should thus be related to a person's age rather than to years of experience. The size of this ageing effect is an empirical issue. It is likely to depend on physiological qualities but also, for instance, on occupation and experience in the labour market. Exposure to a bad working environment might speed up the ageing process. The existence of an ageing effect does not exclude that depreciation is also related to human capital 'vintage'. It might, however, be difficult to distinguish the two empirically.

If experience outside the labour market has little value in market work, one would expect that someone who is old for her experience gets a relatively low wage rate. For instance, women who interrupt market work to stay at home for long periods to nurse and raise children experience a depreciation of the human capital they acquired before they stopped working in the market, and they are at the same time exposed to ageing which might detrimentally affect their ability to invest in the type of human capital which is rewarded by the labour market, when they finally return. Women who interrupt their market work will thus get a lower wage than those who work continuously. They might even get a lower wage than comparable men and women with the same years of experience. Mincer & Polachek (1974) found that married women lost 1.5 per cent for every year they did not work. Gustafsson (1981), however, did not find any net depreciation among female white collar workers in Swedish industry.

Many estimated earnings functions include a seniority variable to capture the return to firm-specific human capital. The estimated effect of seniority might also reflect the common stipulation of labour contracts that wages should increase with increasing seniority, which may or may not be related to the accumulation of firm-specific human capital. An alternative interpretation is, for instance, derived from the incentive scenario of deferred compensation schemes (Lazear, 1981).

Many empirical studies have shown that the shape of log earnings profiles depends on type and level of schooling and on occupation. In general blue collar workers have profiles which just increase a little in the beginning of the career and then level off to a flat profile, while white collar workers, in particular professionals, have steeper and more tilted profiles. Using the national Panel Study of Income Dynamics (PSID) sample from the University of Michigan for the period 1967–77 Lillard and Willis (1978) found a significant interaction between experience and schooling and schooling squared such that people with academic training had a steeper profile. For European evidence see, for instance, Klevmarken (1972, 1980, 1982) and Phelps Brown (1977).

There are also a number of studies which have compared male and female profiles and in general found that the profile of females is below that of males and that it has a flatter, less tilted shape. The extent to which these differences are explained by discrimination against women is an issue of continuing controversy. A problem with this literature is that any unexplained difference is attributed to discrimination, but what is unexplained of course depends on the variables included in the model. One typically finds that the more detailed the occupational classification or preferably job classification used to explain the differences in earnings, the smaller becomes the unexplained gender difference. A major explanation for observed differences in earnings is thus that men and women choose different work careers. In Sweden there are still clearly distinguishable male and female jobs (Leiniö, 1988, *Statistical Year Book of Sweden 1992*, Table 204 and '*Women and Men in Sweden, Equality of the Sexes 1990*', Statistics Sweden).

Profiles also differ in shape between major sectors of the labour market and between industries. For instance, Lillard & Weiss (1979) found that earnings progression with experience was relatively low in the government sector. In an extensive study of the Swedish government sector Gustafsson (1976) got similar results for employees with college or university education, in particular for men. The earnings profiles for women, who on average had less schooling, did not differ much between the government and private sectors. In a later study using Swedish survey data from 1974 and 1981 Zetterberg (1990) found a somewhat steeper profile for women in the private sector compared to women employed by the central government or by a local municipality. The earnings profiles in the private sector showed a stronger curvature, both for males and females, than the profiles of the public sector. In particular, the decrease in earnings after their peak was stronger in the private sector.

These differences are, however, not constant, and are not the same for all countries. In a comparison between Sweden and the United States

Klevmarken (1982) showed that Swedish workers with less than high school had in the 1970s a much flatter log-earnings profile than the corresponding group in the United States, while there was less of a difference for workers with high school or university training. He also demonstrated how the profiles shifted location and changed in shape (see below).

The individual earnings progression with increasing age thus depends on a number of decisions about schooling, career choice, breaks in labour force participation, etc. and these decisions depend on the expected future private return to alternative investments in human capital. The private return is a function of the market return, income taxes and pension benefits, and the market return to investments in human capital is determined by the demand for and supply of various types of skills, but also by wage bill taxes levied on employers to finance, for instance, social security pensions.

To capture all major influences on the location and shape of earnings profiles would thus require a modelling effort which goes far beyond the scope of this paper. We will have to contend with a reduced form type of approach when we now turn to a discussion of the dynamics of earnings profiles. This discussion will concentrate on the effects of a changing age distribution.

3 Changes in the age distribution and the dynamics of earnings profiles

Let us now relax the assumption of a constant earnings structure and let us also introduce the assumption of a general productivity increase which motivates an increase in the average wage rate. The latter assumption makes the distinction between cross-sectional and longitudinal earnings profiles necessary (Klevmarken, 1972; Jonsson and Klevmarken, 1978; Klevmarken, 1980). Figure 7.1 exhibits the difference between the two types of profile. People progress along the solid curves as they age and the curves of new cohorts start at successively higher wage rates due to the general increase in productivity of the economy. When earnings are registered as a function of age in a particular calendar year one observes, however, the dashed cross-sectional profiles. The slope of the cross-sectional profiles gives the return to investments in human capital, while the slope of the longitudinal curves gives the sum of the general increase of productivity and the return to human capital investments.[2]

If the age distribution of the population changes such that the supply of young people who join the labour market increases, one would *ceteris paribus* expect that initial wages are adjusted downward as a response to the increased supply of young people. If the substitution possibilities between inexperienced and experienced labour are small the immediate

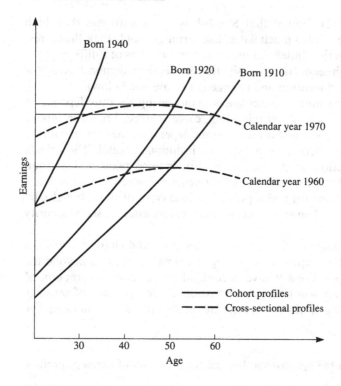

Figure 7.1 Schematic cross-sectional and longitudinal age-earnings profiles

effect is thus that observed cross-sectional profiles become steeper, as illustrated in Figure 7.2. An interesting issue is what will happen to the earnings profile as the large birth cohorts become older. Will these cohorts always keep their relative disadvantage in earnings level?

The answer should at least partly depend on the organization of the labour market and on the type of jobs and investment activities these large cohorts initially get into. If a large share of the big cohorts initially has to take relatively 'simple' jobs which do not offer opportunities to learn new skills of importance for their future career, these employees 'lose' a number of years which could have been used for investment activities. Even if they are able to find jobs later which permit them to invest, they have a disadvantage relative to smaller cohorts which did not have to compete so hard for the good jobs. If in addition the labour market is segmented, with low mobility, and if firm-specific human capital is important and promotion by seniority customary, they might never be able to catch up.

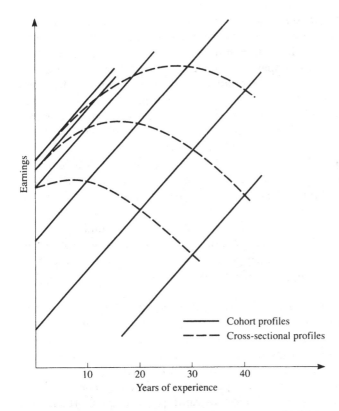

Figure 7.2 Earnings profiles with declining increases of initial earnings

If on the other hand most members of the large cohorts find jobs which involve much learning activity (low initial wages are indicative of investment) they might invest even more than members of small cohorts, which implies that they will catch up in pay as they grow older. Also, if investments in human capital are predominantly of a general character, a difference of a few years in experience might not be important in the later phases of a career. The less steep slope of the earnings profile for experienced people supports this argument.

In the United States the postwar baby boom peaked in 1955–60, which changed the age distribution of the US labour force in the end of the 1960s and the beginning of the 1970s. The number of young persons increased rapidly. Freeman (1979) investigated the impact on the age-earnings profiles of this change. He found that the relative pay of young workers decreased in the period 1968–77, and in an analysis of mean income differences for the period 1947–74, taking variations in GNP (the demand side) and cohort size differences into account, he found that the latter variable had a major impact on the earnings profiles. This was, in particular, the case for college graduates, while as a contrast there was almost no change in the profile of women. He explains this difference in result by the lack of substitution between inexperienced and experienced workers in the kind of jobs held by college graduates and the greater substitution possibilities in typical female jobs.

Welch (1979) got similar results in his study of the same problem. The impact of cohort size was largest for people with four or more years of college. He also distinguished between an entry effect of cohort size and a persistent effect. The entry effect was larger than the persistent effect for all educational groups and the largest difference was found for college graduates. He concluded that much of the downward pressure on earnings was a temporary phenomenon and most important for college graduates. The persistent negative effect was small and not clearly related to schooling.

Berger (1985) criticized Welch's results because he had *a priori* assumed that large and small cohorts proceed through the career from learner to fully vested workers at the same speed. The interaction between cohort size and experience was assumed to be zero after the end of the learning phase, the length of which was *a priori* given for each schooling group. Welch's model thus ruled out the possibility of flatter profiles for large cohorts. Berger (1985) relaxed this constraint, permitting cohort size and experience to interact in the entire experience range, and reestimated the model. He found that larger cohorts experience slower early career growth and flatter earnings profiles than do smaller cohorts. One should note, however, that the marginal effect of the interaction cohort size * experience was assumed to be constant and thus independent of experience. If one gets a negative estimate the model will thus necessarily give a flat profile.

Building on theoretical arguments in Nothaft (1985) and Stapleton & Young (1988), who suggested that large cohorts invest less in human capital and that people in cohorts with large *surrounding* cohorts invest more, Berger (1989) estimated a model which included both the size of the current cohort and those of preceding and following cohorts. The model was estimated for each educational group separately, and cohort size was defined by level of schooling. The model permitted the same type of interaction between experience and cohort size as in his previous work. Preceding and following cohort sizes were also allowed to interact with experience of the current cohort. He found that 'increases in own cohort

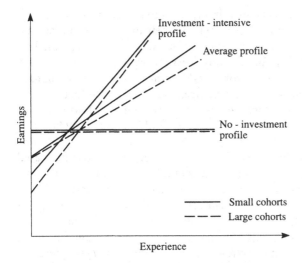

Figure 7.3 Cohort size effects on earnings profiles

size lead to higher beginning earnings but flatter earnings profiles, while increases in the sizes of surrounding cohorts lead to lower beginning earnings but steeper earnings profiles' (p. 319). The interpretations of this result appears to be the following. For a given level of schooling there are jobs with less investment and flatter profiles and jobs with more investments and steeper profiles, cf Figure 7.3. In the first type of jobs there are greater substitution possibilities between less experienced and more experienced workers than in the second kind of jobs. When cohort size increases initial pay in investment-intensive jobs therefore decreases more than in less investment-intensive jobs. In the latter case the whole profile tends to shift in level by a small amount. The result is that the opportunity cost of investments in human capital increases, which will induce relatively more people to choose a career with less investment and a flatter profile. It is, however, hard to understand why the resulting net effect on average initial pay of the increased supply of inexperienced workers and the shift away from investment activities is positive. Another puzzle is the absence of systematic differences in cohort effects between educational groups. By the same argument as above one would have expected stronger effects for higher levels of schooling.

Murphy *et al.* (1988) reanalysed the effects of cohort size on earnings in the United States using a different approach. Average earnings data for males by 4 levels of schooling, 40 years of experience and 16 years from the Current Population Surveys (CPS) were used to estimate a three-factor model. Each factor was interpreted to represent three types of skills, and the corresponding factor weights their marginal productivity. With calendar year as observational unit these weights were regressed on the total quantities of each factor. In this way Murphy, Plant and Welch were able to simulate earnings profiles taking into account both changes in skill composition and systematic changes in marginal product of these skills. They found that earnings were inversely related to cohort size. The initial effect on the earnings of young people could be relatively large, in their simulations as much as 10 per cent, but the effect on lifetime earnings was much smaller, at most 3 per cent. Their results also indicated that a younger work force leads to a small and temporary decrease in the return to college education compared to high school education.

There are also a few studies of cohort size and relative earnings in countries other than the United States. Ben-Porath (1988) analysed the impact of changing fertility patterns and varying wages of immigration on relative earnings of young men in Israel. Using aggregate data he regressed relative earnings of 18–24 and 35–64 year olds on the rate of unemployment of men aged 35–54 years and the relative size of the age groups 18–34 years and 65 + . He found significant negative effects of both the unemployment rate and own cohort size, but also the strange result that the relative size of the age group 65 + had a negative impact on the relative wage of young males.

A similar study also relying on aggregate data is Martin and Ogawa's (1988) analysis of relative earnings in Japan. After a relatively small baby boom immediately after the Second World War fertility rates have shown a declining trend in Japan, which has thus experienced an exceptional ageing of its population and work force. As a result of the small cohorts of young workers, age-earnings profiles have become less steep. Martin and Ogawa (1988) regress the log of relative earnings of 40–49 to 20–24 year olds on the ratio of the labour force sizes of the same age groups and on the deviation of the logarithm of real gross domestic product from its trend. Both variables have significant negative effects, confirming that both demand pressure and decreases in the cohort size of young males and females have increased their relative wages. Changes in demand were, however, relatively more important than cohort size.

Also Ermisch (1988a, b) presents time-series evidence which supports the hypothesis that cohort size depresses earnings. His results are for Great Britain and the period 1952–79. Wright (1991) pools average weekly earnings data from a series of British household surveys covering the period 1973 to 1982 to estimate earnings functions for three educational groups. His model explains the log of weekly earnings by age, age squared, relative cohort size, the interaction between age and cohort size, the current male unemployment rate, the percentage working part-time and a quadratic trend. Cohort size and its interaction with age are insignificant for those who had least educational qualifications, but significant and with the expected signs for the intermediate and high qualifications groups. Increasing cohort size decreases earnings for the young, but not for middle-aged and old workers.

In a study of Swedish graduate engineers, Jonsson & Klevmarken (1978) tested a model which assumed that initial earnings (the shift in the level of cross-sectional profiles) depended on the number of new graduates while the slope of the profiles was assumed to depend more generally on the particular cohort. The model also included a variable measuring the degree of market disequilibrium. Each single cohort estimate was not well-determined, but they showed a very clear decreasing trend from the first cohort of graduates in 1954–57 to the last in 1966–69, which agrees well with the fact that the Swedish baby boom had already reached its peak in 1945 and that university engineers typically graduated at the age of 25–7 years. These results are thus consistent with flatter profiles for larger cohorts.

In a more recent study Tasiran & Gustafsson (1991) studied another occupational group, salesmen and shop assistants in Sweden. With a modest amount of imputations of mean incomes by age and gender they have been able to cover such a long period as 1948–89. With the log of (mean) monthly wages as the dependent variable they estimated earnings functions for males and females which in addition to cohort dummies and age included cohort size, GDP, unemployment rate and social security contributions. They found a clear negative effect on the wages of young people of cohort size and this effect was of equal magnitude for both genders. It disappeared, however, for older salesmen and shop assistants. The interaction between age and GDP per head and between age and the unemployment rate also showed that the wages of young people were sensitive to market changes while there was very little effect on the wages of older people. Tasiran and Gustafsson's finding that earnings profiles are steeper for large cohorts is a little remarkable given that they analysed such a low-skilled group of workers.

4   An empirical application to Swedish panel data

In an attempt to give additional evidence on the effects of cohort size on the earnings profiles an earnings model was estimated using the Swedish HUS-panel data (Klevmarken & Olovsson, 1989; Klevmarken, 1990). HUS is a national sample not limited to the narrowly defined educational or occupational groups many previous studies used. The first wave of

HUS-data was collected in 1984 for a random sample of the Swedish speaking population. Additional waves were collected in 1986 and 1988. The 1986 wave included both old and new respondents, while the 1988 survey was limited to respondents who had participated in 1986. In 1984 all respondents and in 1986 all new respondents were given personal interviews. The panel was interviewed by telephone in 1986 and data were collected by a mail questionnaire in 1988. Responses about earnings were given for a time-span of an hour, a week, a month or a year, whichever was most convenient for the respondents, and they included both earnings from a main job and from any secondary job. Data were transformed into hourly wage rates using responses to questions on normal weekly hours and weeks worked.

The earnings model includes the conventional variables: Years of schooling, labour market experience, age and seniority. Experience is a measure of full-time equivalent labour market experience, i.e. part-time work has been converted to full-time equivalent years. Data come from a sequence of survey questions on number of years worked full-time and part-time respectively. There is thus no linear dependency between the schooling, experience and age variables. The model also includes relative birth (b) cohort size defined by,

$$RCS_{bt} = \frac{\frac{1}{9}CS_{b-2} + \frac{2}{9}CS_{b-1} + \frac{3}{9}CS_{b} + \frac{2}{9}CS_{b+1} + \frac{1}{9}CS_{b+2}}{\text{Size of Swedish population in age range 15–24 years, year } t}$$

and its interaction with years of schooling and age. The Swedish baby booms were not of the same magnitude as the American boom, as shown in Figure 7.4. One might thus expect that any effect of changing cohort sizes would be smaller in Sweden than in the United States. The variation in the size of Swedish birth cohorts is, however, not so small that it would be impossible for this reason to estimate an effect (Figure 7.5).

Sweden is a country which has occasionally experienced relatively large migration. In the beginning of this century there was net emigration and after World War II net immigration, in the 1950s and 1960s predominantly labour immigration from Finland and Southern Europe and in the 1970s and 1980s mostly immigration of refugees and of relatives of previous immigrants. Large net immigration of prime age workers could be expected to influence earnings in approximately the same way as large birth cohorts. There were years when net immigration to Sweden was of the same magnitude as the changes in birth cohort size. Unfortunately it has not been feasible to obtain migration data by year of birth and schooling level, but only totals for each year. Attempts to include these migration varaibles in the earnings function were not successful. They did

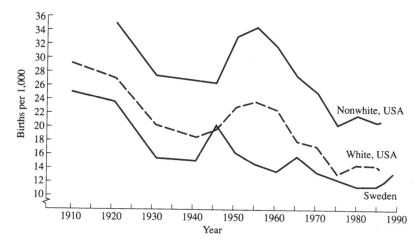

Figure 7.4 Birth rate per 1,000 population in USA and Sweden, 1910–89

Sources: Historical Statistics of the United States, Series B20–21, US Dept. of Commerce, 1960. *Current Population Reports*, US Bureau of the Census. *Historical Statistics of Sweden, I. Population*, Statistics Sweden, Stockholm, 1955. *Population Changes*, Statistics Sweden.

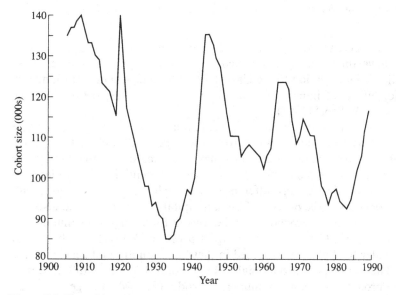

Figure 7.5 Size of Swedish birth cohorts, 1905–89

Sources: Historical Statistics of Sweden, I. Population, Statistics Sweden, Stockholm, 1955, and *Population Changes*, Statistics Sweden.

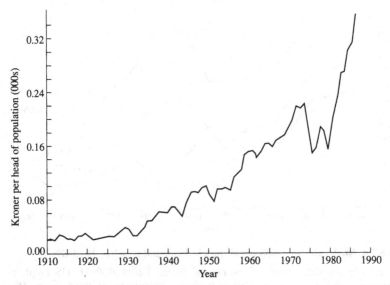

Figure 7.6 Per capita gross investment volume of Swedish industry 1910–89 (1908/09 price level)

Source: Unpublished data from the Department of Economic History, Lund University, and *Statistical Yearbook of Sweden*, Table 259, 1992.

not contribute to the explanation of the dynamics of the earnings profiles, and have thus not been included in the model presented here. Also, studies of immigration to the United States have in general not found any major effects of immigration on the wages of natives, see for instance LaLonde & Topel (1991).

In the literature on life-cycle wages of immigrants one has observed that new immigrants tend to get relatively low wages, but catch up to the wage level of native workers and sometimes even exceed it as the immigrants gain experience in their new country. These differential wage profiles have been explained by cohort differences in initial human capital endowment, by differences in the process of human capital accumulation and also as a result of selection. Depending on the reasons for immigration, immigrants might be a positively selected group of people and this should be true in particular for those who succeed in their new country and decide to stay on. This suggests that one might like to control for these differences in wage progression between immigrants and natives when wage rate functions are estimated. However, because of the difficulty and expense of administering interviews in foreign languages the HUS-surveys only cover the Swedish-speaking population. New immigrants were thus never interviewed, and no attempts were made to control for a different wage profile of former immigrants.

The demand side is captured by the gross investment volume in Swedish industry (Figure 7.6).[3] Two variables are used: the investment volume per head in the year of entry to the labour market, and the change in the investment volume per head from the year of entry to the year of observation.[4] The implicit assumption is that changes in investment volume are indicative of changes in the demand for labour and thus of demand-induced wage changes. Although there might be a problem of timing, investment changes usually precede changes in demand for labour, and a problem with an increasing relative importance of labour-saving investments in the 1970s and 1980s, these variables might serve as good proxies.

To capture the panel character of the data, to allow for data wave-dependent variances[5] and to make it possible to use all observations, not only panel members, the following stochastic structure was assumed,

$$
\begin{bmatrix} y_1 \\ y_2 \\ \cdot \\ \cdot \\ \cdot \\ y_n \end{bmatrix} = \begin{bmatrix} x_1 \\ x_2 \\ \cdot \\ \cdot \\ \cdot \\ x_n \end{bmatrix} \beta + \begin{bmatrix} \epsilon_1 \\ \epsilon_2 \\ \cdot \\ \cdot \\ \cdot \\ \epsilon_n \end{bmatrix} \tag{1}
$$

$$
(y = x\beta + \epsilon)
$$

$$
E(\epsilon\epsilon') = \begin{bmatrix} \Omega_1 & & & 0 \\ & \Omega_2 & & \\ & & \cdot & \\ & & & \cdot \\ 0 & & & \Omega_n \end{bmatrix} \tag{2}
$$

where y_i and ϵ_i are $n_i \times 1$ vectors, and x_i and Ω_i $n_i \times k$ and $n_i \times n_i$ matrices respectively. n_i is 1, 2 or 3 depending on how many times the ith individual participated in the surveys. There is a total of n individuals in the sample. For $n_i = 3$, i.e. for an individual who participated in all three waves,

$$
\Omega_i = \begin{bmatrix} \Omega_{11} & \Omega_{12} & \Omega_{13} \\ \Omega_{12} & \Omega_{22} & \Omega_{23} \\ \Omega_{13} & \Omega_{23} & \Omega_{33} \end{bmatrix} \tag{3}
$$

where Ω_{rs}, $r,s = 1, \ldots, 3$ are scalars. For individuals who only participated in one or two waves the residual variance-covariance matrix is the

Table 7.1. *GLS estimates of an earnings function for males*

	Estimate	Standard error
Intercept	2.8279	0.3528
Schooling	0.0392	0.0118
Schooling squared	− 0.0002	0.0004
Experience, full time equivalent	0.00456	0.0046
Ditto, squared	− 0.0001	0.0001
Schooling * Experience	0.0001	0.0002
Age	0.0202	0.0102
Age squared	− 0.0002	0.0001
Seniority	0.0042	0.0007
Relative cohort size	− 13.6766	14.7726
Rel. cohort size * Schooling 10–15 years	− 0.5475	1.7175
Rel. cohort size * Schooling 16– years	0.4268	2.7915
Investments at career start	0.7204	0.2911
Change in investment since career start	0.6103	0.1999
Investment change * Schooling 10–15 years	0.3508	0.2123
Investment change * Schooling 16– years	0.2190	0.3554
Rel. cohort size * Age	0.3286	0.3280
Born before 1920	− 0.2472	0.0710
$R^2 = 1 - \Sigma e_i^2 / \Sigma (y_i - \bar{y})^2$	0.3196	
No. of cases	2,518	
No. of individuals	1,290	

		1984	1986	1988
Residual variance–covariance matrix	1984	0.0575	0.0343	0.0328
estimated from OLS residuals	1986		0.0667	0.0295
	1988			0.0769

Note: The dependent variable is the log of hourly earnings in 1984 prices. Extremes were eliminated by the rule $\ln(w) - 4.057 < - 3.5 * 0.308$ or $\ln(w) - 4.057 > 4.3 * 0.308$. 7 individuals were dropped.

relevant part of the matrix above. For instance, for those who only participated in the 1988 wave $\Omega_i = \Omega_{33}$.

The model was estimated by feasible generalized least-squares i.e. β was first estimated by OLS and the OLS-residuals used to estimate Ω_{rs}. The feasible GLS estimator then becomes

$$\hat{\beta}_{GLS} = (\Sigma x_i' \hat{\Omega}_i^{-1} x_i)^{-1} \Sigma x_i' \hat{\Omega}_i^{-1} y_i \tag{4}$$

with variance-covariance matrix

$$Var(\hat{\beta}_{GLS}) = (\Sigma x_i' \hat{\Omega}_i^{-1} x_i)^{-1} \tag{5}$$

The results are displayed in Table 7.1.

The estimates for the human capital variables come out more or less as expected. The return to another year of schooling is 4%. The second-degree term is negative but small and insignificant. The estimates for full-time equivalent experience have the expected signs but they are insignificant. The age variable comes out much stronger than the experience variable, and it shows the conventional reversed U-shape with the log of earnings. There is no significant interaction between schooling and experience. The return to an additional year of seniority is 0.4%, which is a rather well-determined estimate.

All cohort variables are insignificant. There is thus no support for or rejection of the hypothesis that cohort size influences the dynamics of Swedish earnings profiles. It might have been too optimistic to believe that cohort effects could be estimated with good precision from only three waves of data.

The demand side is, however, estimated with much greater precision. The demand effect at career start is somewhat higher than for those who have been in the market for some time, at least for those who have only compulsory schooling. The interaction effects with schooling are positive as expected, but P-values are relatively high. There is thus only a weak indication of a higher sensitivity of earnings to demand changes with increasing schooling.

Those who were born before 1920 had already reached pension age in 1984. This is thus a selected group of retirees who have reported some market work. The negative estimate indicates that they have lower-paid jobs.

We thus have to conclude that there is a diversity of results which does not lead to a clear consensus about the effects of cohort size on the earnings profiles. An evaluation of the literature suggests, however, that the earnings of university-trained and professional workers react more strongly to changes in cohort size than those of workers with less schooling, and that the wages of inexperienced workers are more sensitive to market changes than those of experienced workers. None of these conclusions are, however, supported by the empirical results of this paper. Another result, supported both by this and previous studies, is that earnings profiles are more sensitive to changes in demand than to supply side changes.

5 Earnings mobility

Define mobility as movements away from or towards an average earnings profile. Mobility is thus a residual property of the earnings function. It is, however, not necessarily measured by the residual variance, because a large share of this variance might have been generated by permanent but unobserved individual differences in earnings (heterogeneity).[6] The degree of mobility is thus measured by those parameters of the residual process which determine how much an individual changes his position relative to the average earnings profile. It is obvious that the properties of this residual process and thus also the properties of earnings mobility will depend on the specification of the average profile. It will also depend on the time unit used.[7]

With a few exceptions the literature on earnings mobility has not much to say about any dependence of mobility on age. As already noted, human capital theory suggests, however, that people with a given level of schooling who join the labour force can choose between jobs which offer a relatively low initial wage, rich investment opportunities and relatively high future wages, and jobs which pay relatively good wages already from the beginning but offer less investment opportunities and thus slower wage progression. This theory thus predicts first a movement towards the mean and then away from it. It follows that the variance of earnings around the average profile will first decrease towards a minimum relatively early in the career, the so called 'overtaking point', and then increase. In his study of the fine structure of earnings Hause (1980) took advantage of this theory and assumed that unobserved individual deviations from the average profile were linear functions of experience with negatively correlated random intercept and slope coefficients. Lillard and Weiss (1979) estimated a similar but somewhat more restricted model.

The accumulation of firm-specific human capital suggests that job mobility will decrease as people age. If job mobility is motivated by a desire to increase one's earnings or for other reasons associated with changes in pay, earnings mobility should also decrease when people age. In a study of job mobility and subsequent wages in Sweden Björklund and Holmlund (1989) found that those who quit their jobs on average gained about 8 per cent in pay per hour during the two-year period studied, somewhat more for young and somewhat less for old employees, while the change in pay for those who were laid off did not significantly differ from the average change. In another study of longitudinal wage growth, Zetterberg (1990) investigated wage rate changes associated with moves between the private and public sectors.[8] He estimated a wage-growth equation of fixed effect type with the conventional human capital variables and dummy variables indicating if an individual had moved from one sector to another. For females he found that a move from the private to the public sector gave a wage increase above average, in particular for young females. The mobility gain decreased with increasing age. For males the results were not as strong, but they indicated that males who moved from the central government to a job with local government and from such a job to a job with a private employer got a smaller wage gain than average. This loss in wage gain was larger for young employees than for old. There are clearly many reasons for job mobility not directly related to pay. When asked about their reasons for moving to another job, only a small minority mentioned 'too low pay' or 'wanted higher pay' (Björklund and Holmlund, 1989; Klevmarken and Olovsson, 1989). In his study Zetterberg (1990) claimed that males who moved from the private to the public sector obtained mobility gains in the form of a better work environment, rather than in the form of wage increases, (which was not the case for females).

In addition to the trivial type of mobility when people temporarily leave the labour force or become unemployed – they move to and from zero pay – a long spell of unemployment or absence from market work might result in a net depreciation of human capital and thus a lower wage rate when market work starts again. young people are more likely to experience unemployment than old because decisions about lay-offs usually follow seniority rules. Young females more frequently than middle aged and old stay at home to have children and give them care. Young people are thus most likely to experience this type of earnings mobility.

To explore the pattern of residual mobility as a function of age Klevmarken (1992) fitted an earnings function to panel data for males from the Swedish HUS-data set. The model was written in the following form,

$$ln(w_{it}) = x'_{it}\beta + \delta_i + v_{it} + z_{it} \tag{6}$$

$$v_{it} = \rho v_{it-1} + \epsilon_{it} \tag{7}$$

$$E(\delta_i) = E(v_{it}) = E(\epsilon_{it}) = E(z_{it}) = 0 \tag{8}$$

$$E(\delta_i^2) = \sigma_\delta^2 \tag{9}$$

$$E(\epsilon_{it}^2) = \sigma_\epsilon^2 \tag{10}$$

$$E(z_{it}^2) = \sigma_{zT}^2 \quad T = 1984, 1986, 1988 \tag{11}$$

$$E(\delta_i \epsilon_{it}) = E(\delta_i z_{it}) = E(\epsilon_{it} z_{it}) = 0 \tag{12}$$

where i indexes individuals and t years of labour market experience, x_{it} is a vector of variables which explain the average earnings profile, δ_i is a random heterogeneity component which determines each individual's 'normal' distance from the average profile and v_{it} is a temporary deviation from this distance. It was assumed to follow a first-order autoregressive process. z_{it} is a measurement error, the variance of which depends on the particular wave in which data were collected. Because personal interviews were used in 1984, telephone interviews in 1986 and a mail questionnaire in 1988, one might expect that measurement errors in the wage rate variable increase from one wave to another. (For a more detailed discussion see Klevmarken, 1992). All variance components were assumed independent of the x-variables.

With a maximum of three observations per respondent, all parameters of the covariance matrix were unfortunately not identified. One constraint was needed, and $\sigma^2_{\bar{z},84}$ was constrained to zero. This implied that the heterogeneity variance could not be distinguished from the measurement error variance for 1984.

Separate estimates were obtained for three disjunct age groups, -35, $36-50$ and $51-64$. For the reasons already given above we should expect that,

$\sigma^2_{\bar{\delta}}$ increases with age except possibly in the very beginning of the career,

σ^2_{ϵ} decreases with age,

ρ increases with age.

From human capital theory it follows that $\sigma^2_{\bar{\delta}}$ should decrease until the 'overtaking point' and then increase. The first age-interval was, however, so wide that it probably covered both the initial decreasing phase and part of the increasing phase. The estimates of $\sigma^2_{\bar{\delta}}$ showed an increase with age.

The model has now been reestimated on the same data set but with cohort size and demand indicators included. Extreme values were eliminated as in the case of GLS estimation in Table 7.1. The model was estimated by the maximum likelihood method under the assumption of normal errors, and all observations were permitted to contribute to the likelihood function. The sample was *not* truncated to those who had contributed observations for all three years.

The estimates are presented in Table 7.2. The first two columns give the parameter estimates and corresponding estimated standard errors for all age groups. The following three pairs of columns are the estimates for each age group separately.

When the model is estimated for all age groups, we find that the variance of the heterogeneity component is 2.6 times that of the temporary component. Measurement errors are most important in the last wave (mail questionnaire). The estimate of ρ is significantly negative. The same result was obtained in Klevmarken (1992) and in that case also when different starting values were tried. This implies that people tend to alternate between positions above and below their 'normal' earnings level.

Lillard & Willis (1978) who estimated a similar model on PSID-data for the years 1967–73 obtained rather different results. The variances of the

Table 7.2. Maximum likelihood estimates of earnings functions with a specified covariance structure

Variable	All males	Males aged		
		−35	36–50	51–64
Intercept	2.3646 (0.1579)	1.8209 (0.6579)	2.7997 (0.6789)	−0.3042 (2.0523)
Schooling	0.0562 (0.0087)	0.0154 (0.0208)	0.0558 (0.0138)	0.0500 (0.0199)
Schooling squared	−0.0007 (0.0003)	0.0000 (0.0008)	−0.0007 (0.0005)	−0.0004 (0.0008)
Experience, full time equivalent	0.0069 (0.0038)	0.0061 (0.0085)	0.0105 (0.0079)	0.0283 (0.0102)
Ditto, squared	−0.0001 (0.0000)	−0.0007 (0.0004)	−0.0003 (0.0002)	−0.0004 (0.0002)
Age	0.0281 (0.0065)	0.0631 (0.0343)	−0.0129 (0.0344)	0.0843 (0.0693)
Age squared	−0.0003 (0.0000)	−0.0008 (0.0006)	0.0004 (0.0004)	−0.0009 (0.0007)
Seniority	0.0038 (0.0005)	0.0034 (0.0026)	0.0030 (0.0010)	0.0033 (0.0011)
Relative cohort size	−0.4022 (4.0925)	14.3066 (19.9250)	7.2657 (7.5811)	80.7547 (45.6357)
Investments at career start	0.6497 (0.3101)	1.4985 (0.3762)	1.1182 (0.7788)	2.2883 (1.8788)
Change in investments since career start	0.9423 (0.1210)	1.7146 (0.2186)	0.5350 (0.2939)	1.3642 (0.7482)
ρ	−0.2680 (0.0778)	−0.1463 (0.2070)	0.6644 (0.1635)	−0.5610 (0.1186)
σ^2_δ	0.0435 (0.0017)	0.0211 (0.0032)	0.0375 (0.0058)	0.0625 (0.0065)
σ^2_ν	0.0173 (0.0007)	0.0204 (0.0032)	0.0199 (0.0047)	0.0149 (0.0035)
$\sigma^2_{-.86}$	0.0104 (0.0010)	0.0296 (0.0058)	0.0039 (0.0041)	0.0032 (0.0069)
$\sigma^2_{-.88}$	0.0192 (0.0018)	0.0049 (0.0049)	0.0175 (0.0044)	0.0228 (0.0071)
σ^2_ϵ	0.0160 (0.0012)	0.0199 (0.0033)	0.0111 (0.0026)	0.0102 (0.0036)
n	1,290	382	580	300
Mean ln L	−2.21038	−2.00236	−2.19204	−2.18978

Note: Data and variable definitions are the same as in Table 7.1. Extreme values have been removed. For 'all males' the covariance matrix of the parameters was computed from the inverse of the cross-products of the first derivatives, while the inverse of the matrix of second-order derivatives was used for each separate age group.

heterogeneity and temporary components were almost equal and p was estimated as 0.35. The specification of the average earnings profile was, however, richer than the one used here. When they limited the number of explanatory variables to years of schooling, experience, experience squared and time dummies, the p-estimate increased to about 0.4 and the heterogeneity variance became 50% larger than the variance of the temporary component.

A comparison of the estimates for the separate age groups shows that the heterogeneity variance increases with age and the variance of the temporary component is largest for the youngest age group, as expected. The p-estimates show an unexpected pattern. When the model was estimated without demand and supply indicators in Klevmarken (1992) they were all negative and increasing with age in absolute value, which implies that alternating behaviour is more pronounced among older people. In Table 7.2 the estimate for the youngest age group is insignificantly negative, for middle aged men it is positive and for the oldest group it is significantly negative. The weak dependence on past wages in the youngest age group is easy to accept, but the switch in sign between the two older groups is harder to explain. The positive p of the middle age group might be interpreted as the result of a career pattern. Those who have chosen to make a career and are successful increase their relative earnings position while those who do not make a career decrease theirs. After the age of 50 most people have reached the peak of their career and their wages increase slowly if at all. Wage increases for this age group are more dependent on general and negotiated increases than on increases due to promotion compared to the younger age group. Considering the nature of the local negotiations and wage revision process it is conceivable that people tend to have an alternating pattern around *their own* relative earnings position, with major wage increases every second year and no or small increases in the meantime.

This interpretation of the results in Table 7.2 is not altogether implausible, but it should be admitted that it is not an easy task to estimate a variance-covariance structure from only three waves of data. The lack of robustness in the results might indicate remaining specification errors.

The estimates of the average profiles conform more or less with previous results. We again find that the age variable dominates the experience variable. The effect of seniority is a robust 0.3–0.4 per cent return to another year with the same employer. The estimated effect of relative cohort size has a very low precision, while the estimates of wage changes due to demand shocks are significantly positive when the model is estimated for all males, but become less reliable when the data set is divided into age groups. A comparison coefficient by coefficient shows that most differences between the age groups could be random.[9]

6   Conclusions

Human capital theory suggests that wages level off at the end of a career and even decline if there is depreciation of human capital. Individuals do not necessarily experience a decline as they grow old. If there is a sufficiently high general productivity increase in the economy the resulting wage increases might dominate any decrease in human capital. In general we thus find that old people have high wages but declining wage increases. The first-order effect of an ageing workforce therefore becomes an increasing wagebill. If wages are proportional to the marginal productivity of people, as assumed by the human capital theory, this is not necessarily a problem, but if the high wages of old employees are the result of a deferred compensation scheme, wages will exceed marginal productivity and adjustments in the pay structure or in the rules for retirement are likely.

A second-order effect might arise as a result of an adjustment of the structure of wages to changes in the age distribution. Although the results from the studies of cohort size effects on earnings profiles do not all tell the same story, an evaluation of the literature suggests that wages of young people are more sensitive to changes in cohort size and to market changes in general, than those of more experienced people. A lasting effect of cohort size cannot be excluded, but it is probably smaller than the initial effect. The results also indicate that the sensitivity to changes in supply and demand is much greater for the relatively small groups of university-trained people and other professionals than for people with less schooling in occupations which do not require much investment on the job. For this reason cohort size changes might only have small effects on the average age-earnings profile for the entire labour force.[10] Indeed, the empirical results of this study have not been able to support any effect at all of cohort size on Swedish wages.

The difficulty in capturing a cohort size effect might at least partly be the result of contemporaneous changes in the demand for labour. The increased supply of young inexperienced workers from the postwar baby boom should according to most previous studies have exerted a downward pressure on wages. These cohorts, however, came out of school to join the labour market in the 1960s and beginning of the 1970s when there was still relatively high economic growth and a high demand for labour. The smaller cohorts which followed the baby boom cohorts faced the opposite situation. Their small size should *ceteris paribus* make initial wages adjust upward and result in relatively flat profiles, but they have entered the labour market at a time with low demand, and in many western countries, high unemployment which might have neutralized the effect of a small cohort size.

When the post-war baby boom cohorts retire in the first decades of the 21st century there will be a relative shortage of experienced workers. The future market situation for young inexperienced workers is less clear because there are now indications of an increased fertility rate (cf. Figure 7.4). Although it would seem less likely that we would get another large baby boom, which would increase the supply of young workers at about the same time the post-war baby boom cohorts retire, a mild increase in the slopes of the earnings profiles might be expected. If the average age at retirement is increased it should to some extent reinforce this change.

If there is any noticeable effect of cohort size on wages at all, observed and expected future changes in cohort size might thus in the next few decades first give a tendency to flatter and then to steeper profiles. Because the profiles of skilled people have a higher propensity to adjust to market changes than the profiles of unskilled workers there will also be changes in wage dispersion. The dispersion for young workers will first increase then decrease. Changes in dispersion are likely to be smaller for experienced workers but they should go in the opposite direction. For each level and type of schooling a small supply of new graduates implies a smaller wage dispersion in the beginning of the career and thus smaller investment costs. Investment on the job should thus increase, which will eventually make profiles steeper again.

It is obvious that these conclusions are of the *ceteris paribus* type. Changes in supply other than cohort size changes, for instance increased immigration, and major demand changes could make the profiles shift and change in shape in a different way. We have noted that demand changes tend to dominate any effects of cohort size.

Because the bunch of earnings profiles for all educational and occupational groups radiate with increasing age, there is a mobility away from the average earnings profile. With the exception of the first part of the career there is no reason to believe that the degree of mobility would increase with age; on the contrary, when profiles flatten out mobility away from the mean declines. As we have seen above mobility caused by temporary changes in pay also decreases with age. The major net effect of an ageing labour force is thus a decline in earnings mobility.

In this review human capital theory has served as a framework in interpreting age-earnings profiles. It might be a case of negligence not to rely more on modern theories of union wage bargaining and efficiency wages. Although they are basically micro theories they appear to have been developed and used primarily to analyse macro issues.

Most studies have focused on the earnings profiles of males. Although the estimation of female earnings profiles will put a higher demand on good data and econometric technique to cope with the problems of female mobility into and out of market work, future research should focus more on women. Do we get the same results of changes in cohort size, etc. or are these effects completely dominated by the general increase in female labour force participation? Another aspect of female labour force participation is that the post-war increase in female market work might not only have influenced the earnings of females but also the earnings of males.

NOTES

Constructive comments on previous drafts from Axel Börsch-Supan, Björn Gustafsson, Rolf Ohlsson and Klaus F. Zimmermann are gratefully acknowledged.

1　All those cases when age is a substitute variable for years of experience for lack of a better measure are disregarded.
2　It is assumed that the curves are in real wages.
3　This variable is expressed in the 1908/09 price level. I am grateful to Rolf Ohlsson who made this series available to me.
4　Year of entry was estimated by birth year + 7 + years of schooling.
5　For a discussion see Klevmarken (1992).
6　Part of the residual variance might in addition be caused by measurement errors in the earnings variable.
7　For a discussion of this approach and a review of the literature see Klevmarken (1992); for a more general survey of the literature on earnings mobility see Atkinson *et al.* (1992).
8　Chapter 3, in particular Table A4 pp. 139–40.
9　A chi-square test rejects the hypothesis that all age groups follow the same model. The test statistic is 172.79 with 32 degree of freedom. In calculating this test statistic the upper age limit of the oldest age grup was extended to include people above the age of 64 to conform with the null hypothesis that the wages of all males are generated by the same model.
10　To the extent that the share of 'skilled' jobs increases the sensitivity to changes in the supply of inexperienced workers will gradually increase.

REFERENCES

Atkinson, A.B., F. Bourguignon and C. Morrisson (1992) 'Empirical Studies of Earnings Mobility', in *Fundamentals of Pure and Applied Economics*, Chur: Harwood Academic Publishers.

Becker, G.S. (1962) 'Investment in Human Capital: A Theoretical Analysis', *Journal of Political Economy* **70**, S9–49.

　(1964) *Human Capital: A Theoretical and Empirical Analysis, with Special Reference to Education*, for National Bureau of Economic Research, New York: Columbia University Press.

Ben-Porath, Y. (1988) 'Market, Government, and Israel's Muted Baby Boom', in R.D. Lee, W.B. Arthur and G. Rodgers (eds.), *Economics of Changing Age Distribution in Developed Countries*, Oxford: Oxford University Press, 76–86.

Berger, M.C. (1985) 'The Effect of Cohort Size on Earnings Growth: A Reexamination of the Evidence', *Journal of Political Economy* **93**, 561–73.

(1989) 'Demographic Cycles, Cohort Size and Earnings', *Demography* **26**, 311–21.

Björklund, A. and B. Holmlund (1989) 'Job Mobility and Subsequent Wages in Sweden', in J. van Dijk *et al.* (eds.), *Migration and Labor Market Adjustment*, Dordrecht: Kluwer Academic Publishers.

Ermisch, J. (1988a) 'Fortunes of birth: The impact of generation size on the relative earnings of young men', *Scottish Journal of Political Economy* **35**, 266–82.

Ermisch, J. (1988b) 'British labour market responses to age distribution', in R.D. Lee, W.B. Arthur and G. Rodgers (eds.), *Economics of Changing Age Distribution in Developed Countries*, Oxford: Oxford University Press, 12–38.

Freeman, R.B. (1979) 'The Effect of Demographic Factors on Age Earnings Profiles', *Journal of Human Resources* **14**, 289–318.

Gustafsson, S. (1976) *Lönebildning och lönestruktur inom den statliga sektorn* (Determination and Structure of Salaries in the Government sector of Sweden), for Industriens Utredningsinstitut (IUI), Uppsala: Almqvist & Wiksell International.

(1981) 'Male-Female Lifetime Earnings Differentials and Labor Force History', in G. Eliasson, B. Holmlund and F. Stafford (eds.), *Studies in Labor Market Behaviour: Sweden and the United States*, for IUI, Stockholm: Almqvist & Wiksell International.

Hause, J.C. (1980) 'The Fine Structure of Earnings and the On-the-Job Training Hypothesis', *Econometrica* **48**, 1013–29.

Jonsson, A. and N.A. Klevmarken (1978) 'On the Relationship between Cross-Sectoral and Cohort Earnings Profiles', *Annales de l'INSEE*, 331–53.

Klevmarken, N.A. (1972) *Statistical Methods for the Analysis of Earnings Data*, Stockholm: Almqvist and Wiksell.

(1980) *Ålders-, kvalifikations och befordringstillägg. En studie av industritjänstemännens lönebildning*. Statistiska institutionen, Göteborgs Universitet, Skriftserie nr 17, Almqvist & Wiksell International (Also available in an English translation: *Age, Qualification and Promotion Supplements. A Study of Salary Formation for Salaried Employees in Swedish Industry*, Research Report 1980:3, Department of Statistics, Gothenburg University).

(1982) 'On the Stability of Age-Earnings Profiles', *Scandinavian Journal of Economics* **84**, 531–54.

(1990) 'Household, Market and Nonmarket Activities (HUS). Design, Field Work and Nonresponse', Memorandum No. 144, Department of Economics, Gothenburg University.

(1992) 'Wage Rate Mobility and Measurement Errors: An application to Swedish Panel Data', Memorandum No. 167, Department of Economics, Gothenburg University, forthcoming in M. Casson and J. Creedy (eds.), *Industrial and Economic Inequality: Essays in Honour of Peter Hart*, Edward Elgar.

Klevmarken, N.A. and P. Olovsson (1989) *Hushållens ekonomiska levnadsförhållanden (HUS). Teknisk beskrivning och kodbok*, Department of Economics, Gothenburg University.

Klevmarken, N.A. and J.M. Quigley (1976) 'Age, Experience, Earnings, and Investments in Human Capital', *Journal of Political Economy* **84**, 47–72.

LaLonde, R.J. and R.H. Topel (1991) 'Labour Market Adjustments to Increased Immigration', in Abowd, J.M. and R.B. Freeman (eds.), *Immigration, Trade and the Labor Market*, Chicago: University of Chicago Press.

Lazear, E.P. (1981) 'Agency, Earnings Profiles, Productivity, and Hours Restrictions', *American Economic Review* **71**, 606–20.

Leiniö, T.L. (1988) 'Sex and Ethnic Segregation in the 1980 Swedish Labour Market', *Economic and Industrial Democracy*, London, Newbury Park, Beverly Hills and New Delhi: SAGE, vol. 9, pp. 99–120.

Lillard, L.A. and Y. Weiss (1979) 'Components of Variation in Panel Earnings Data: American Scientists, 1960–70', *Econometrica* **47**, 437–54.

Lillard, L.A. and R.J. Willis (1978) 'Dynamic Aspects of Earning Mobility', *Econometrica* **46**, 985–1012.

Martin, G.M. and N. Ogawa (1988) 'The Effect of Cohort Size on Relative Wages in Japan', in R.D. Lee, W.B. Arthur and G. Rodgers (eds.), *Economics of Changing Age Distribution in Developed Countries*, Oxford: Oxford University Press, 59–75.

Mincer, J. (1958) 'Investment in Human Capital and Personal Income Distribution', *Journal of Political Economy* **66**, 281–302.

(1962) 'On-the-Job Training: Costs, Returns and Some Implications', *Journal of Political Economy* **70**, S50–79.

(1970) 'The Distribution of Labour Incomes: A Survey with Special Reference to the Human Capital Approach', *Journal of Economic Literature* **8**, 1–26.

(1974) *Schooling, Experience and Earnings*, New York: National Bureau of Economic Research.

Mincer, J. and S. Polachek (1974) 'Family Investments in Human Capital: Earnings of Women', *Journal of Political Economy* **82**, S76–108.

Murphy, K., M. Plant and F. Welch (1988). 'Cohort Size and Earnings in the United States', in R.D. Lee, W.B. Arthur and G. Rodgers (eds.), *Economics of Changing Age Distribution in Developed Countries*, Oxford: Oxford University Press, 39–58.

Nothaft, F.E. (1985) 'The Effect of Cohort Size on Human Capital Investment and Earnings Growth', Working Paper 42, Washington, D.C.: Board of Governors of the Federal Reserve System.

Phelps Brown, H. (1977) *The Inequality of Pay*, Oxford: Oxford University Press.

Schultz, T.W. (1961) 'Investment in Human Capital', *American Economic Review* **51**, 1–17.

Stapleton, D.C. and D.J. Young (1988) 'Educational Attainment and Cohort Size', *Journal of Labor Economics* **6**, 330–61.

Tasiran, A. and Gustafsson, B. (1991) 'The Monthly Wage Earnings of Salesmen and Shop Assistants', Working Paper, Department of Economics, Gothenburg University.

Weiss, Y. and L.A. Lillard (1978) 'Experience, Vintage and Time Effects in the Growth of Earnings: American Scientists 1960–70', *Journal of Political Economy* **86**, 427–47.

Welch, F. (1979) 'Effects of Cohort Size on Earnings: The Baby Boom Babies' Financial Bust', *Journal of Political Economy* **87**, S65–97.

Wright, R.E. (1991) 'Cohort size and earnings in Great Britain', *Journal of Population Economics* **4**, 295–305.

Zetterberg, J. (1990) 'Essays on Inter-sectoral Wage Differentials', Dissertation, Department of Economics, Uppsala University.

178 Discussion by Axel Börsch-Supan

Discussion

AXEL BÖRSCH-SUPAN

Anders Klevmarken has delivered an ambitious paper in which he first reviews the state of our knowledge of the dependency of earnings on age and then adds new evidence on age-earnings profiles and earnings mobility drawn from Swedish panel data. The core of his paper is an attempt to separate the effects of individual ageing from the effects of a changing population age structure, measured in terms of changing relative birth cohort sizes. Klevmarken's econometric approach is diligent and skillful. It is thus all the more disappointing that the crucial variable which measures changes in the age distribution remains insignificant. My comments all centre on why this may be the case.

There are essentially three reasons for not measuring effects in an econometric analysis: the model may be inappropriate, the data may be too weak, or there is simply no effect. The rules of statistical reasoning prohibit the last conclusion, and I would not give up on searching for real effects so quickly. What about the second reason? The Swedish HUS-panel is a rich data set which features detailed work and schooling histories for a reasonable number of observations. It is good data on which a number of successful empirical labour studies have been based. However, there are only three waves of data. This time span might simply be too short to sufficiently separate the influence on earnings of variables which depend on individual age from variables which depend on birth cohort.

Although I would consider this is an important reason for not being able to detect cohort size effects, it is not a very interesting one. Let me therefore comment on the appropriateness of Klevmarken's econometric model. I admire Klevmarken's careful econometric approach. In the earnings section, he applies general GLS which takes care of heteroscedasticity as well as autocorrelation, in particular the typical random effect structure of panel data. In the section on earnings mobility, he combines random effects and contemporary disturbances with autoregressive errors in an imaginative variance decomposition. Klevmarken also recognizes the unbalancedness of the panel in accommodating single waves of data rather than chopping his data to the least common period. All this should be applauded. Klevmarken certainly gives the stochastic part of his equations – reduced form equations, as he states at the end of Section 2 – the best econometric treatment. But can you make a silk purse from a sow's ear, as a drastic American saying has it? Couldn't we get better specifications of the deterministic part of the equations?

I therefore want to focus my comments on the theoretical background of Klevmarken's estimated model. Anders Klevmarken takes the human capital theory as his point of departure. At the end of the second section, he summarizes what he thinks we can learn from human capital theory about the specification of empirical age-earnings profiles. Klevmarken's answer is rather general: 'The individual earnings progression with increasing age thus depends on a number of decisions about schooling, career choice, breaks in labour force participation etc.,' and on 'the expected future private return to investment in human capital' as 'determined by the demand for and supply of various types of skills but also by wage bill taxes.'

This is too general to be of much help. This reasoning furnishes a list of variables to be included in a reduced form estimate in which earnings (and earnings mobility) are related to supply and demand variables. But doesn't the rational decision-making process postulated by the human capital theory give us more structure than Klevmarken suggests? I am alluding basically to two kinds of structural restrictions on functional forms of empirical age-earnings profiles.

First, the long-run, life-time rational decision process underlying the human capital theory implies a dynamic programming structure. In cross-sectional data, this structure may be irrelevant because we cannot identify a dynamic structure from cross-sectional data. But we also cannot separate age and cohort-related effects from each other. This is very different for time-series or panel data, the only data that properly identifies age effects not confounded by cohort shifts. A dynamic programming structure, however, puts restrictions on the analysis and is crucial for the proper interpretation of the longitudinal data.

Second, because human capital theory is intrinsically a life cycle theory, it has implications on what is exogenous and what is endogenous. Specifically, the choice of career paths is endogenous as well as schooling, labour force participation, and therefore experience. Hence, almost all of the variables in Table 7.1 which Klevmarken terms 'supply variables' are endogenous from a life cycle perspective.

If we believe in the life-time rational decision making suggested by human capital theory, we should make use of these structural restrictions on functions relating education, age, and earnings. This is not an easy task and certainly requires a modelling effort beyond the scope of a conference paper, as Klevmarken correctly remarks at the end of section 2. Rather, I am proposing a research agenda to get away and beyond the Mincer-type fairly agnostic and atheoretical regressions of earnings on age, occupational or dummy variables, and schooling because we just cannot claim that they are deduced from human capital theory. Failure or success of these reduced form equations do not tell us anything about the validity of the human capital theory because they do not impose the rational, foresighted choice behaviour that is the essence of human capital theory.

It would also be helpful to mention in this theoretical background part some of the alternative theories which try to explain age-earnings profiles – Kotlikoff and Wise's work on productivity comes to my mind, and Edward Lazear's work on seniority. These papers have rather different approaches to age-earnings profiles. Do they imply age-earnings profiles similar to the human capital theory? It appears an important task to sort out these theories and to test their relative validity before one can claim that the estimated regressions are derived from human capital theory and can be interpreted according to it.

Klevmarken summarizes his empirical results of section 4 as follows: 'We thus have to conclude that there is a diversity of results which does not lead itself to a clear consensus about the effects of cohort size on earnings profiles.' Notwithstanding the serious problem of a very short panel duration, I think that we can only extract information about this highly complicated problem by imposing more economic structure. Since the kind of reduced form equations which Klevmarken estimates can be attributed to many kinds of structural forms, and since different structural forms may have various implications on different reduced form equations, we appear to be in a classical identification problem which can only be resolved by theory.

By the way: considering the difficulties in identifying first-order parameters, I would not dare to structurally interpret the estimated variances and correlation coefficients. It is extremely hard to identify second moments of residuals in any case, but certainly here. The negative rho in the earnings mobility equation, Table 7.2, is strange, to say the least, and it may rather indicate specification errors than the biennial wage increases that Klevmarken suggests. In any case, such a structural interpretation should then be checked against other evidence.

The paper says little about structural adjustments of age-earnings profiles to population ageing. Longer life spans due to better health are likely to shift the age-productivity profiles, thus also the age-earnings profiles. The increasing pressure to finance social security systems with even larger dependency ratios than now may spur productivity and technical progress. There is obviously little we can say about these adjustments at this point because they are not measurable in the three waves of the HUS panel data, but these adjustments may be larger than the first round supply effects due to different cohort sizes.

Once again, these points are certainly beyond the scope of Klevmarken's paper. They are suggestions for more research departing from his work. Good papers inspire the phantasy, and this paper certainly did.

8 Age, wages and education in The Netherlands

JOOP HARTOG, HESSEL OOSTERBEEK and COEN TEULINGS

1 Introduction

Throughout the postwar period, the age composition of the Dutch labour force has shown large changes. And according to demographic predictions, the driving force behind these developments has not yet come to an end. In this paper we study some consequences by looking at historical developments, and we use our findings for some speculation about future developments. Throughout the paper, we will distinguish labour by level of education, since this is one of the most obvious sources of heterogeneity. We will study the changes in the educational composition of the labour force and we discuss possible explanations. We will consider labour force participation behaviour, as it is a vital step between population and labour force. And we will analyse the consequences for the structure of wages of a changing composition of the labour force, by age and education (including the impact of variations in cohort size). This latter analysis will be conducted against the background of generally claimed rigidity in the Dutch wage structure, originating in institutionalization of wage determination and supported by the welfare state.

In the next section, we characterize the nature and history of the Dutch labour market. In section 3, we document changes in labour force composition; in section 4 we discuss causes and consequences, based on theory and available research. In section 5, we present our own contribution to empirical analysis, focussing on Mincerian earnings equations estimated for 14 cross-sections between 1962 and 1989. In section 6, we investigate the role of cohort size in determining earnings. In section 7, we collect our conclusions and speculate about possible future developments.

2 A brief history of the Dutch labour market

The relation between wages, education and experience has not developed in a vacuum, but should be interpreted against the background of the

182

general labour market situation. To provide that perspective, we will start with a very brief introduction to the postwar history of the Dutch labour market (details are given in Hartog & Theeuwes, 1991).

Crudely, and without bothering too much about exact boundaries, one might distinguish four periods; the early reconstruction years (late forties), the golden-growth period (fifties and sixties), the interval of decelerating growth and accelerating problems (the seventies, in particular after the first oil crisis in 1973) and the period of mixed recovery, after a deep slump (the eighties).

The first years after the Second World War were years of construction and restoration of normal economic life. Strong growth continued into the late sixties, with unemployment falling to below 1% in the years 1960 to 1965. The labour shortage affected migration, and after 1960, Holland changed from a net emigration into a net immigration country. A large inflow of Mediterraneans developed after 1960, induced by a shortage of unskilled labour that resulted from a simultaneous increase in demand and a decrease in national supply. Up to 1972, this exerted substantial downward pressure on the wage structure for blue-collar males, stabilizing the skill differential in the face of initial excess demand (the female unskilled relative wage rose strongly). After 1972, the skill differential probably narrowed, due to deliberate redistributive government policies (see Hartog & Vriend, 1989). However, the statistical series on the skill differential was discontinued, so we cannot substantiate this.

During the seventies, labour market problems became manifest, with unemployment rising from 1.1% in 1970 to 5.1% in 1979. Employment growth was low, and in particular, female labour supply grew strongly by international standards. The worst period in the Dutch labour market was the mid-eighties, with the official ('registered') unemployment rate rising to 17.3% in 1984. The late eighties showed recovery, with strong employment growth.

From the late sixties on, the welfare state was developed, with particular relevance for workers at the lower end of the income distribution, with a legal minimum wage, a generous disability insurance programme and a Social Assistance Law ('welfare') that used a relative norm for its benefits, rather than an absolute one (see Hartog, 1989, for details). The highly institutionalized process of wage determination (see below) was allowed *de facto* to determine minimum wage rates for a large segment of the labour force, and a legal minimum wage, with even wider coverage, was introduced in 1969. It was raised substantially in 1974 but during the eighties lagged behind average wage development. The disability insurance programme that started in 1967 absorbed many workers who would otherwise have been unemployed (it even explicitly allowed the extent of an individual's disability to be determined taking local labour market

conditions into consideration). Unemployment benefits, disability benefits, and social assistance all came to use the same net minimum level,
equal to the net minimum wage for a male with a dependent family, and to
70% of this net minimum wage for single wage earners. The high levels of
unemployment that developed after the early seventies fell disproportionately on the less educated and on 'guest workers'. At the same time these
individuals experienced most protection from minimum wage legislation,
the general social welfare programmes and early retirement schedules.
The causal relation between inactivity and the welfare state has been
extensively debated. There is a good deal of consensus that the welfare
state contributed much through benefits and reduced effective supply and
through taxes and premiums that reduced labour demand (see Hartog &
Theeuwes, 1991, for details).

Interest in distributional matters has been very strong in the Netherlands
throughout the postwar period. There always have been many government interventions aiming at a flatter income distribution, especially
between the late sixties and the early eighties. During the eighties,
national consensus about the desirability of small income differences
diminished, but even now, most government policy proposals are most
vehemently debated in terms of their consequences for the income distribution, especially for the lowest incomes. Unions participate in such
debates, and in some periods there have been explicit union policies to
reduce wage differentials. In the early seventies, for example, unions
demanded (and obtained) wage rises in equal nominal amounts rather
than in percentages, and minimum nominal wage increase for given
percentages of vacation allowances and cost-of-living adjustments. There
is no good time-series information on earnings inequality among individuals in the Netherlands, due to the absence or incomparability of
information about particular years. The best source for a series based on
comparable data is Van de Stadt (1988), on 'disposable income' (which
includes social security transfers received and subtracts premiums and
taxes paid); the income unit is either a single person or the joint household
of a married couple. Between 1959 and 1984, the Theil coefficient for
employees has fallen by 36%. The reduction took place almost entirely in
the period 1964–75; before and after these years, inequality was virtually
stable (Van de Stadt, 1988, p. 29).

Wage determination is highly institutionalized in the Netherlands. For a
long time there was strong government intervention with special boards
for consultation and negotiation. From 1945 to 1954, collective agreements required government approval, and they were tested against norms
for wage increases, with little room for differentiation. Up to 1959, there
were upper limits to wage increases, rather than binding norms, but in

practice, the limit became the actual increase. After 1959, official policy admitted differentiation by industry, depending on productivity growth. After 1963, the government lost authority and formal influence, but consultations at the central level were continued. In 1982, unemployment rose quickly. The government, trade unions and employers organizations reached a general agreement ('Stichtingsakkoord') to combat unemployment by moderation of wage claims and working time reduction. This agreement has had large effects on the outcome of the process of wage formation and these effects lasted for several years. However, it was the last time that official negotiations at the central level took place. Since then wage contracts have been negotiated at the industry level, mainly due to pressure of employers' organizations. Formal union influence on wage growth and the wage structure has always been very strong, through the highly developed system of centralized consultation, the instrument of the collective agreement and the policy of general extension of an agreement to all firms (and workers) in an industry. At present, union membership is about 24%, but some 80% of the labour force is covered by a collective agreement. About 18% of covered workers have company agreements; the other 82% are covered by industry-wide collective agreements.

It is often claimed that the wage structure in the Netherlands is weakly responsive to labour market conditions. This would be caused by the high degree of institutionalization of wage setting and by welfare state programmes, which maintain a solid floor to the wage structure through the social minimum (minimum wage and related social benefits) and support the wage structure itself through high replacement ratios in unemployment and disability insurance. We will keep this claim in mind in the analyses that follow.

3   The composition of the labour force by age and education

3.1   Age

The development of the age composition of the labour force is given in Table 8.1, for males and females separately. Among males, the share of the young diminishes steadily, and there is a small decline in the share of the old, mostly of those above the state-pension age (65). The share of prime-aged males rises considerably, from 54% in 1947 to 68% in 1989. Among females, there are similar trends, but much more pronounced. The share of the young falls dramatically and that of the prime-aged increases by about 50%, from 40% in 1947 to 60% in 1985. Jointly, the total development can be summarized as a modest decline in the share of

Table 8.1. *Dutch labour force composition by age, 1947–89 (%)*

Year	15–24	25–49	50–64	65+
Males				
1947	23.9	53.6	18.5	3.9
1960	20.9	54.1	22.2	2.8
1971	21.5	55.6	21.1	1.9
1975	17.8	60.3	20.5	1.4
1979	16.6	63.2	19.3	1.0
1985	16.1	65.8	17.4	0.7
1989	15.7	68.4	15.9	0.0
Females				
1947	46.4	39.7	11.4	2.4
1960	52.1	33.9	12.5	1.5
1971	48.1	37.4	13.2	1.4
1975	39.7	46.5	12.8	1.1
1979	35.0	52.3	12.2	0.6
1985	28.6	60.4	10.6	0.3
1989	24.0	65.6	10.4	0.0
Total				
1947	29.4	50.2	16.8	3.6
1960	27.9	49.6	20.0	2.5
1971	28.3	50.9	19.1	1.7
1975	23.9	56.5	18.4	1.3
1979	22.1	59.9	17.1	0.9
1985	20.5	63.9	15.1	0.6
1989	18.8	67.3	13.8	0.0

Source: See Table 8.2.

the old, a strong decrease in the share of the young and an equally strong increase in the share of the prime-aged.

These developments resulted in part from changes in the age composition of the population. In the entire postwar period, the ratio of the population aged over 65 to that aged 20–64 has increased, from 13.4 per 100 in 1947 to 20.7 per 100 in 1989. The ratio of the population aged under 20 to that aged 20–64 initially increased, from 55.5% in 1947 to a maximum of 72.5% in 1963, and then started a long and rapid decrease to 42.8% in 1989 (*Tachtig Jaren Statistiek*, p. 21 and *Statistisch Zakboek 1991*, p. 37).

More important are changes in participation behaviour. The young increasingly stayed in school. For males, the participation of those below 20 fell from 66.0% in 1947 to 25.8% in 1975, for females the drop was from 57.5 to 28.4%. Participation rates for older individuals behaved differently

Table 8.2. *Participation rates, 50–64 year-olds, 1947–89 (%)*

Year	1947	1960	1971	1975	1979	1985	1989
Males	89.5	91.1	85.1	79.2	72.9	64.7	60.1
Females	16.9	13.5	17.0	17.4	18.2	19.9	23.6

Sources: 1947–1975 *Tachtig Jaren Statistiek in Tijdreeksen,* C.B.S., p. 67.
1979 *Statistisch Zakboek 1983,* p. 120.
1985 *Statistisch Zakboek 1987,* p. 159.
1989 *Statistisch Zakboek 1992,* p. 97.

for males and females (see Table 8.2). The participation rate for older males dropped about 30 points in the last 30 years, with an acceleration after 1971, when unemployment started to increase. For females, it diminished between 1947 and 1960 but then started to increase. This development reflects the strong increase in labour force participation for married females. Married females were virtually absent from the labour market in 1947, barely participated in 1960 (6.4%) and then started to catch up with those in neighbouring countries: from 15.6% in 1971 to 45% in 1989. Much female participation is part-time, however. We can now summarize the changes in the labour force composition by age as follows. Both for males and females, the share of the 'prime-aged' increased strongly between 1947 and 1985: by about a quarter for males, and by half for females. The share of the young diminished for males up to 1975 and then more or less stabilized, for females dramatically and continuously. Both for males and females, there was a reduction in the share of the old. For the young, the share diminished for demographic reasons (after 1963), and because of increased participation in education. Older males rapidly disappeared from the labour market, when unemployment started to increase. Older females increased their participation during the seventies and eighties, in spite of the high unemployment rates. This development is associated with the strong increase in labour force participation of married females.

3.2 Education

There is no neat time series of the labour force by education in the Netherlands. The first observation only dates back to 1960 (before, an individual's education was not included in the Census). Moreover, the educational system has changed and some school types disappeared, while new ones were created. In Table 8.3 the best available information is

Table 8.3. *Composition of the Dutch labour force by education, 1960–90* *(%)*

Year	1960	1975	1979	1990
Males				
Lower	56.7	34.4	22.9	13.8
Extended lower	32.5	40.2	29.0	25.6
Intermediate	6.8	13.9	31.8	40.1
Semi-higher	2.4	7.1	9.5	12.4
Higher	1.6	3.7	4.1	7.6
Females				
Lower	54.1	32.4	20.5	11.8
Extended lower	36.6	39.4	34.6	28.1
Intermediate	8.3	18.8	28.5	39.7
Semi-higher	0.5	7.6	10.3	15.6
Higher	0.5	1.5	1.6	4.2

Note: Figures do not add up to 100% due to missing information on the level of education of some workers. For 1979 only, students are not attributed to any level, leading to totals substantially further below 100%.

Sources: 13e *Algemene Volkstelling,* 31 mei 1960, tabel 25A.
   Arbeidskrachtentelling 1975, staat 8.
   Arbeidskrachtentelling 1979, staat 13.
   Enquête Beroepsbevolking 1990, staat 64.

collected, using the standard classification of education levels. The pattern is quite straightforward: a general, monotonic and very strong increase in the level of education of the labour force.

Although there can be no doubt about this general trend in the level of education, some care should be exercised when interpreting the data in Table 8.3. In principle each level represents three years of education. However, in applying this principle to the practical classification of various types of education, some arbitrary assumptions must be made. These assumptions are changed in the course of time as the system of education itself has been changed. In particular, the Central Bureau of Statistics tries to account for courses followed later on during a labour market career. This effort causes an artificial increase in the level of education. The recoding of types of education is a more or less continuous process which makes data hard to evaluate. A major recoding took place between 1975 and 1979, explaining the large shift in composition in this period reported in Table 8.3.

Of course, the changes in the composition by age and education interact, with the changes in educational behaviour first manifesting themselves among young school leavers, and re-entering married females. We will refrain from presenting such detailed tables of interaction, as there would quickly be too much information to digest. However, this cohort effect enables us to be positive about future developments: a further rise of the average level of education is to be expected, especially for females.

4   Explaining changes in labour force composition

We will take the demographic developments for granted and study two questions:
– Why did the demand for education increase?
– What caused the change in participation behaviour?
Understanding the causes of these developments will be helpful for speculating about future developments, as we do briefly in the concluding section.

4.1   Increased demand for education

Obviously, the increased level of education of the labour force results from two effects; an inflow of young entrants with above-average levels of education, and an outflow of older workers with below-average levels of education. The increased enrolment in higher education has been the subject of several previous studies (De Jong et al., 1990; Huijsman et al., 1986). These studies typically use a time-series framework. They suggest that both consumption and investment motives play their role in explaining high enrolment rates in recent years. Government intervention is important, through supply of education facilities (private schools are virtually absent) and by influencing financial conditions.

Throughout the postwar period, participation in extended education increased almost year by year. If education were just a consumption good, one might find an explanation in prices and incomes. From growing parental incomes and a positive income elasticity of demand, one would indeed predict increased participation. Statements about the effect of the price of education are less easily derived without empirical research, because it is not immediately clear what happened to the price of education. The price consists of tuition fees, the wage foregone while at school, the tax treatment of schooling expenditures and government subsidies.

Ritzen (1985) has extensively documented the government contribution to the individual cost of schooling. Tuition fees, until recently, were levied only for higher education. From 1950 to 1971 they declined in real terms; they rose sharply in 1972 but fell again in 1973 (after strong student protest); from 1973 till 1980 they declined steadily, and since 1980 we observe an increase.[1]

Financial aid to students has been complicated and subject to drastic changes over time. Before 1986, governmental support consisted of child allowance and child tax deductions for students and of loans and grants. Loans and grants were only available in the case of parents with income below a threshold; above that, allowance and deduction applied. In 1954, the age limit for allowance and deduction was raised from 21 to 27; from 1963, students were counted twice, since 1966 three times. In 1978, child deductions were abandoned, and child allowances were raised.

After 1986, the system of child allowances was abandoned altogether and replaced by a new system of financial support for students (the old system of loans and grants was given up at the same time). In the current system all students up to 27 years old receive a basic grant. Depending on their parents' income some students can obtain an interest-bearing loan and, as children of poor parents, an additional grant.

If all these developments are lumped together in an index of financial aid to students (based on the maximum grant and the after-tax value of allowances and deduction, weighted by the share of grant-receiving students) we observe a pattern similar to the tuition index: an improvement from 1950 to 1970, a deterioration thereafter.[2]

To calculate the price of education, one should add the opportunity wage, and this no doubt has risen in real terms through most of the period. This suggests that between 1950 and 1970, the price of education might have fallen (if fee reduction and financial aid improvement outperformed increased opportunity cost), thus contributing to increased participation. But after 1970, the price will certainly have increased, and hence, cannot be the basis for explaining the continued growth of participation.

If we apply the human capital view that education is an investment, expected returns should also be relevant for the participation decision. However, participation increased without indication of substantial changes in the expected earnings structure (and in section 5 we will show that the actual return to education even has fallen). Combined with the (crude) observations above on the price of education, this suggests that the simple human capital model with a perfect capital market cannot explain the strong increase in enrolment in higher education. Capital market imperfections, in particular, the reduced rationing of investment funds, may be very important.[3] With an imperfect capital market, some individuals are unable to reap the benefits of education and returns contain an element of rent. Rising parental incomes and more generous government subsidies (up to 1970) would then provide an explanation for increased participation. If this explanation holds, increased participation, *ceteris paribus*, should reduce the rate of return by competing away the rent component.

4.2 Changes in labour force participation

Reduced participation for the young does not need any special attention, as it just mirrors increased participation in education. Reduced participation for older males does not seem to pose great problems either. Increased demand for leisure, based on rising wages (for males, the income effect tends to dominate the substitution effect) and improved (state) pensions has been long observed. On top of that, the explanation can be found in the financial incentives provided by disability insurance and early retirement schemes developed by the government and in collective bargaining when high unemployment rates persisted. Disability programmes and early retirement schemes have been quite generous in the Netherlands and easily explain the accelerated male labour force withdrawals observed in Table 8.2.

Changes in participation behaviour of married females are a more complicated matter, if one wants to find an explanation without arbitrarily invoking changes in preferences. A convincing explanation would combine, in a life-cycle perspective, changes in education, fertility and participation behaviour, based on changes in wage rates, household technology and availability of contraceptives. Increased labour productivity in the household, due to increased capital-intensity, would lead to more market activity, if the volume of household production is considered fixed. Improved birth control methods may reduce family size, also freeing time for market activity.[4] A strong substitution effect of increased female wages and a weak negative income effect for female and male wages (which are usually found in empirical research) similarly lead to increased market activity.[5] But no doubt, other effects, such as reduced rationing and discrimination against females in the labour market, and more equal treatment by the government (in taxes and in the law) also have played their part. While there have been many analyses of female labour supply in the Netherlands, the postwar developments have not yet been completely explained and decomposed within an estimated econometric model.

Participation rates will also be affected by the conditions of labour demand. In this perspective, it is remarkable that during the shortage of unskilled labour in the sixties employers in the manufacturing sector did not attempt to hire females, but turned to imported labour (Hartog & Vriend, 1989). This may be attributed to discrimination (and/or to 'statistical discrimination') or to the impact of labour legislation, such as laws forbidding female night and shift work. The recent strong shift of employment towards the service sector, with its increased latitude for part-time work and flexible hours did come to be associated with rising female participation rates. The relation between female labour force participation and the nature of job opportunities is underresearched in the Netherlands.

5   The wage structure

In the next two sections of the paper, we will present novel empirical work of our own, focussing on changes in the wage structure. We will begin with a brief excursion into theory to get some feel for what might be expected when the labour force composition by age and education changes. Thereafter we present our empirical analyses.

5.1   Labour force composition and wage structure

Predictions on the consequences of a change in the composition of the labour force for the wage structure can formally be derived from a set of supply and demand equations for each education-age group. With supply and demand each depending on all wage rates and some exogenous variables, changes in equilibrium wages, under perfect competition, can be solved for changes in the exogenous (supply and demand) variables. Crucial for the outcome would be the cross-effects, or, stated differently, the responses to changes in relative wages by supply and demand (substitution elasticities).

Only strong restrictions allow unambiguous predictions. If human capital theory is interpreted as a theory of the long-run equilibrium wage structure, the structure of demand (for different education levels) would not be relevant. The wage structure would be shaped by the equilibrium rate of return. With a horizontal supply curve of capital, it would be constant; with an increasing supply curve, increased participation in education (induced by an outward shift of the demand curve for educated labour) would lead to higher rates of return. If the supply curve for human capital were to shift downward over time (due to increased supply of parental wealth or more generous government scholarships), educational expansion could be associated with falling rates of return to investment in human capital. A downward shift in parental supply curves of funds for investment in human capital seems a plausible assumption.

If the supply of funds for human capital investment is not horizontal, the demand for educated labour in response to relative wages is also relevant for determining the location of the equilibrium. With perfect substitutability of educated labour (among all categories), demand would dominate the wage ratios: they would equal the fixed ratios of productivity. Perfect substitutability (i.e. the efficiency units assumption) is not commonly assumed, but agreement on the exact magnitude of elasticities of substitution is weak.

Implicit in the above interpretation is the notion of educated labour as a homogeneous factor with equilibrium price formation in the (related) factor markets. It may be that there is not so much a system of markets for labour of different levels of education, but that education serves to allocate labour to jobs. In the short run, the structure of jobs and job wages may be given, and a given supply of labour by education may be distributed across jobs, with the best jobs going to the most highly educated. Increased supply of highly educated labour will lead to lower average wages for this category, because graduates are pushed into lower paid jobs. This will imply increased wage dispersion for the more highly educated workers (they will now extend into lower job levels) and reduced wage dispersion for the least educated group (they are expelled from higher job levels). Predictions on dispersion for intermediate levels of education cannot be made without further restrictions, as they will depend on the range of job levels covered before and after the shift.[6] Job wage rigidity and top-down rationing of individuals to jobs would also imply that unemployment falls disproportionately on the less educated.

Predictions on the wage effects arising from changes in the age composition of the labour force are not straightforward either.[7] Age or experience can be taken as an index for separate production factors, for which (related) supply and demand relations hold. As before, changes in the equilibrium wage structure by age will depend on the substitution elasticities of supply and demand. Empirically, wage profiles by age (experience) slope upward initially, with a decreasing slope, and may fall towards the end of working life. The curvature of such profiles is stronger, the higher the level of education.

Human capital theory explains the profiles from investment in on-the-job training, which gives rise to productivity growth initially beyond and later below depreciation of human capital. The analyses available in the literature seem to assume that the demand side of the labour market (supply of training opportunities) will accommodate any preference by labour supply, thus generating equilibrium wage profiles that reflect the desired rate of return. If this is so, changes in the age composition of the labour force should not affect age-wage profiles, other than through a change in the desired (equilibrium) internal rate of return. Can one meaningfully speculate about the relation between changes in the age composition and the required rate of return? Note that if the supply curve of training opportunities (related to the rate of return) is not horizontal, this supply curve will also affect the equilibrium outcome (and changes therein). In the analysis of effects of cohort sizes, one sometimes assumes perfect foresight on age-specific equilibrium wage rates and then predicts optimum investment profits given the pattern of relative wages. This also presupposes an accommodating supply of training opportunities.

Other explanations of the upward sloping age-wage profile have been put forward. One type of explanation refers to the effect of imperfect information. Employers are not fully informed about worker qualities, workers are not fully aware of job requirements (and their own talents). Mobility and job shopping gradually improve the match and hence, wages. We are not aware of models that develop the implications of changed labour force composition along these lines, and we have not attempted to develop one ourselves. It may be that more young entrants create something like search congestion, but it is not clear what that means for the wage structure.

Upward sloping profiles have also been interpreted as an incentive mechanism under imperfect observation of individual effort (Lazear, 1979). The worker is underpaid in the initial stages of his career, and will only catch up through later overpayment if not caught cheating. Whatever the value of this argument (in the face of temporary rather than lifetime worker-firm attachments), it would seem that the argument implies stable age-wage profiles when the labour force composition changes: why would the incentive structure have to respond to such changes? If anything, this is an easy prediction to test.[8]

So, where does this brief exercise in theory lead us? With a human capital explanation of the wage structure by education, we would postulate upward sloping supply curves for investment funds (higher opportunity cost for ever more investment). And we would assume these curves to move outward over time, due to growing parental wealth and increased government subsidies (up to 1970). That would lead us to a prediction of increased participation in higher education at falling rates of return. In the model with fixed job wage rate and top-down rationing, it is not quite clear what would happen to calculated rates of return to education if individuals take up more education. The average wage rate for the most highly educated falls, but this also occurs for the least educated. And for intermediate education, it is not clear what will happen. But the model has two other, unambiguous predictions: increased wage dispersion for the most highly educated, reduced wage dispersion for the least educated, and unemployment disproportionately for the least educated.

Age-income profiles will not be sensitive to changes in the age composition of the labour force, if Lazear's moral hazard explanation holds, or if on-the-job training is governed by a given required internal rate of return and perfectly elastic supply of training opportunities. If one takes age groups as exogenous supply of separate production factors, large cohorts depress earnings, small cohorts increase earnings. This latter type of approach will be further discussed in section 6.

5.2   Data on the structure of wages

Our analyses are essentially based on six cross-tabulations for 1962, 1965, 1972, 1979, 1985 and 1989. Entries of these tables are attained level of education and age-group. The data allow us to distinguish 5 different levels of education and 6 to 10 age groups. The classification into levels of education is formally the same as that discussed in section 3.2, although in practice data from both sources may be not fully consistent. For each education-age group the tables contain the mean and standard deviation of the gross hourly wage rate, and the number of observations. The tables for 1962, 1965 and 1972 refer to male white-collar workers in manufacturing, construction and the banking sector, the tables for 1979, 1985 and 1989 are based on samples of full-time working male employees. The data are collected directly from the administration of employers, which makes the information on gross wages highly reliable. Also, the sample size is 10,000 or more. This generates enough information for reasonably precise measurement of wages.

In addition to the information contained in the cross-tabulations, we also have four other (smaller) datasets available, with which it is possible to estimate the Mincerian earnings equation. These datasets are based on surveys collected in 1982, 1985, 1986 and 1988.[9] Information on wages from these surveys is less precise than the wage information from the cross-tabulations. On the other hand, whereas in the cross-tabulations people are grouped into 5-years age groups, the surveys provide age by year.

5.3   The Mincerian earnings function

In this section we present results for the standard Mincerian earnings equation (Mincer 1974):

$$ln\, w = \beta_0 + \beta_1 s + \beta_2 t + \beta_3 t^2 + u$$

with w the wage rate, s the amount of education, t working experience, u an i.i.d. disturbance term with expectation zero, and β_i parameters to be estimated.[10] Given our datasets estimation of the earnings equations proceeds as follows.

(i) Assuming that w follows a lognormal distribution, $\ln w = N(\mu, \sigma^2)$, $E(w) = exp(\mu + \frac{1}{2}\sigma^2)$ and $V(w) = exp(2\mu + 2\sigma^2)-exp(2\mu + \sigma^2)$ (Mood et al. 1974, p. 540). With these expressions we can calculate the means and standard deviations for $\ln w$.[11]

(ii) The amount of education is expressed in years by translating levels of education into the number of years that is normally required for a particular level.

(iii) Working experience is approximated by potential experience which is equal to the midpoint of an age group minus 6 (age at entrance to primary education) minus the number of educational years calculated under (ii).

(iv) To gain efficiency the grouped data are analysed by weighted least squares instead of ordinary least squares.[12]

Results obtained from the cross-tabulations and the surveys are all presented in Table 8.4. Because all coefficients are highly signficant we do not present t-values. Lack of data precludes analysis of female wages. Because the data for different years are not fully comparable some care is needed when interpreting the results. First, we concentrate on the regressions based on cross-tabulations (marked c). The results before 1979 are based on a sub-sample of the working males (white-collar employees only). The analysis in Appendix A suggests that due to this selectivity bias the return on human capital is underestimated by 2%. Thus, before 1979, β_1 should be raised by 0.02. The results suggest the return on human capital has fallen steadily, from 13% in 1962 to 7% in 1985. Since then it seems to have stabilized or maybe risen slightly (comparing 1985 c to 1989 c, β_1 increases from 0.072 to 0.073; comparing 1985 and 1988 s, n, h, the return increases from 0.050 to 0.055).

Apparently, the Dutch experience differs from that of the US, UK and Australia, where the return on human capital has increased during the eighties. The Dutch experience looks more like what happened in France (Katz and Loveman, 1992; Borland, 1992). We return to this issue later on.

The experience profiles remain remarkably stable. The shift between 1972 and 1979 is probably due to differences in the sample discussed before.[13] Inspection of the results in Appendix A shows that this selectivity bias can account for the shift in the relevant coefficients. Again, this finding contradicts the experience of the US, UK and Australia, where the return on experience increased during the eighties.

We ran some alternative regressions, to test the robustness of our findings. First, we looked at the potential effect of the civil servants' salary freeze evoked by the large budget deficit. The wage index for the

Table 8.4. *Estimation results for the Mincerian earnings equation for males, 1962–89*

Year	Type	Wage	Sample	β_0	β_1	β_2	β_3
1962	c	g, h	w, 25 +	− 0.324	0.110	0.059	− 0.00077
1965	c	g, h	w, 25 +	0.095	0.102	0.057	− 0.00076
1972	c	g, h	w, 25 +	0.838	0.093	0.056	− 0.00080
1979	c	g, h	a, 25 +	1.450	0.089	0.038	− 0.00054
1982	s	g, h	a, 25 +	2.062	0.073	0.034	− 0.00041
1982	s	g, h	a, n	1.904	0.078	0.048	− 0.00050
1982	s	n, h	a, n	1.283	0.074	0.040	− 0.00050
1985	c	g, h	a, 25 +	1.740	0.072	0.038	− 0.00052
1985	s	n, h	a, n	1.480	0.050	0.040	− 0.00060
1986	s	n, h	a, n	1.624	0.048	0.032	− 0.00040
1988	s	g, h	a, 25 +	2.085	0.059	0.034	− 0.00040
1988	s	g, h	a, n	1.971	0.061	0.042	− 0.00050
1988	s	n, h	a, n	1.410	0.055	0.040	− 0.00050
1989	c	g, h	a, 25 +	1.740	0.073	0.040	− 0.00056

Notes: Type refers to the kind of data source employed; c for cross-tabulation and s for survey. Wage refers to the wage concept; g for gross, n for net, a for annual and h for hourly. Sample refers to characteristics of the sample employed for the regression; w for white collar workers only, a for all workers, 25 + if only individuals older than 25 are included and n for no age restriction. All coefficients are significantly different from zero at the 5%-level.

public sector lagged behind that for the private sector by 15% at the end of the eighties. Hence, one can expect that running separate regressions for the public and the private sector will affect the results, especially because the majority of highly educated workers is employed in the public sector. However, the empirical results run counter to this intuition. The coefficients for a regression for workers in the private sector do not differ significantly from the results for all workers together.

Second, we extended our specification by adding cross-terms for education and experience (st) and for education and experience squared (st^2), and estimated this extended equation with the data from the cross-tabulations. For none of the years we can reject the restrictions that the usual Mincer-equation imposes on this extended equation. This is quite important, as it indicates tht our finding of stable age-wage profiles is not an artefact of an unduly restricted specification.

Mincer's monograph also offers a framework for analysing the dispersion of earnings within age-education groups. This framework has been applied and extended by Dooley & Gottschalk (1984). In its simplest form the analysis comes down to running a regression with the within-group

Table 8.5. *Regressions for within age-education group variances of log earnings, males only, 1962–89*

	γ_0	γ_1	γ_2	$\gamma_3/1{,}000$	R^2
1962	− 0.0607	0.0057	0.0045	0.0289	0.4682
	(1.61)	(3.63)	(1.86)	(0.62)	
1965	− 0.0101	0.0052	0.0006	0.0317	0.4709
	(0.34)	(4.14)	(0.30)	(0.87)	
1972	0.0232	− 0.0002	0.0031	0.0053	0.8145
	(0.10)	(0.27)	(2.34)	(0.21)	
1979	− 0.0115	0.0049	0.0016	− 0.0180	0.2285
	(0.56)	(3.80)	(1.12)	(0.66)	
1985	− 0.0225	0.0048	0.0012	0.0271	0.2303
	(0.54)	(2.18)	(0.42)	(0.51)	
1989	− 0.0413	0.0076	0.0027	− 0.0177	0.4855
	(1.89)	(5.73)	(1.87)	(0.59)	

	a_0	a_1	a_2	a_{85}	a_{89}	R^2
Lower	0.1068	− 0.0053	0.00008	0.0208	0.0320	0.1108
	(3.1)	(2.0)	(1.8)	(1.1)	(1.7)	
Extended lower	0.1014	− 0.0064	0.00014	0.0595	0.0255	0.1066
	(2.1)	(1.6)	(1.8)	(1.9)	(0.8)	
Intermediate	0.0437	0.0015	0.00001	0.0098	0.0119	0.2400
	(1.8)	(0.7)	(0.1)	(0.6)	(0.7)	
Semi-higher	0.0209	0.0051	− 0.00008	− 0.0144	0.0389	0.5667
	(1.2)	(3.1)	(2.1)	(1.1)	(2.9)	
Higher	0.0098	0.0067	− 0.00011	0.0064	0.0447	0.4199
	(0.4)	(2.7)	(1.8)	(0.3)	(2.5)	

variance of the log wage rate as the dependent variable. We perform this analysis twice. First, separately for each year, the explanatory variables in that case are schooling and experience. The equation estimated reads

$$\sigma^2_{\text{year}} = \gamma_0 + \gamma_1 s + \gamma_2 t + \gamma_3 t^2 + e$$

Then we pool the observations for the years 1979 to 1989, and repeat the analysis separately for each level of education. The regression equation then runs

$$\sigma^2_s = a_0 + a_1 t + a_2 t^2 + \Sigma a_i d_i + v$$

with d_i dummy variable for year i ($i = 85$ and 89); this allows for a nonlinear trend. Estimation results are summarized in Table 8.5

The prediction from human capital theory with respect to the life-cycle profile of the variance of log earnings among persons with the same amount of schooling (initial earnings capacity) is that of a U-shaped profile. At the so-called point of overtaking the variance is at the minimum (in fact zero), before that point individuals who invest more than average earn less than average; after the overtaking year, the reverse holds.[14] Whether the same profile holds if groups with different initial earnings capacities are compared depends on the correlation between the initial earnings capacity and the rate of investment. If those with a larger initial capacity also invest a larger portion, the mean log earnings profiles of different groups diverge, and hence the between-group variance increases (cf. Dooley & Gottschalk, 1984, p. 61–2, who find strong support for such U-shaped profiles in the US).

The results in the bottom part of Table 8.5 are mixed regarding the theoretical predictions. For the lower and extended lower educated we find (at the margin of significance) the predicted U-shaped profile. The value of the coefficients suggest a minimum variance of log wages after more than 20 years of experience. This result is close to the findings reported by Dooley & Gottschalk. For workers with intermediate levels of education the profile of variance of log wages with respect to experience seems to be flat, whereas it increases (at a decreasing rate) for the semi-higher and higher educated. In the context of on-the-job training profiles this latter result can only be explained by heterogeneity within schooling groups. Those who have the greatest initial earnings capacity within their schooling group can invest more than average while receiving the highest initial earnings. The heterogeneity argument is supported by our analysis of a homogeneous sample: all Dutch economists.[15] For this group, the U-shape is confirmed, and it may very well be that the difference between the results for the US as reported by Dooley & Gottschalk and our findings for the Netherlands is due to different organization of the data rather than to real differences. The matter calls for further research.

The upper part of Table 8.5 shows that for all years, with the exception of 1972, the within-group variances of the log wages increase with the level of education and do not depend on the amount of experience. For 1972 the opposite holds. From 1962 to 1985 the within-group variances for higher educational levels decrease, after 1985 they increase, and in 1989 the impact of education on the within-group variances reaches its highest level.[16] These results are also captured by the estimates for a_{89} in the bottom part of the table.

Table 8.6 gives a decomposition of the changes of the variance of log wages between 1979 and 1989. The total variance in this period did not change, but there was a substantial shift from between-group to within-group variance. The drop in between-group variance is mainly due to the

Table 8.6. *Decomposition of changes in the variance of log wages for males, 1979–89*

	Within-group[1]	Between-group[2]	Total
1979	0.0586	0.1134	0.1620
Changes in the distribution over groups	0.0028	− 0.0248	
Changes of the group means and variances	0.0240	0.0091	
1989	0.0835[3]	0.0787[3]	0.1622

Notes:
[1] Group: 10 age categories × 5 educational levels.
[2] For a description of the method see Borland (1992).
[3] Columns do not add up due to neglect of cross-terms.

narrowing of the age distribution of the work force: the shares of both the younger low wage workers and the elderly high wage workers have declined. The compensating effect comes from the larger variances within each subgroup. This effect can probably be interpreted as the result of a relaxation of the control of trade unions over relative wages and a decrease in the importance of collective agreements. Relative wages are more closely related to market conditions, nowadays.[17] For the (semi-) higher educated the increase of the within-group variances can be explained by a model with fixed job wage rates and top-down rationing.

The constancy of the total variance of log wages is remarkable in international perspective. Table 8.7 gives an overview of the development of the 10%–90% log wage differential for the US, the UK, France, and the Netherlands. The Dutch and the French experience clearly deviates from that of the US and the UK. In Australia also wage dispersion is rising. Katz and Loveman (1992) suggest that the French experience may be due to the rise of the minimum wage as compared to the average wage rate (from 61% in 1980 to 69% in 1987). However, this factor cannot account for the low wage dispersion in The Netherlands, as the following figures show:

index 1989, 1979 = 100
hourly minimum wage for adults (> 23 years)   117
hourly minimum wage for youngsters[18]   100
average hourly wage   127
average hourly wage for the age group 25–29   122
with only primary education

Table 8.7. *Income dispersion and participation rates for various countries, for males, 1980–90*

Year Age group	10%–90% log wage differential[1]		Labour force participation[2]			
			1980		1990	
	1979	1989	55–59	60–64	55–59	60–64
US	1.18	1.29[3]	80.9	59.8	79.1	54.9
UK	0.86	1.10	90.1	71.2	81.0	54.4
France	0.97	1.00[3]	80.9	47.6	67.7	22.7
The Netherlands	1.01	1.01	74.8	48.8	66.3	22.7

Note:
[3] 1987.

Sources:
[1] US, UK and France: Katz and Loveman (1992). Netherlands: own calculation based on cross-tabulations.
[2] Jacobs and Rein (1992).

Maybe the final columns of Table 8.7 offer a better explanation for the observed pattern. Both France and the Netherlands are characterized by a large fall of the rate of labour force participation of elderly male workers.

To the extent that early retirement is concentrated among low-skilled workers, this has two effects on the distribution of wages. Firstly, it reduces inequality due to the elimination of the lower tail of the distribution. Secondly, it reduces labour supply of the lowest skill-level, leading to an upward pressure on wages.

6   The influence of cohort sizes

Since the pioneering work by Freeman (1976, 1979) and Welch (1979), it has been recognized that the level of an individual's earnings might be affected by the size of the cohort to which s/he belongs. Welch reports that persons born duing a boom experience lower earnings in the beginning of their career. This effect becomes smaller with experience but it never vanishes completely. The findings of Welch have been criticized by Berger (1985) and Connelly (1986), the major point being the specification of the production technique, e.g. the substitution elasticities between younger and older workers. Berger shows that Welch's specification of the earnings equation imposes several restrictions on the parameters of the terms that are of special importance when one wishes to examine the

Table 8.8. *Earnings equations with cohort-size effect, males only 1979, 1985 and 1989*

	Level of education				
	Lower	Extended lower	Intermediate	Semi-higher	Higher
Intercept	− 27.659	− 20.911	− 17.212	1.014	− 40.104
	(3.4)	(2.7)	(3.6)	(0.3)	(0.4)
exp	0.861	0.693	0.703	0.313	0.848
	(2.8)	(2.2)	(3.3)	(1.3)	(0.2)
expsq	− 0.0015	− 0.0014	− 0.0015	− 0.0012	− 0.0035
	(3.6)	(3.3)	(5.2)	(3.5)	(0.4)
cohort	2.192	1.703	1.446	0.117	3.117
	(3.6)	(3.0)	(4.1)	(0.3)	(0.4)
cohort*exp	− 0.058	− 0.046	− 0.047	− 0.019	− 0.046
	(2.6)	(2.0)	(3.1)	(1.1)	(0.1)

Notes: t-values in parentheses. Regression equations also include dummies for 1985 and 1989.

effects of cohort size. Allowing for a more general form, Berger concludes by rejecting the restrictions imposed by Welch, and moreover, he concludes that the earnings loss of belonging to a larger cohort remains stable over the career.

Table 8.8 reports results from estimating Berger's general specification with Dutch data. The variable 'cohort' is constructed as the logarithm of the number of males within a particular age group. Unlike some other possible measures, this measure is really exogenous; it neither depends on labour force participation decisions nor on schooling decisions. Figure 8.1 shows the sizes of male birth cohorts in the periods 1910–75. The results in Table 8.8 are based on the cross-tabulations for 1979, 1985 and 1989. Earnings equations are estimated for each level of education separately. Note that we do not have independent information on experience in these datasets, so that in fact we use age as a proxy.

The results deviate from the findings reported by Welch (1979) and Berger (1985). Whereas these authors report a negative effect of own cohort size on earnings we find a positive effect for the lower three levels of education. This positive effect declines with experience. For the two higher educational levels own cohort size does not affect earnings.

The results for the lower levels suggests that the larger the cohort to which someone belongs, the higher the (initial) wage rate. This result runs counter to economic intuition. To shed some more light on this 'hard to

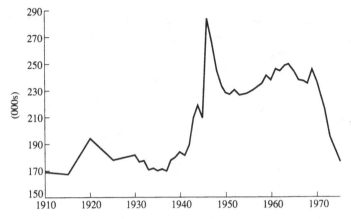

Figure 8.1 Cohort sizes of Dutch males, 1910–75

accept' result, we performed an additional analysis with our 1988-cross-section survey. The advantage of this dataset is that both age and experience are observed directly.

We experimented with several specifications of the earnings equation. Results are reported in Table 8.9. 'Cohort' in this table is again measured as the logarithm of the size of one's birth cohort. The results in Table 8.9 show that the conclusion regarding the effect of cohort size on earnings crucially depends on whether experience (squared) or age (squared) is included as a regressor. With age (squared) included we obtain a neutral effect of cohort size on earnings and with (real) working experience (squared) included we obtain the theoretically correct negative effect. These outcomes hold irrespective whether schooling is included as a regressor or not (rows 4 and 5). Leaving out the schooling variable from the regression is a (albeit, not very sophisticated) method to purge the results for the possible endogeneity bias of schooling. A preferable method would be to instrumentize the schooling variable but this requires data on social background and/or ability, which are not available in the dataset.

The results in Table 8.9 are puzzling. There is no theoretical argument in favour of any one of the specifications. The best that we can do is therefore, to rely on the specification that is superior on statistical grounds. As all other equations are special cases of equation 3, we can test whether the implied restrictions can be rejected or not. It turns out that in each case we have to reject the restriction, hence we prefer equation 3. Therefore our tentative conclusion is that in the Netherlands, cohort size has no effect on earnings.

Table 8.9. *Earnings equations with cohort-size effect, survey data, 1988*

Run	Schooling	Cohort	exp	expsq	age	agesq
1	0.047	− 0.51	0.039	− 0.0007		
	(11.0)	(4.2)	(6.9)	(5.5)		
2	0.042	− 0.08			0.062	− 0.0006
	(10.0) .	(0.4)			(6.3)	(4.0)
3	0.040	− 0.09	0.003	− 0.0002	0.054	− 0.0004
	(9.4)	(0.5)	(0.5)	(1.4)	(4.6)	(2.5)
4		− 0.68	0.04	− 0.0009		
		(5.4)	(7.5)	(6.8)		
5		− 0.069			0.075	− 0.0007
		(0.4)			(7.3)	(4.9)

Notes:
t-values in parentheses.
Dependent variable is gross hourly wage rate.
Number of observations: 1,269.

7   Conclusions and speculations

Since 1960, the level of education of the labour force has increased
continuously. Regressions for Mincerian earnings functions indicate that
the rate of return to education for males continuously dropped, from
about 13% in 1962 to 7% in 1985, and then seems to have stabilized (if
not risen). The observations until 1985 can be interpreted as increased
investment due to better access to investment funds (rising parental
wealth, improved government support) and competitive reduction of a
rent component in the rate of return. It is not clear why the rate of return
stabilized after 1985, while there was no indication of a slowdown in the
rise of levels of education.

The age composition of the labour force has also changed continuously,
with both young and old participants disappearing. For males, this implies
that the share of the prime-aged (25–49) increased from 54% in 1960 to
68% in 1989. The impact on earnings structure seems to be quite modest,
however, and certainly not unequivocal. We have to be cautious, though,
because our observations in cross-tabulations are restricted to workers
older than 24. But the results at least suggest that the (casual) observation
of reduced starting salaries in the eighties was indeed restricted to the
youngest section of the labour force only. These findings are consistent
with the apparent irrelevance of cohort size for earnings structure.

If the wage structure by age is rigid, one would expect this to lead to an unequal burden of unemployment by age groups. This expectation is borne out by the data collected in Salverda (1992, Table A.9). He presents a time series of unemployment by age, relative to the 25–49 age group. Young males initially were underrepresented, i.e. had lower unemployment rates. But when unemployment started to rise after the mid-sixties, they became overrepresented, at an increasing rate until the peak of unemployment in the early eighties. The overrepresentation was strongest for the youngest group (14–18), suggesting that the adjustment in wages that has occurred was not sufficient.

Stability of the wage structure by age is consistent with Lazear's moral hazard explanation of upward sloping profiles. Stability can also be upheld by the facilities of the welfare state. High replacement ratios and a legal minimum wage put a bottom in the market. Wage rates and earnings for older workers can be maintained if disability and early retirement programmes take these workers off the market in periods of excess supply. (Redundant workers over 50 do not end up in unemployment statistics; they are increasingly underrepresented after 1979 according to Salverda's time series of relative unemployment rates.) Cooperation of employers with such programmes is more in line with overpayment according to the moral hazard argument than with underpayment due to a shared investment in specific human capital (although this latter argument can be saved by pointing to market and technology shocks that make some investments obsolete).

Turning to some speculation about the future, we take it for granted that the demographic trend continues, and that birth rates remain low, leading to relatively small cohorts of entrants. There may be compensation from immigration, but if we assume that this will be insufficient to make up for the difference, what will be the consequences for the labour market? First of all, the choice of education for the new cohorts will be relevant. There are reasons to expect continued rise in desired levels of education. Educational ambitions and rising parental wealth will maintain this process. If the rate of return to education were to rise, this would be a further stimulus. But there is a relevant policy question here, at least in the Netherlands. Student subsidies are now quite generous, and there are indications that cutbacks are being considered. Also, the balance between formal and on-the-job training may have been lost. There are large subsidies to formal education, barely any to on-the-job training and evidence that the rate of return to the latter is very high (Groot *et al.*, 1992). This suggests that a shift from formal to on-the-job training might well be efficient, and perhaps some day politicians will make the adjustment.

The second aspect concerns participation decisions in the future. Participation rates of married females do not seem to have reached satiation levels yet, so additional female labour supply can continue to make up (in part) for smaller sizes of future cohorts. Participation behaviour of older (male) individuals might also change in the future. Increased leisure at higher ages may follow from strong individual preferences, using increased wealth to finance non-participation. But in the last decade, non-participation of older individuals has been stimulated by early retirement schemes in collective agreements and sometimes supported by government subsidies. Pensions may deteriorate in the future, especially in case of pay-as-you-go systems (such as the Dutch state pension). Employer resistance to costly early retirement schedules is now increasing. So, it is possible that participation rates for older individuals will increase in the future, as there is no longer the drive to 'reduce' unemployment by buying out older workers.

Speculation on the future earnings structure is perhaps even more difficult. We found the (male) earnings structure to be sensitive to the educational composition of the labour force, but not to the age composition. If a shift from formal education to on-the-job training were to occur, this might have complicated effects. And if the provisions of the welfare state that now seem to play a role in maintaining age-wage profiles are to be changed, this may well lead to greater responsiveness of wages to the age composition of the labour force.

Appendix A: Data

The data on gross wages by education and age are derived from different sources and apply to different populations: to all employees for 1979, 1985, 1989 and to white-collar employees only for 1962, 1965 and 1972.

In order to make the regression results for different years comparable we try to determine to what extent these differences in the sample affect the regression coefficients. For three years we have data for both the full sample and white collar workers only. For 1982 and 1988 the survey data allow for making a distinction between white and blue-collar workers. For 1972 a separate cross-tabulation for blue-collar workers was available. Combining these data with those for white-collar workers and making some assumptions on the level of education of blue-collar workers, the wage structure for the full sample can be reconstructed.

By running regressions for each of these three years both for all workers and for white-collar workers only we get an impression of the selectivity bias. The results are listed in Table 8A.1. We find that by using the data for white-collar workers only the return on human capital is consistently

Table 8A.1. *Selection bias in the wage equation due to differences in sample composition*[1]

Data from cross-tabulations	1972	
	White-collar[2]	All
Education (years)	0.092 (17.4)	0.113 (19.7)
exp	0.055 (9.3)	0.055 (8.5)
expsq	−0.0008 (6.0)	−0.0009 (6.0)

Survey data	1982		1988	
	White-collar[2]	All	White-collar[2]	All
Education (years)	0.053 (3.4)	0.073 (11.2)	0.038 (3.2)	0.059 (13.2)
exp	0.041 (2.5)	0.033 (6.3)	0.018 (1.1)	0.034 (5.5)
expsq	−0.00056 (1.9)	−0.00041 (4.5)	−0.00002 (0.1)	−0.00040 (3.2)

Notes:
[1] OLS-regression of log gross hourly wage rates of males with minimum age of 25 years (*t*-values in brackets).
[2] White-collar workers in manufacturing, construction and the banking sector.

underestimated by 2%. For the coefficients for experience the results are mixed.

Appendix B: The price of education

Table 8A.2. *The price of education (real 1975 Dutch guilders)*

	1950–4	1955–9	1960–4	1965–9	1970–4	1975–9	1980–3
% students with government grants	9.8	22.6	32.3	32.6	33.9	34.6	37.5
Tuition	880	520	460	360	700	520	590
Maximum grant	5,420	5,540	6,000	7,230	7,400	7,500	7,240
Child allowance and deduction (after tax value)	770	1,610	2,110	4,850	5,450	5,300	3,100
National income per head	4,500	5,570	6,920	8,420	9,850	10,620	10,350

Source: Ritzen (1985) p. 22.

NOTES

Comments of conference participants (especially by our discussant Bob Wright) and by Dan Hamermesh and Jules Theeuwes are gratefully acknoweldged.
1 The index of tuition fees for higher education, in real terms, for selected years was: 1950 = 100, 1960 = 46, 1970 = 30, 1980 = 43 and 1987 = 95 (see De Jong *et al.*, 1990, p. 39).
2 For the same years as in Note 1, the index of financial aid equals 100, 222, 499, 373 and 364; see also Appendix B.
3 Huijsman *et al.* (1986) applied a regression analysis to a time series (1950–82) for first-year enrolment in higher education. For males the financial variables came out with the right sign; the largest elasticity referred to per capita income (about one).
4 Groot and Pott-Buter (1991) suggest a large sensitivity of the timing of children to male and female wages, and a low sensitivity of zero versus non-zero number of children.
5 Hartog & Theeuwes (1985) estimate a female participation model on a cross-section for 1979; inserting mean values for the explanatory variables in 1947, 1960 and 1971 traces the actual participation rate quite closely, with the female market wage by far the most important variable. Groot and Pott-Buter (1992) conclude that changes in reservation wages are more important than changes in market wages to explain changes in female participation between 1979 and 1987. Such a decomposition hinges critically on the variables used to explain the unobserved reservation wage.

6 From data for 1960, 1971, 1977 and 1985, based on job grading in 7 levels of complexity, one may (cautiously) conclude that the average job level has decreased for all levels of education. Dispersion mostly increased between 1960 and 1971 (with the exception of semi-higher and higher education). Between 1977 and 1985, dispersion was stable for the three lower levels of education, and increased for the two highest levels. Sources: Huijgen 91989, pp. 44–45) and Hartog (1980, pp. 167–170).

7 In the wake of the baby boom generation reaching labour market age, a discussion has emerged on the labour market effects of cohort size. We will deal with that in section 6.

8 Until recently, employers in the Netherlands tended to be rather cooperative in setting up early retirement schemes. Such behaviour is easier to understand from incentive-based overpayment at high ages than from the underpayment that results from a shared investment in specific human capital. Employers are now attempting to demolish early reitrement schemes, or at least reduce their generosity.

9 The data for 1982 are collected by the National Program for Labor Market Research (NPAO). Estimation is based upon 475 observations. The data for the other years are collected by the Organization for Strategic Labor Market Research (OSA). The number of observations varies around 1,200. The cross-tabulations for 1979, 1985 and 1989 are available from the Central Planning Bureau (CPB). The data for 1962, 1965 and 1972 are documented in Hartog (1980).

10 We deliberately refrain from adding any other explanatory variable, and let the estimated coefficients function as a summary of changes over time.

11 $$\sigma^2 = ln(E^2(w) + V(w)) - 2\,lnE(w)$$

$$\mu = 2\,ln\,E(w) - \tfrac{1}{2}ln(E^2(w) + V(w))$$

12 The weights are the square root of the quotient of the numbers of observations and the variances in the cross tabulations.

13 Theeuwes *et al.* (1985) apply the Rosen model of optimal investment in on-the-job training to samples of white-collar workers only. They combine the 1962 with the 1972 observations ('sixties') and the 1972 with the 1979 observations ('seventies') to unravel cohort and experience effects. They conclude that the minimum internal rate of return to on-the-job training, between the sixties and the seventies, was stable for university educated workers in the private sector, but dropped in the public sector. The reverse held for higher vocational education. For secondary education, returns in the private sector fell and in the public sector they increased. The vintage growth rate fell strongly for all categories.

14 We excluded the cross-tabulations for 1962 to 1975 from the analyses of the variance per level of education, because our data for these years contain no information for persons aged under 25. As the point of overtaking typically occurs after 10 years of experience this omission makes these years less suitable to trace out the U-shaped profile.

15 If we first regress log wage on age, age squared, gender, public/private sector, grade average and business economics/general economics and then regress the absolute value of the residual on experience t, we get (t-values in brackets):

$$|u| = 0.403 - 0.011t + 0.0033t^2 \quad R^2 = 0.002$$
$$\quad\ (8.7)\quad\ (1.84)\quad\ (2.10)$$

16 The increase in λ_1 after 1985 echoes increased job level variance at the highest levels of education between 1977 and 1985 (see note 6). However, from increased job level dispersion, one would have expected a higher λ_1 in 1985 in any case.

17 Numerical evidence for this assertion can be found in the decomposition of wage growth in the rise in contract wages and wage drift. In the eighties wage drift was more important than before (see various issues of the *Macro Economische Verkenningen*, a yearly publication of the Central Planning Bureau).

18 The reported figure is calculated as a weighted average of the minimum wage reductions for subgroups, see Mot and Teulings (1990).

REFERENCES

Berger, M.C. (1985) 'The effect of cohort size on earnings growth: A reexamination of the evidence', *Journal of Political Economy* **93**, 561–73.

Borland, J. (1992) 'Wage inequality in Australia', paper for the NBER confernece 'The labor market in international perspective', 10–11 April.

Connelly, R. (1986) 'A framework for analyzing the impact of cohort size on education and labor earnings', *Journal of Human Resources* **21**, 543–63.

Dooley, M.D. and P. Gottschalk, 'Earnings inequality among males in the United States: Trends and the effect of labor force growth', *Journal of Political Economy* **92**, 59–89.

Freeman, R.B. (1976) *The overeducated American*, New York: Academic Press.

— (1979) 'The effect of demographic factors on the age-earnings profile in the U.S.', *Journal of Human Resources* **15**, 124–42.

Groot, W., J. Hartog and H. Oosterbeek (1992) 'Wage and welfare gains of within company training', mimeo.

Groot, W. and H.A. Pott-Buter (1991) 'The timing of maternity in The Netherlands', working paper, University of Amsterdam.

— (1992) 'Why married women's labor supply has increased', Research Memorandum 92.01, CRPE, Leiden University.

Hartog, J. (1980) *Tussen vraag en aanbod*, Leiden: Stenfert Kroese.

— (1989) 'Distribution policies in the Netherlands', in F. Muller and W.J. Zwezerijnen (eds.), *The role of economic policy in society*, Rotterdam: UPR.

Hartog, J. and J. Theeuwes (1985) 'The emergence of the working wife in Holland', *Journal of Labor Economics* **3**, S235–55.

— (1991) 'Postwar unemployment in the Netherlands', Paper prepared for the VSB Masterclass on Unemployment, The Hague, December 1991 (an abridged version will appear in the *European Journal of Political Economy*).

Hartog, J. and N. Vriend (1989) 'Post-war international labor mobility: The Netherlands', in I. Gordon and A.P. Thirwall (eds.), *European factor mobility*, London: Macmillan.

Huijgen, F. (1989) *De kwalitatieve structuur van de werkgelegenheid in Nederland, deel III*, OSA Voorstudie V 33, Den Haag: DOP.

Huijsman, R., T. Kloek, D.A. Kodde and J.M.M. Ritzen (1986) 'An empirical analysis of college enrollment in The Netherlands', *De Economist* **134**, 181–90.

Jacobs, K. and M. Rein (1992) 'Ageing and employment trends: A comparative analysis for OECD countries', this volume.

Jong, U. de, H. Oosterbeek, J. Roeleveld, C.N. Teulings and H.D. Webbink

(1990) *Wel of niet verder studeren?* Vooronderzoek naar deelname aan hoger onderwijs, Wetenschappelijk onderzoek 26, Ministerie van Onderwijs en Wetenschappen.

Katz, L. and G. Loveman (1992) 'An international comparison of changes in the structure of wages: France, the United Kingdom, and the United States', paper for the NBER conference 'The labor market in international perspective', 10–11 April.

Lazear, E.P. (1979) 'Why is there mandatory retirment?' *Journal of Political Economy* **87**, 1261–84.

Mincer, J. (1974) *Schooling, experience, and earnings*, NBER.

Mood, A.M., F.A. Graybill and D.C. Boes (1974) *Introduction to the theory of statistics*, Singapore: McGraw Hill.

Mot, E.S. and C.N. Teulings (1990). *Minimumjeugdloon en werkgelegen heid*, OSA werkdocument W 75, 's-Gravenhage.

Ritzen, J.M.M. (ed.) (1985). *Menselijk kapitaal en conjunctuur; een voorstudie*, Erasmus Universiteit, Rotterdam.

Salverda, W. (1992) 'Youth unemployment', PhD thesis draft, Rijksuniversiteit Groningen.

Van de Stadt, H. (1988) 'The dynamics of income and welfare', PhD thesis, University of Amsterdam.

Theeuwes, J., C. Koopmans, R. van Opstal and H. van Reyn (1985) 'Estimation of optimal human capital accumulation parameters for the Netherlands', *European Economic Review* **239**, 233–57.

Welch, F. (1979) 'Effects of cohort size on earnings: The baby boom babies' financial bust', *Journal of Political Economy* **87**, S65–97.

Discussion

ROBERT E. WRIGHT

Numerous studies in the United states have confirmed that individuals born into large cohorts, *ceteris paribus*, tend to have lower earnings in the labour force compared to individuals born into small cohorts (see for example, Berger, 1985; Freeman, 1976; Welch, 1979). However, only limited attention has been directed towards examining the relationship between cohort size and earnings in other nations. This apparent lack of interest is surprising given that most industrialized nations, like the United States, have experienced significant changes in age structure due primarily to fluctuations in fertility rates (see Calot and Blayo, 1982; Wright, 1989). Therefore, one would expect that such changes would have an impact on earnings, unemployment and other labour-market related variables in these countries. In this sense, the paper by Hartog, Oosterbeek and Teulings makes an important contribution to a neglected area of research by examining carefully the relationship between age structure, education and earnings in the Netherlands.

Currently, fertility is well below the replacement level in the Netherlands. If fertility remains low (which seems likely), the Dutch population will 'age' rapidly, in the sense that an accelerating proportion of the population will concentrate in the older age groups. Population ageing will place a heavy financial burden on Dutch society. There will have to be massive increases in public expenditure if existing social welfare programmes aimed at accommodating the elderly population are to be maintained. There is serious concern that the Dutch economy will not be able to meet this challenge. The Netherlands' poor economic performance in the 1980s, coupled with little expected improvement in the 1990s, will make this difficult. Given this pessimistic forecast, issues relating to the labour market implications of population ageing are of paramount importance and deserve considerably more attention than they have received in the past in the Netherlands. This paper is an important step in this direction.

In order to place the findings of Hartog *et al.* in perspective, it is useful to briefly describe the various mechanisms by which changes in age structure can affect earnings. As Welch (1979) points out, it is useful to divide an individual's working life into two 'career phases'. The first is an inexperienced or 'learning phase'. The second is a senior or 'experienced phase'. In simple terms, individuals in the learning phase tend to be younger with less work experience while individuals in the senior phase tend to older and have more work experience. Younger inexperienced workers are *complementary* to older more experienced workers – the former assist the latter thereby gaining experience. As most economic activities use a mix of inexperienced and experienced workers in production, the productivity of older workers depends on the productivity of young workers and *vice versa*.

The law of diminishing returns implies that an increase in the size of one group, relative to the other, will reduce its productivity relative to the other. For example, an increase in the number of younger workers relative to older workers will lower the productivity of younger workers but raise the productivity of older workers – there will be more inexperienced workers to assist more experienced workers. On the other hand, an increase in the number of older workers relative to younger workers will increase the productivity of younger workers but lower the productivity of older workers – there will be fewer inexperienced workers to assist more experienced workers. Therefore, if earnings are a positive function of productivity, *ceteris paribus*, one would expect changes in the number of younger workers relative to older workers to affect their relative earnings.

The results of analysis of the effect of cohort size on earnings performed by Hartog *et al.* 'deviate from the findings reported by Welch (1979) and Berger (1985)'. First, they find that individuals from larger cohorts have *higher*, not lower earnings on entry to the labour market. Second, they find that this apparent 'advantage' declines as individuals grow older and gain more work experience. Clearly, these findings are very hard to interpret within the context of the Welch's 'career-phase' model. The authors attempt to elaborate on this 'hard to accept result' by estimating alternative specifications of the underlying wage equations, but in the end provide little rigorous evidence for what they believe to be theoretically correct effects.

Are the findings of Hartog *et al.* really 'hard to accept'? A recent paper by Berger (1989) suggests that this may not be the case. He argues that an individual's 'own cohort size' and his/her position in the 'demographic cycle' must both be considered in order to understand the effects of cohort size on earnings. Berger argues that the shape of age-earnings profiles will differ depending on the demographic cycle because individuals make different decisions concerning investment in education. In other words, cohort size affects schooling and education choices (see also Connelly, 1986; Nothaft, 1985; Stapleton and Young, 1988). He shows that individuals who enter the labour market before or after the peak of a baby boom have depressed earnings but faster earnings growth. In his earnings equations, Berger includes both measures of own cohort size and the size of surrounding cohorts. He finds that: 'Increases in own cohort lead to higher initial earnings but slower early career earnings growth, whereas increases in the size of surrounding cohorts are associated with lower earnings at the start of the career but faster earnings growth' (Berger, 1989, p. 311). In other words, it is possible for large cohorts to have enhanced earnings on entry into the labour market, as Hartog *et al.* find. In this sense, their findings may be a result of specification error which confounds these two effects, since they fail to model position in the demographic cycle in their estimation.

Increased cohort size can also affect unemployment. Numerous empirical studies have demonstrated that cohort size affects unemployment (see for example, Bloom *et al.*, 1987; OECD, 1980; and especially Zimmermann, 1991). However, Hartog *et al.* choose not to explore this possibility in detail. They do, however, cite an (unpublished) study where this 'expectation is born out' (Slaverda, 1992). If we accept the conclusion that

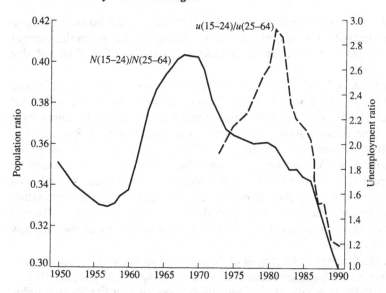

Figure 8A.1 Population-unemployment age ratios in The Netherlands, 1950–90

cohort size has little effect on earnings in the Netherlands, then attention should be shifted towards examining the effect of cohort size on unemployment.

To examine this hypothesis further, I have plotted a measure of relative cohort size against a measure of relative unemployment for the Netherlands (see Figure 8A.1). Relative cohort size is the ratio of the size of the male population age 15 to 24 to the population age 25 to 64. Upward movement in this ratio indicates an increase in the number of 'young' men relative to 'older' men, and can be thought of as a crude index of the ratio of younger to older workers. Relative unemployment is the ratio of the unemployment rates of men age 15 to 24 to that of men age 25 to 64. An increase in this ratio, indicates a relative increase in 'youth' unemployment. If cohort size affects unemployment, we would expect these two ratios to exhibit a positive correlation and move closely together through time.

Unfortunately, I was not successful in finding age-specific unemployment data for the period prior to 1971. Nevertheless, the picture that emerges for the 1970 to 1990 period is not simple or clear-cut. In the 1970s the two variables moved in opposite directions, which is contrary to the hypothesis that larger cohorts suffer from higher relative unemployment. However, in the 1980s the two measures moved in the same direction, which is consistent with view that population ageing has contributed to a relative reduction in youth unemployment. Needless to say, the visual inspection of two time-series is a crude test of this central hypothesis and more detailed analysis is required before any confident conclusions can be reached.

Bloom *et al.* (1987) argue that it is useful to think about the effect of changes in cohort size as a 'trade-off' between an earnings effect and an employment effect. They believe that in some countries large cohorts reduce relative earnings, while in other countries large cohorts increase relative unemployment, and still in others both occur. The paper by Hartog *et al.* is a solid examination of the effect of changing age structure on earnings. However, to understand the labour market implications of Dutch population ageing fully, the determinants of age patterns in unemployment must be analysed with the same degree of rigour.

NOTE

The assistance of Stephen Callender is gratefully acknowledged.

REFERENCES

Berger, M. (1985) 'The Effect of Cohort Size on Earnings: A Reconsideration of the Evidence', *Journal of Political Economy* **93**, 561–73.
(1989) 'Demographic Cycles, Cohort Size, and Earnings', *Demography* **26**, 311–21.
Bloom, D., R. Freeman and S. Korenam (1987) 'The Labour Market Consequences of Generational Crowding', *European Journal of Population* **3**, 131–76.
Calot, G. and C. Blayo (1982) 'Recent Course of Fertility in Western Europe', *Population Studies* **36**, 349–72.
Connelly, R. (1986) 'A Framework for Analyzing the Impact of Cohort Size on Education and Labor Earnings', *Journal of Human Resources* **21**, 543–62.
Freeman, R. (1976) 'The Effects of Demographic Factors on Age-Earnings Profiles', *Journal of Human Resources* **14**, 289–318.
Nothaft, F. (1985) 'The Effect of Cohort Size on Human Capital Investment and Earnings Growth', Working Paper No. 42, Washington, D.C.: Board of Governors of the Federal Reserve System.
OECD (1980) *Youth Unemployment: The Causes and Consequences*, Paris: OECD.
Stapleton, D. and D. Young (1988) 'Educational Attainment and Cohort Size', *Journal of Labor Economics* **6**, 330–61.
Welch, F. (1979) 'Effects of Cohort Size on Earnings: The Baby Boom Babies' Financial Bust', *Journal of Political Economy* **87**, S65–97.
Wright, R. (1989) 'The Easterlin Hypothesis and European Fertility Rates', *Population and Development Review* **15**, 107–22.
Zimmermann, K. F. (1991) 'Ageing and the Labor Market: Age Structure, Cohort Size and Unemployment', *Journal of Population Economics* **4**, 177–200.

9 Ageing and unemployment

CHRISTOPH M. SCHMIDT

1 Introduction

Ironically, just as the economic problems created by population ageing have been identified as a matter of most imminent concern for the majority of advanced economies, anxiety has arisen about the flood of immigration these countries are expecting in the near future. While it appears at first glance that these problems might be offsetting, a closer look reveals that neither the economic effects of population ageing nor the economic effects of immigration are well understood. Will larger cohorts experience dismal labour market outcomes as they move through their life cycle? Will workers in the same age bracket as incoming migrants suffer from migrant inflow?

Previous research has found cohort size to have an important impact on the relative labour market outcomes of the very young. For the US economy, there is strong evidence that the large 'baby boom' cohorts experienced relatively low earnings and high unemployment upon labour market entry. It appears that workers of different ages are not perfectly substitutable in production and thus a large cohort is likely to face depressed labour market conditions. Since workers can influence their prospects via their human capital investments, the persistence of adverse cohort effects over the life cycle is a matter of empirical and theoretical controversy.

Labour market imperfections might create an additional potential for the persistence of adverse cohort size effects over the life cycle. This study analyses the effects of changes in a population's age composition on the relative unemployment experience of workers in different age brackets when wage adjustments are hampered by the presence of a strong monopoly union. Germany appears to be a model case of such an economy. Collective bargaining is performed by a strong union organization on behalf of virtually the whole labour force and it usually targets the level of aggregate wage growth, but leaves the relative wage structure largely unchanged.

If cohort sizes were indeed to be found to substantially affect relative unemployment rates in corresponding age brackets, this would raise two issues of serious concern for an ageing German economy. First, in addition to the burden arising for the younger cohorts from the support of the retired elderly there would be an additional burden arising from the support of the unemployed elderly, even if the apparent trend towards early retirement could be halted. Second, if Germany elected to solve its problem of an ageing labour force by permitting young immigrant labour to enter, this would involve the cost of raising the relative unemployment rates of the young.

The German population has aged substantially in recent decades, mainly as a result of a drastic decline in fertility. In addition, it is demonstrated here that immigration has already been an important determinant of the German age structure in the past. In fact, the presence of young immigrant labour prevented substantial ageing from taking place earlier, especially for males; the stop in guest worker recruitment in 1973 then added to the steep increase in German average age. German age-specific unemployment rates have moved in close accord with aggregate unemployment rates in the past. Yet there are marked differences. While young workers experienced, in general, higher unemployment rates than older established workers, this pattern appears to have reversed in recent years.

The estimation results presented here confirm that variations in the age structure play an important role for the relative unemployment experience of different age groups. The empirical analysis shows, however, that it is only for a few sex-age groups that a strong positive relationship between the size of a cohort and its relative unemployment experience can be established from the available data. It appears that for most sex-age groups a description of the impact of changes in the age structure on relative labour market outcomes has to take into account issues of participation and union representation.

Section 2 reviews the empirical literature on the labour market consequences of variations in cohort sizes, section 3 contains a brief formalization of the underlying ideas and derives the empirical implications stemming from the existence of a large monopoly union. Section 4 presents the empirical results. The concluding section 5 discusses the impact of the empirical findings for economic policy.

2   Ageing, migration and labour market outcomes

The age structure of advanced societies has changed drastically over recent decades. This development has triggered massive research on the problems of ageing societies (see the surveys by Clark, 1989, Clark *et al.*, 1978, and Hurd, 1990). In virtually all Western economies, birth rates appear to have declined permanently and have led to projections of shrinking populations coupled with higher expectations of life and, thus, with a higher fraction of elderly among the population. A sizeable part of the literature concentrates on the problems created by this development for the support of the elderly by the young via social security. Old-age dependency ratios and their projections have risen dramatically while economic growth will apparently be stagnating at low rates. These forecasts raise doubts about the economic and political feasibility of existing transfer schemes, since in most countries social security is financed as a pay-as-you-go scheme (see for example Keyfitz, 1988, or Börsch-Supan, 1991).

Apart from the purely technical consequence that a rising average age means that an increasing fraction of the population has to be supported by a decreasing fraction of the population, research has been devoted to behavioural consequences of population ageing. First, individual consumption and savings patterns appear to vary with age, and – depending on the underlying model – are found to potentially have important consequences for economic growth (see Clark, 1989). Second, ageing affects the development of the labour market. There will, in general, be labour market consequences of ageing both in terms of aggregate labour market outcomes and their distribution across age.

Some studies try to capture the effect of variations in the age structure on the level of aggregate economic variables. Fair and Dominguez (1991) investigate the impact of the US age structure on different types of aggregate consumption and investment expenditures, on aggregate money demand and on the labour force participation within different sex-age groups. Zimmermann (1991) analyses the development of the unemployment rates of different German sex-age groups in response to the age structure of the population. He finds no clear relation between the age structure and age-specific unemployment rates in the long run, but an impact of the age composition on short-term dynamics. Here I will take a different perspective and ask how the relative behaviour of the unemployment rates of different sex-age groups compared to the aggregate unemployment rate responds to variations in cohort sizes.

Analyses of age structure effects on relative labour market outcomes have previously concentrated on the structure of earnings and wages (see for example Freeman, 1979, Welch, 1979, and Berger, 1985). It is a well recognized fact that workers of greater age or experience earn more than young labour market entrants. Viewed from the perspective of labour demand theory, it can be argued that workers in different age or experience brackets perform different tasks and are thus separate factors of production with a limited amount of substitutability. Technically, the amount employed of a factor of production has an effect on its marginal productivity. In a competitive economy, marginal productivities are reflected in factor prices and, thus, since all factors are fully employed, factors more readily available generate lower returns: the technology determines the structure of wages. Variation in the availability of factors will then lead to responses of this relative wage structure.

The main motivation for empirical analyses has been the arrival of the US baby boomers of the 1950s on the US labour market that has led to the apparent twist of empirical age-earnings profiles to the disadvantage of the younger workers at the beginning of the 1970s. How pronounced these effects are over the life-cycle is a matter of debate, however. The development of a cohort's post-entry labour market outcomes depends crucially on the amount of time invested in human capital when young. Welch (1979) found that the earnings of workers in large cohorts will catch up to the earnings of workers in smaller cohorts over the life-cycle; opposite results have for example been found by Berger (1985).

The focus of the US studies on the sensitivity of wage outcomes to cohort sizes is a reflection of the paradigm of competitive labour markets that describes the US labour market relatively well. In contrast, European labour markets seem to be characterized by a lower degree of competition: in Germany, most collective bargaining is undertaken on a regional and industry level by industry unions that are members of one large head organization, the *Deutsche Gewerkschaftsbund* (DGB). These bargaining agreements cover virtually the whole labour force (see, for example, the discussions in Franz, 1987, and Schmidt and Zimmermann, 1992).

The effects of the availability of workers of different age will, in general, be reflected – via union choices of bargaining strategy – both in wage and in unemployment adjustments. These ideas will be formalized in section 3. I will argue that the relative wage structure in Germany is relatively stable over time and will concentrate on the structure of relative unemployment by age. For the US, Bloom *et al.* (1987) surveyed a number of studies in which age-specific unemployment rates of young workers were regressed on a reference rate and, among other things, on cohort size. Most studies found a significant effect of cohort size on the unemployment experience of the young. Imperfect labour markets create the possibility that large cohorts will experience higher relative unemployment rates as they mature.

Thus, questions of ageing relate to the consistent body of evidence on the effects of individual age on turnover and job tenure. Hall (1982) found a large fraction of long-term jobs in the US economy: young workers typically spend a certain amount of time searching for a good match and older workers – typically having found such a match – stay in their jobs for a longer period. Coupled with given matching rates this evidence argues for higher unemployment rates among the young workers. The evidence is supported by results on job turnover, in which age is generally found to reduce turnover propensities (see Ehrenberg, 1980). The question raised here is whether these relations vary systematically with changes in the population age structure. To motivate the empirical analysis, the next section develops a simple model of wage determination in which age-specific unemployment rates are driven by age structure variations.

3   A formal model and its empirical implications

To demonstrate the effects of (own) cohort sizes on marginal productivities and thus wages in a full employment economy, Welch (1979) used a model of career phases in which workers follow a given career path independently of cohort size. In this section, an extension of Welch's model is used to formalize effects of cohort size on the incidence of unemployment over the life-cycle. In contrast to the original model, here a large economy-wide monopoly union sets wages above the full employment level for all imperfectly substitutable groups of labour input. When bargaining mainly targets the level of aggregate wages while leaving the structure of relative wages unchanged, differences in cohort sizes will translate into differences in the relative unemployment experience of cohorts.

It will be assumed that the production process can be summarized in an aggregate production function $f(N, Z)$ where N denotes total labour efforts used in production and Z captures all other factors that are taken to be fixed in the short run and capture the state of the economy. Unlike Welch (1979) I do not distinguish between individuals with different levels of schooling. N itself is a function of the employed workers of several groups $i = 1, 2, \ldots$:

$$N = g(N_1, N_2, \ldots) \tag{1}$$

Firms face the problem of choosing levels of labour input N_i in each worker group, given the level of Z and group-specific wages w_i

$$\max_{\{N_i\}} f(N, Z) - \sum_i w_i \cdot N_i \tag{2}$$

leading to a system of first-order conditions

$$f_N \cdot g'_{N_i} = w_i \tag{3}$$

which upon solving will yield a system of demand equations, giving labour inputs demanded as functions of wage rates for all groups and of aggregate activity

$$N_i^* = h_i(w_1, w_2, \ldots, w_i, \ldots, Z) \tag{4}$$

It is the basic idea of the career phase model that any worker's career consists of the transition between distinct activities as the worker ages (the original model was cast in terms of experience). As soon as phase i is entered, at age x_i, the worker begins a transition into the phase $i + 1$. During the time spent in i, the proportion of time supplied to activity i, p_i, decreases monotonically from unity to zero, while its residual, $1 - p_i$, is supplied to activity $i + 1$. Let $m(x)$ denote the number of workers of age x. Then the number of workers supplying their labour to activity i is given by

$$M_i = \int_{x_{i-1}}^{x_i} [1 - p_{i-1}(x)] \cdot m(x) dx + \int_{x_i}^{x_{i+1}} p_i(x) \cdot m(x) dx \tag{5}$$

A comparison with the actual number of workers employed in this activity, N_i, will yield activity-specific unemployment rates

$$UR_i = \frac{M_i - N_i}{M_i} \tag{6}$$

These rates can be used to calculate age-specific unemployment rates

$$UR(x) = p_i(x) \cdot UR_i + [1 - p_i(x)] \cdot UR_{i+1} \tag{7}$$

for x falling into phase i. Thus, the unemployment rate in each age group is determined simultaneously by wages set for all activities, by the number of workers in each age group, and by the state of aggregate activity.

Wages are set by a large monopoly union that organizes the work force of the whole economy. This union maximizes preferences defined over both wages and unemployment

$$\max_{\{w_i\}} V(w_1, N_1, w_2, N_2, \ldots, w_i, N_i, \ldots) \tag{8}$$

subject to (4), the system of solutions to the employers' problem. Union preferences could for example be parameterized by the sum over group-specific wage bills $\Sigma_i w_i \cdot N_i$ that explicitly trades off higher wages for employed workers with lower employment. Upon solving the resulting system of first-order conditions

$$V'_{w_i} + \sum_j V'_{N_j} N'_{j, w_i} = 0 \tag{9}$$

and as a result of (4) for interior solutions the optimal wage choices are functions of aggregate activity, $w_i^* = w(Z)$, but not of the number of workers in each age group. Thus, the resulting activity-specific or age-specific unemployment rates are in turn functions of the number of workers in each age group. The construction of a smooth transition between career phases will lead to a smooth variation of age-specific unemployment rates with age.

The influence of the age structure upon the chosen wages and the corresponding age-specific unemployment rates can take a more complicated form, however, when unemployment is weighed negatively in the union objective as well. In this case the union will solve the trade-off between the wage bill for the N_i employed members of this activity group and the number of unemployed workers $M_i - N_i$, taking into account the spillover effects to the employment outcome of other activity groups. Consider an exogenous increase in the cohort size $c(x)$ of age-group x, defined as the fraction of workers of a given age x in the population of workers, holding the population size constant. With x falling into career phase i, relatively many workers will stay unemployed for any given wage w_i, an incentive to choose a low wage for this activity. As the number of workers in each group i varies systematically with the number of workers at each age x, optimal wages can also be seen as functions of the number of workers at each age. The reasoning might again be made more complicated, if cohorts of different size receive different weights in the union objective function.

While the aggregate unemployment rate UR is a function of the state of aggregate activity, age-specific unemployment rates UR_i will systematically deviate from the aggregate rate following variations in the composition of the labour force according to age. Clearly, the effect of a change in the age structure of the labour force is twofold. It will determine the level of overall economic activity and thus the overall level of unemployment. And it will also influence the relative unemployment burden borne by different age groups. In its empirical implementation, the paper focuses on the second effect and uses linear approximations to the true relations in the data. Age-specific unemployment rates are taken as linear functions of the aggregate unemployment rate and of the size of the own and adjacent cohorts, c_{i-1}, c_i and c_{i+1}:

$$UR_i = \gamma_0 + \gamma_1 \cdot UR + \sum_{j=-1}^{1} \delta_j \cdot C_{i+j} + \epsilon_i \qquad (10)$$

The next section analyses whether such equilibrium relationships between these variables can be found in German data.

4 Data and empirical results

4.1 Data and unit root tests

In the empirical analysis, age-specific unemployment rates for the Federal Republic of Germany will be investigated for the period before unification. Do age-specific unemployment rates vary systematically together with the aggregate unemployment rate, and is this variation related to cohort size? I will utilize information on the number of inhabitants of the Federal Republic of Germany by age as of the 31st of December of each year between 1950 and 1989, provided by the *Statistisches Bundesamt*, and information on unemployment rates in seven age groups (15–19, 20–24, 25–34, 35–44, 45–54, 55–59 and 60–64) between 1967 and 1989, provided by the *Institut für Arbeitsmarkt und Berufsforschung der Bundesanstalt für Arbeit*.

First, I will present a description of the underlying series, including tests for the presence of a unit root in the univariate representation. Augmented Dickey-Fuller (ADF) test procedures are used to test the null hypothesis of a single unit root estimating the two regression specifications

$$\Delta y_t = \mu + a y_{t-1} + \sum_{i=1}^{k} 0_i \Delta y_{t-i} + u_t \qquad H_0: \mu = 0, a = 0 \qquad (11)$$

$$\Delta y_t = \mu + \beta t + a y_{t-1} + \sum_{i=1}^{k} 0_i \Delta y_{t-i} + u_t \qquad H_0: \mu = 0, \beta = 0, a = 0 \qquad (12)$$

The t-statistic analogue of the regression coefficient of the lagged endogenous variable, $\hat{a}$, that is tabulated in Fuller (1976), p. 373, Table 8.5.2 for model (11) as $\hat{\tau}_\mu$ and for model (12) as $\hat{\tau}_\tau$, is the central statistic in ADF tests. Moreover, Dickey and Fuller (1981) proposed joint tests of the following form; for model (12) the null hypothesis $\mu = \beta = a = 0$ is tested by estimating a restricted model

$$\Delta y_t = \sum_{i=1}^{k} 0_i \Delta y_{t-i} + u_t \qquad (12')$$

and using the resulting restricted sum of squared residuals (SSR) together with the SSR of the original specification to form a likelihood-ratio test statistic ϕ_2 whose distribution is tabulated in Dickey and Fuller (1981), p. 1063, Table V. The results of Perron (1988) suggest to use a testing strategy that starts with the most general model one wishes to consider under both null and alternative hypotheses, say model (12). In this first step the null hypothesis $a = 0$ is tested using the t-statistic on $\hat{a}$. If a rejection of the hypothesis occurs, one stops here. If no rejection is possible, this might be due to the low power of the procedure.

Therefore one would like to go to the estimation of a model without the trend term β, model (11). The estimate of a in model (11) is not invariant to the presence of a drift term, however. Therefore one has to check first whether in the estimation of (12) the joint null hypothesis $\mu = \beta = a = 0$ can be rejected via ϕ_2. If not, one can estimate model (11) and test again the null of a unit root using the t-statistic on $\hat{a}$. In each step of this testing procedure the number of lagged difference terms in the regressions will be determined as the outcome of an iterative procedure that starts with two difference terms and reduces the number one at a time working from longer to shorter lags (see Perron, 1989). The specification chosen for analysis is the first of these specifications whose longest lag has a significantly high t-statistic.

4.2 Age-structure, migration and cohort size

The development of the German age structure is depicted in the equiscaled graphs contained in Figures 9.1(a) and (b) for male and female inhabitants of the Federal Republic of Germany, respectively. In each figure, the distribution of inhabitants by age is shown in 10-year intervals, starting with 1950, and for the end of the pre-unification period, 1987. Quite obviously, these graphs do not show a population in steady state: there are pronounced troughs and peaks, whose origins mostly appear to be well understood.

Let us turn first to events influencing the number of births in the pre-sample period. There was a marked decline in births during World War I that can easily be followed over time; for example in 1950, these are the individuals in their early thirties. In the Weimar Republic births obviously stayed at lower levels (abstracting from differences in mortality). They then appear to have peaked in 1940, only to be followed by another marked decline at the end of World War II. The development after 1950 parallels to a certain degree that in the United states, with a delay of a few years. In the middle of the 1950s the number of births started to rise in the German 'baby boom', with the peak in 1964. They then declined dramatically to unprecedented low levels in a German 'baby bust', at which they stayed from about 1973 until the middle of the 1980s. Since then, roughly 30 years after the onset of the baby boom, births have increased again. It is mainly the drastic regression of births during the baby bust that – as in the United States – has triggered the debate about the German ageing problem. Average age rose by roughly 5 years during the sample period, from 34 in 1950 to 39 in 1987.

In the comparison between men and women three major facts are apparent. First, slightly more boys are born than girls. Second, and more important, for higher ages the stock of men deteriorates faster than that of women, i.e. women have lower mortality rates. Third, one can see from the graphs documenting the age distributions by gender in 1950 that the male population of birth-year 1927 and older was strongly decimated compared to the female population by the events of World War II. All three reasons work in the direction of raising the average age of women compared to that of men during the whole sample period. The average age of women rose from 35 to 41 years, that of men from 33 to 37 years from 1950 to 1987. Since 1987, both average ages stagnated at these levels, apparently as the effect of the inflow of young migrants after the onset of German unification. But an additional pattern emerges. During their lifetime, the population of men of a given birth-year tends to grow, much more so than the population of women born in a given year.

Figures 9.2(a) and (b) describe the development of selected birth-cohorts over time in equi-scaled graphs, starting with birth-year 1930 and proceeding in five-year intervals until birth-year 1965 for men and women separately. The data only allows us to follow a given birth-cohort over a window of maximal 40 years and this window is over different intervals in the life-cycle of different cohorts. Nevertheless, these graphs are able to stress that the variation in births is not the only important factor determining the size of a given birth-cohort in the population. Special attention should be paid to the distinction between men and women: While the profiles of women stay relatively flat, male birth-cohorts are augmented considerably by immigration in the course of their ageing process. In effect, the population of men was 'artificially' kept younger than that of women by the inflow of young immigrants. This phenomenon partly accounts for the rise in the spread of average ages between men and women from about 2 years to about 4 years in the last 40 years. It is also consistent with the higher concentration of the age distribution of men around its mean, i.e. its lower standard deviation, and for the higher skewness of the male distribution. These patterns are documented in the bottom panels in Figures 9.1(a) and (b).

Overall patterns of male and female immigration evolve quite parallel, however, although all swings are more pronounced for men. Around 1955 there was a major inflow, immediately followed by a strong decline, and it affected the populations of birth-years before 1940 most: the time around 1970 was a period of especially strong inflow, and all but the older birth-cohorts grew significantly following the breakdown of the iron curtain at the end of the 1980s. Moreover, immigrants tend to be young, mainly between 25 and 35. In recent years their average age was declining.

These observations have consequences for the fraction of a given age group in the population of age 15 to 64, henceforth referred to as *cohort*

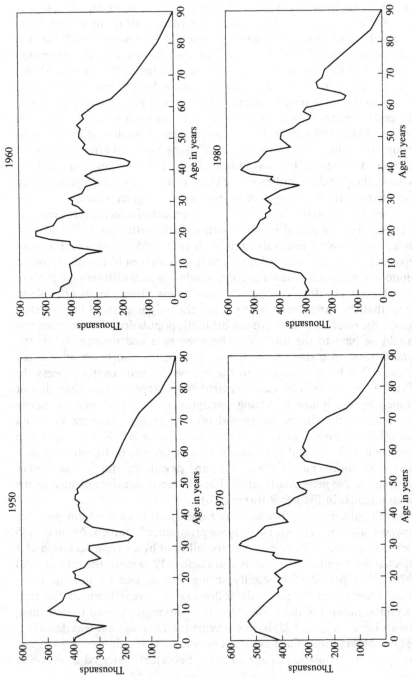

Figure 9.1(a) Germany's age structure: male inhabitants of the FRG, 1950–87 (at 31 December each year)

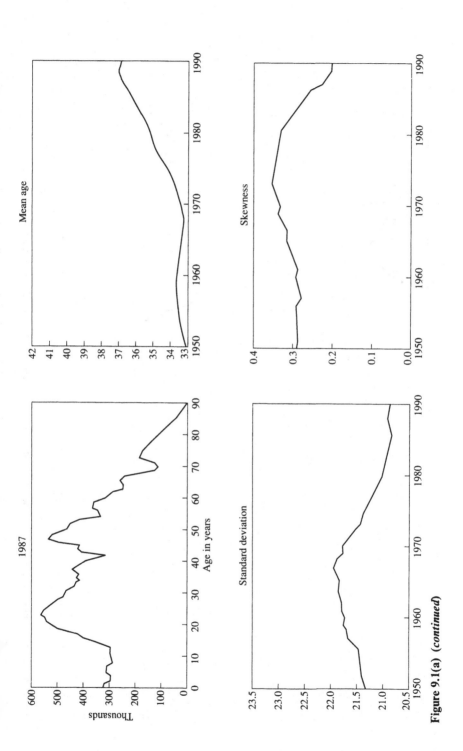

Figure 9.1(a) *(continued)*

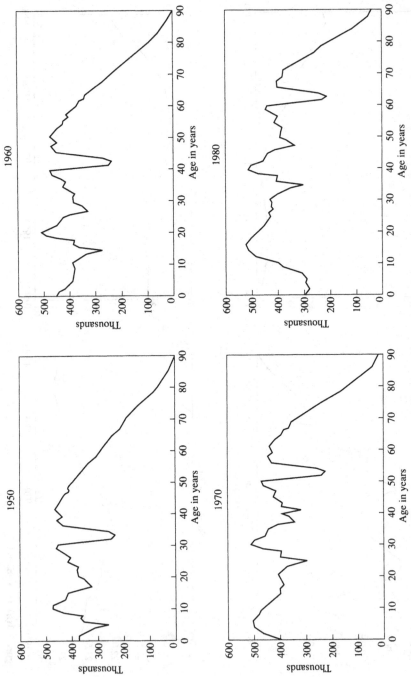

Figure 9.1(b) Germany's age structure: female inhabitants of the FRG, 1950–87 (at 31 December each year)

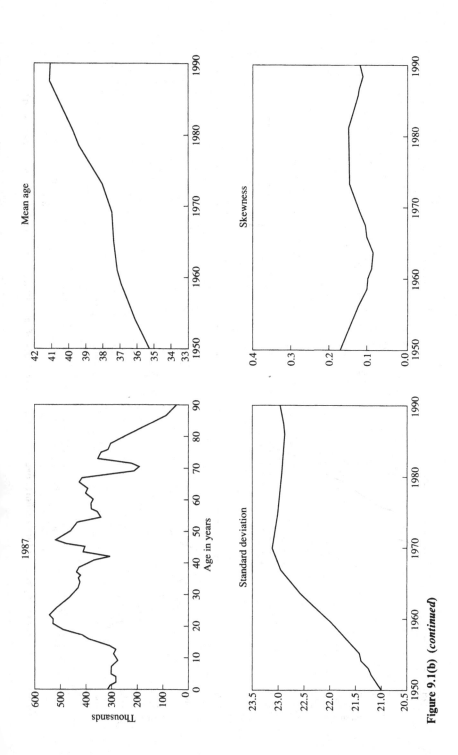

Figure 9.1(b) *(continued)*

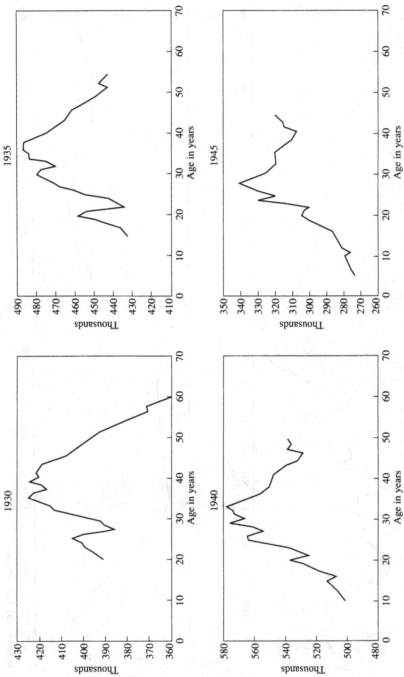

Figure 9.2(a) The development of birth-cohorts over time: male inhabitants of the FRG, 1950–89 (at 31 December each year)

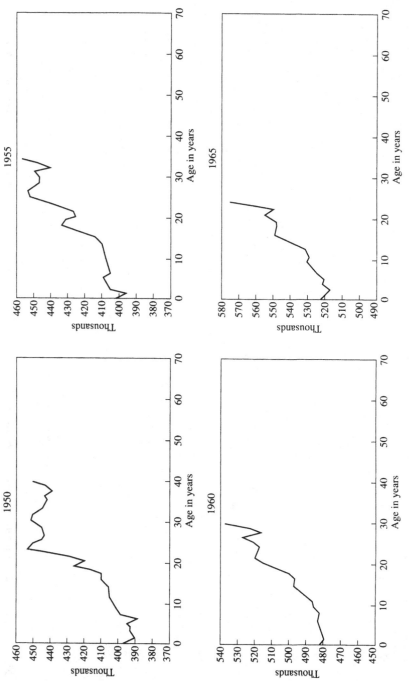

Figure 9.2(a) *(continued)*

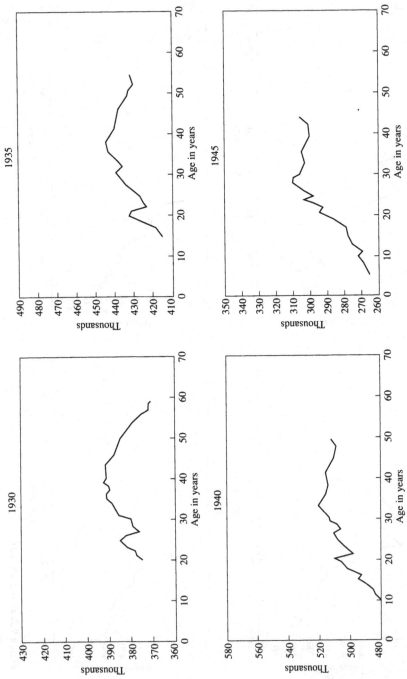

Figure 9.2(b) The development of birth-cohorts over time: female inhabitants of the FRG, 1950–89 (at 31 December each year)

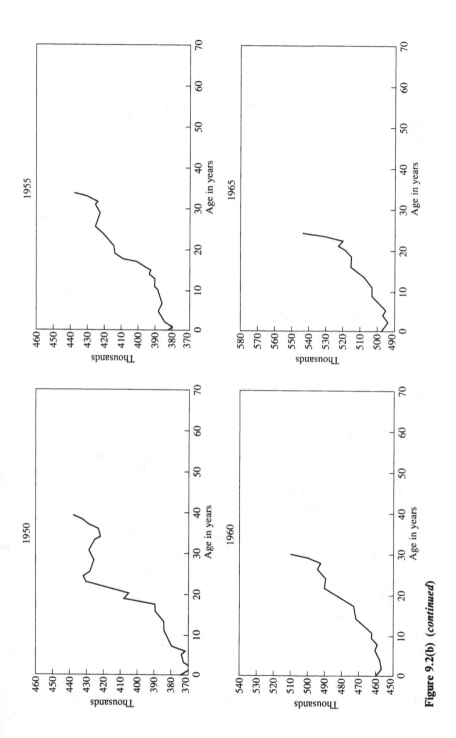

Figure 9.2(b) *(continued)*

size: Cohort size is determined not only by births but also – mainly for men – by migrant inflow. Indeed, young male cohorts and old female cohorts are comparatively large, and the swings in the male cohort size series are more pronounced. Note that these cohort size measures are not the ones constructed by Zimmermann (1991) who used the ratios of the numbers and of the average ages of young individuals to those of old individuals to capture the German population age structure.

Unit root tests for these cohort size series are shown in Table 9.1, columns 1–3. For most series the null hypothesis of a unit root is rejected at the 5% level. There are strong exceptions, however: for the oldest cohort, a unit root cannot be rejected in the univariate representation of all three series, men, women and men and women together. The same holds for the age group 25 to 34. It is mainly the latter phenomenon that relates to the discussion about migrant inflow presented above. At the beginning of the 1970s recruitment of foreign workers into Germany was abruptly halted, and – since guestworkers generally fell into these younger age brackets – the population fraction of individuals between age 25 and age 34 had to shrink dramatically and persistently. It is questionable whether it is conceptually sensible to model some cohort sizes as integrated while others are viewed as trend-stationary, in particular when considering that these tests have been based on a very small sample size. The final set of estimations presented here will therefore impose a unit root on all the cohort size series.

4.3   Unemployment by age group

The development of age-specific unemployment rates between 1967 and 1990 is shown in equi-scaled graphs in Figure 9.3 for men and women together. After staying at very low levels throughout the 1960s, the aggregate unemployment rate experienced two major increases, one after OPEC I in 1973 and one at the beginning of the 1980s. Both after 1975 and after 1983 it stayed at the same level for an extended period of time. At the end of the sample period, a modest decline seems to have started. These overall patterns are also present in the age-specific unemployment rate series. There are marked differences, however.

Two phenomena are apparent: First, over long sub-sections of the sample period, some of these rates stayed consistently below and some stayed consistently above the realization of the aggregate series. Second, since the beginning of the 1980s the position of the very young (less than 20 and 20–24) and that of the old (55–59 and 60–64) relative to the aggregate rate has changed dramatically. Ratios of the age-specific to the aggregate unemployment rate peaked for the very young in 1970 and

Table 9.1. *Unit root tests*

	Cohort sizes			Unemployment rates		
	All	Men	Women	All	Men	Women
15–19	−5.02 (1)	−4.53 (1)	−4.28 (1)	−2.31 (1)[c]	−2.87 (1)[c]	−1.74 (1)[c]
20–24	−3.89 (1)	−3.44 (1)	−4.30 (1)	−2.93 (1)[c]	−3.35 (1)[c]	−2.32 (1)[c]
25–34	−0.04 (1)	1.07 (0)	−0.10 (1)	−2.66 (1)[c]	−2.96 (1)[c]	−2.28 (1)[c]
35–44	−3.47 (1)	−3.47 (1)	−3.30 (1)[r]	−3.12 (1)[c]	−2.95 (1)[c]	−3.29 (1)[c]
45–55	−5.17 (1)	−3.73 (1)	−4.69 (1)	−3.05 (1)[c]	−2.93 (1)[c]	−3.11 (1)[c]
55–59	−3.20 (2)	−2.86 (2)[r]	−6.58 (1)	−3.12 (1)	−3.00 (1)[c]	−3.29 (0)
60–64	−1.19 (2)[c]	−0.63 (2)[c]	−1.69 (2)[c]	−3.20 (0)[c]	−2.79 (0)[c]	−3.54 (0)
All	—	—	—	−3.01 (1)[c]	−3.06 (1)[c]	−2.72 (1)[c]

Notes:

Cell entries are t-statistics of $\hat{\alpha}$ in ADF regressions including both a constant and a trend,

$$\Delta y_t = \mu + \alpha y_{t-1} + \sum_{i=1}^{k} \theta_i \Delta y_{t-i} + u_t.$$

The entries in brackets report the number k of included lagged difference terms. k was chosen as the outcome of a sequence of estimations in which the number of lagged difference terms has been reduced in steps of 1 starting with 2 included lagged differences and stopping at the first specification in this sequence in which the highest included lag coefficient is significant at the 5% level (1.96). The 5% critical asymptotic value is −3.41.

[c] The joint test statistic ϕ_2 warranted a regression without trend term; the unit root null hypothesis was not rejected at the 5% level.
[r] The joint test statistic ϕ_2 warranted a regression without trend term; the unit root null hypothesis was rejected at the 5% level.

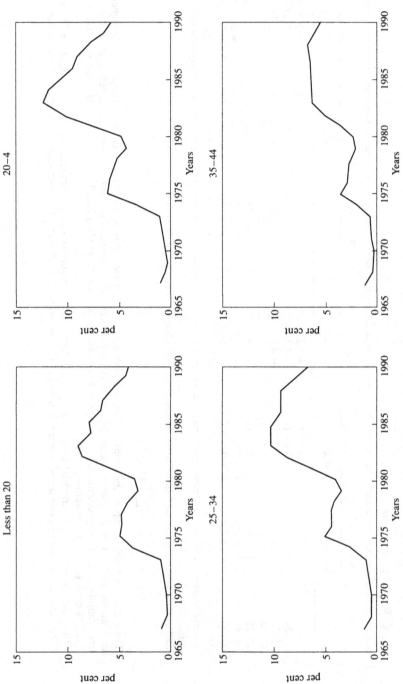

Figure 9.3 German age-specific unemployment rates: a comparison with the aggregate unemployment rate, 1966–90 (at 30 September each year)

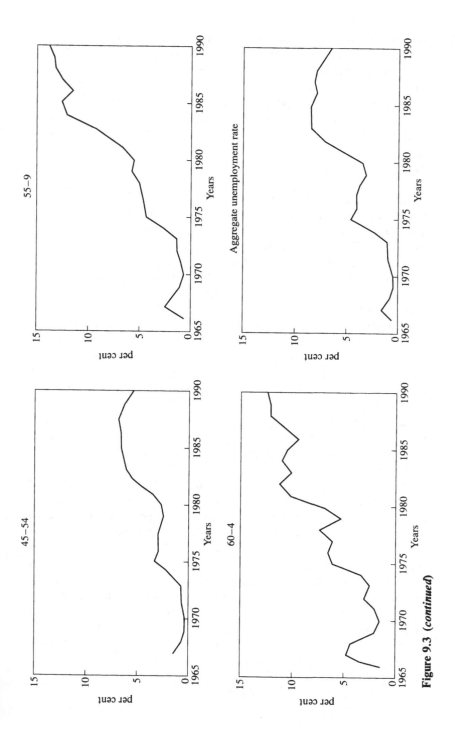

Figure 9.3 (*continued*)

1973, but declined towards the end of the sample period, and are even smaller than unity for the most recent periods. In contrast, for the two oldest age-groups the development runs from a steady decline throughout the early sample period until the early 1980s to a steep increase towards the end of the sample period. There are also important differences between some of the ratio series of men and of women. Most significantly, middle-aged (35–44) men experienced an increase of their unemployment rate compared to the male aggregate rate, while this ratio declined steadily for women in the same age group.

Nelson and Plosser (1982) found the unemployment rate to be the only economic variable of major interest for which a unit root could be rejected in the univariate representation. For Germany, some evidence indicates that unemployment rates might contain a unit root (Schmidt and Zimmermann, 1992). Unit root tests for the unemployment rate series considered here are shown in Table 9.1, columns 4–6. For no series but the unemployment rate of women of age 60 to 64 one is able to reject the null hypothesis of a unit root at the 5% level.

The lack of reliability of unit root tests when analysing small samples is demonstrated by a comparison of these clear cut results with a previous version of this paper: using only one data point less (1967 to 1988), the unit root test statistics derived there diverge remarkably from those found here. Nevertheless, the further analysis will presume all unemployment rate series to contain a unit root. Cointegration theory tells us, however, that integrated series might be linearly related in the long run and that deviations from this long-run equilibrium will themselves be stationary. Thus, in a first set of estimations I ask the question whether there exists such a long-term equilibrium relationship between the age-specific and the aggregate unemployment rates.

To test for the presence of cointegration given two or more integrated variables, one simply runs a static *cointegrating regression* between the levels of these variables using least squares (see Engle and Granger, 1987). One of the variables has to be designated the dependent variable. It generally does not matter for the consistency of the coefficient estimates which is chosen due to the special convergence properties of least squares regressions when all the variables involved are integrated. Here, the age-specific unemployment rate is always chosen. If the equilibrium relationship of the variables might change over time, one should include a deterministic trend into the regression. The residuals from the cointegrating regression are then investigated for the presence of a unit root, using an ADF regression without trend and without a constant

$$\Delta u_t = \rho \cdot u_{t-1} + 0 \cdot \Delta u_{t-1} + e_t \tag{13}$$

(I will restrict the coefficient θ to 0 when its absolute t-statistic is smaller than 1.96). A rejection of the null hypothesis of a unit root in the residual means that the null hypothesis of non-cointegration between the integrated variables has been rejected and a long-run relationship has been established. The critical values for this test differ according to the number of variables and whether a time trend was included in the cointegrating regression (see MacKinnon, 1991). To describe the short-term dynamics, first differences of age-specific unemployment rates would then be regressed in an *Error Correction Model* (ECM) on own lagged differences, the lagged residuals of the corresponding cointegration regression (the *equilibrium error*) and lagged differences of the other integrated variables.

In all regressions discussed below the unemployment rate of a given sex-age group will be regressed on the corresponding sex-specific aggregate unemployment rate. Cohort size measures for a sex-age group will always reflect the fraction of individuals of that sex-age group in all individuals of the same sex and between ages 15 and 64. Only for women in the age group 25 to 34 can the null hypothesis of non-cointegration be rejected at the 5% level. In the regression without a trend the estimated coefficient of the aggregate unemployment rate is 1.24 and the residual-based test statistic is − 3.43 (the 5% critical value is − 3.34). All other age-specific unemployment rates do not appear to be cointegrated with the corresponding aggregate unemployment rate. Obviously the long-term relationship between these unemployment rates – if it exists at all – is driven by the long-term development of at least one more integrated variable. The next section will investigate whether the cohort size series can be used to establish such long-run equilibria.

4.4 Unemployment rates and own cohort sizes

Three sets of regressions analyse the impact of the size of the own cohort on the relative unemployment rates in different sex-age groups. A first set of estimations includes own cohort size in the cointegrating regression. Only for three sex-age groups can the corresponding test of non-cointegration be rejected. For men of age 15 to 19 the estimated coefficients of the aggregate unemployment rate are 1.05 and 0.91, the estimated coefficients of cohort size are 0.49 and 0.51, and the residual-based test statistics are − 4.30 (critical 5% value − 4.12) and − 4.22 (critical 5% value − 3.74) in the regressions with and without trend, respectively. For women of age 15 to 19 the regression with a trend term included leads to estimated coefficients for the aggregate unemployment rate of 1.17 and for cohort size of 0.59, and to a residual-based test statistic of − 4.18 (critical 5% value − 4.12). Finally, for men of age 55–59 the regression with a trend yields coefficient estimates of 0.88 on the aggregate unemployment rate and of 0.67 on cohort size, and a test statistic of − 4.34 (critical 5% value − 4.12).

In this set of estimations, no clear pattern emerges for the relationship between cohort sizes and unemployment rates. For the two younger age groups, 15 to 19 and 20 to 24, and for the age group 55 to 59 are the estimated cohort size coefficients positive for both men and women. They are negative for men and positive for women of ages 25 to 34 and 45 to 54, and both negative for men and women of ages 35 to 44 and 60 to 64. The t-statistics from the cointegrating regression cannot be used for inference, since in the case of integrated variables the distribution of the coefficients is nonstandard. Thus, I will not discuss which of these effects are significant.

A second set of regressions redefines the cohort size measure. The sum of own cohort size and of the cohort sizes of the younger and the older adjacent cohorts is included in the cointegrating regression. For the age groups 15 to 19 and 60 to 64 the only adjacent cohort sizes included are those of the older and of the younger cohorts, respectively. Unit root tests for these redefined cohort size series indicate that the null hypothesis of a unit root cannot be rejected at the 5% level for women of age 15 to 19, and for men of ages 20 to 24, 25 to 34, 45 to 54 and 55 to 59. For these four age groups a unit root is also not rejected at the 5% level for the series combining the cohort sizes of men and women. Thus, these tests confirm the indeterminacy of the unit root tests presented for cohort sizes on the narrow definition of section 4.2.

In this set of estimations, a cointegrating relationship can be established for 5 sex-age groups. For men and women of age 15 to 19 the cointegrating regressions with included trend term lead to coefficient estimates of 1.03 and 1.17 on the sex-specific aggregate unemployment rate, and 0.43 and 0.58 on the broad measure of cohort size, and to residual-based test statistics of − 4.19 and − 5.01, respectively (critical 5% value − 4.12). For women of ages 25 to 34 the coefficient estimates in the cointegrating regression with a trend term are 1.17 on the sex-specific aggregate unemployment rate and − 0.24 on the broad cohort size measure. The residual-based test statistic is − 5.32 (critical 5% value − 4.12). Finally, for men and women together and for men of age 55 to 59 the coefficient estimates are 0.61 and 0.76 on the corresponding aggregate unemployment rate series, and 0.60 and 0.55 on the series capturing the broad definition of cohort size, and the residual-based test statistics are − 4.49 and − 6.30, respectively (critical 5% value − 4.12).

As for the narrow definition of cohort size, no clear pattern emerges from this set of regressions for the relationship between unemployment rates and the broader cohort size definition. Only for age groups 15 to 19 and 55 to 59 is the same set of relationships found with both measures of cohort size. Opposite signs are taken by the cohort size coefficients of age groups 25 to 34, and 35 to 44, by male cohort size in the age group 20 to 24, and by female cohort size in the age groups 45 to 54 and 60 to 64. Thus, it appears that neither cohort size measure is able to capture the substitutivity relations in the economy's technology sufficiently well.

One might argue that unemployment rates and cohort sizes cannot be integrated variables by construction, despite the evidence on unit root tests presented above. In that case, modelling the relations between the variables in levels is appropriate, and the usual asymptotic normality results apply. In effect, t-statistics can be used for inference on the significance of the variables. However, in contrast to the case of integrated variables, the issues of simultaneity bias and serial correlation will play an important role. Since each age-specific unemployment rate is a component of the corresponding aggregate unemployment rate, the aggregate unemployment rate cannot be treated as an exogenous variable and instrumental variable techniques are called for.

A similar argument applies to the measures of cohort size. US studies on the earnings effects of larger cohorts usually treat the cohort size as exogenous: potential parents are generally not seen as being influenced in their fertility decisions by the fertility decisions of other parents. Given stable participation rates across age, in empirical studies, fluctuations in cohort sizes can thus be treated as exogenous variations in labour supply (see Connelly, 1986). This view is no longer valid when labour force participation rates within age groups or migration decisions are endogenous. Thus, in general, instrumental variable techniques should be employed in empirical analyses.

In a third set of regressions, these arguments are taken up. Using again the narrow definition of own cohort size, the level regressions are repeated using two stage least squares with corrections for serial correlation (implemented by an iterative CORC procedure) and varying the set of included instruments. In one subset of regressions the aggregate unemployment rates are instrumented for by the age-specific unemployment rates of all the age-groups other than the one investigated in the regression. In a second subset of regressions, additional instruments include the lagged values of the dependent variable and of the explanatory variables and the inflow of immigrants into Germany lagged one year.

The coefficient estimates on both the aggregate unemployment rates and on the cohort size series stay remarkably close to those achieved in the simple least squares regressions, whether serial correlation in the error term is controlled for or not. Several estimations with serial correlation correction do not converge, and for some others the estimated serial correlation coefficient is close to unity. I take the stability of the parameter estimates and these convergence problems as a further indication for the importance of the nonstationarity in the investigated series. Endogeneity issues do not seem to matter.

4.5   Unemployment rates, own and adjacent cohort sizes

A final set of estimations is documented in Tables 9.2–4. In addition to the narrow measure of own cohort size, the narrow measures of the cohort sizes of the younger and the older adjacent cohorts are separately included in the cointegrating regression. As coefficient estimates of the aggregate unemployment rates again differ only slightly from those achieved in the regressions presented above, they will be discussed in detail only in this section. The same holds for the description of the short-term dynamics.

For both men and women one finds a clear break in the relationship between age-specific unemployment rates and the corresponding aggregate unemployment rate. For the young age groups 15 to 19, 20 to 24 and 25 to 34, the coefficient of the aggregate unemployment rate is larger than unity, for the older age groups it is smaller. The only exception to this uniform behaviour is the coefficient of the aggregate unemployment rate of men aged 60 to 64 which is roughly unity. For the same age group it is also exceptionally low for women. Overall, taking into account the age structure of the population helps to establish behaviour that is consistent with the studies on individual job tenure and job turnover discussed above. Clearly, the age group that has the most sensitive relative unemployment rate is the age group 20 to 24, followed by the age group 25 to 34. The age groups that are least sensitive in terms of relative unemployment experience are those aged 45 to 54 and 55 to 59. The results on the relationships between cohort sizes and the unemployment rate series partly conflate opposite effects for men and women and will therefore be discussed separated by sex.

For men one can only establish a cointegrating relationship between the male unemployment rates and cohort size measures for the age group 55 to 59. A positive long-term relation between own cohort size and the relative magnitude of the unemployment rate can be found for age groups 15 to 19, 25 to 34, 35 to 44, 45 to 54 and 55 to 59. A large magnitude of the older adjacent cohort appears to be correlated in the long run with high relative unemployment for age groups 25 to 34, 35 to 44, 45 to 54 and 55 to 59. The same holds for the size of lower adjacent cohorts for age groups 20 to 24, 25 to 34 and 35 to 44. Only for the age group 45 to 54 will a large cohort size of men of age 35 to 44 lead to a lower unemployment experience in the long run. In the regressions for men trend terms do not appear to play an important role in long-term relationships between unemployment rates and cohort sizes.

For women in the four youngest age groups, 15 to 19, 20 to 24, 25 to 34 and 35 to 44, one is able to establish a long-term relationship between cohort sizes and unemployment rates. Unemployment rates in the age groups 15 to 19, 20 to 24, 35 to 44 and 60 to 64 compared to the female aggregate unemployment rate are higher when the own cohort and the adjacent cohorts are large. Only for the age group 25 to 34 does own cohort size reduce relative unemployment. For this age group the cohort size of 20 to 24 year-old individuals appears to influence relative unemployment substantially: the larger this adjacent cohort, the smaller is the relative unemployment experienced by women aged 25 to 34. For most of the regressions the inclusion of a trend term appears to be important.

For all sex-age groups I proceed to describe the short-term dynamics in terms of error correction models, whether a cointegrating relationship can be established or not. With a few exceptions, short-term dynamics appear to be exclusively driven by adjustments to the long-run path. This impression is mainly due, however, to the high correlation of changes in age-specific and aggregate unemployment rates. The tables document a set of regressions that restrict the coefficients of the aggregate unemployment rate and of all cohort size measures to zero. The corresponding F-test is only rejected for a single sex-age group: for women of age 45 to 54 changes in the size of the own cohort and in the size of the adjacent older cohort lead to significant downward adjustments in their unemployment rate. In general, adjustments of age-specific unemployment rates are driven negatively by deviations from the corresponding long-run relationship and positively by own past changes.

Why does one fail to establish long-term relationships for such a large fraction of sex-age groups? First, it might be that the age groups are chosen too narrowly given the small number of observations. Second, the separate treatment of men and women and the lack of disaggregation by skill might lead to the omission of important substitution possibilities from the analysis. Third, the population cohort size might not be the correct cohort size measure to describe the behaviour of age-specific unemployment rates relative to the aggregate unemployment rate. The behaviour of the fraction of individuals in a given age group in the population might deviate over time from that of the fraction of workers in this age group in the labour force.

A related question is why one does not find an even more consistent

Table 9.2. *Unemployment rates and cohort sizes (men and women)*

Age group	15–19	20–24	25–34	35–44	45–54	55–59	60–64
Cointegrating regressions[1]:							
Constant	−8.850	−11.33	2.992	−10.83	−12.00	−32.68	−0.361
	(2.32)	(2.03)	(0.44)	(5.87)	(7.85)	(5.83)	(0.11)
Trend	−0.137	−0.170	−0.029	−0.011	0.048	0.200	0.124
	(1.99)	(3.08)	(0.92)	(0.93)	(3.42)	(2.50)	(1.17)
Aggregate UR	1.085	1.487	1.128	0.802	0.635	0.636	0.859
	(12.2)	(22.6)	(20.3)	(28.6)	(32.5)	(6.75)	(4.01)
Adjacent younger cohort	—	0.694	0.236	0.227	−0.039	1.182	0.414
		(4.28)	(1.04)	(4.85)	(2.11)	(3.96)	(1.79)
Own cohort	0.598	0.396	−0.162	0.086	0.615	1.077	−0.174
	(6.77)	(1.28)	(1.38)	(2.05)	(10.0)	(6.93)	(0.72)
Adjacent older cohort	0.285	0.004	−0.088	0.214	0.299	0.321	—
	(0.68)	(0.03)	(0.86)	(5.39)	(7.68)	(2.71)	
DW	1.411	1.064	1.162	1.522	1.553	1.480	1.322
Adjusted R-squared	0.972	0.992	0.998	0.998	0.998	0.989	0.908
ADF[2]	−4.02[3,4]	−3.66	−4.42	−4.37	−3.50[4]	−7.23	−4.42[3]
Error correction models[5]:							
Constant	0.025	0.084	0.168	0.189	0.111	0.236	0.023
	(0.12)	(0.33)	(0.75)	(1.41)	(1.04)	(1.57)	(0.08)
Equilibrium error$_{t-1}$	−1.957	−1.355	−1.926	−3.537	−3.460	−1.224	−1.186
	(2.69)	(1.28)	(0.95)	(2.51)	(2.75)	(3.91)	(2.91)
Δ age-specific UR$_{t-1}$	0.964	0.705	0.565	0.327	0.504	0.545	0.588
	(3.70)	(3.66)	(2.50)	(1.74)	(3.03)	(3.57)	(2.21)
F-test	2.33	2.34	2.40	0.87	0.86	0.47	0.58
	(3.29)	(3.06)	(3.06)	(3.06)	(3.06)	(3.06)	(3.29)

DW	1.872	1.520	1.513	1.680	1.803	1.845	1.828
Adjusted R-squared	0.368	0.364	0.175	0.323	0.407	0.513	0.247

Notes:

[1] Static regressions of age-specific unemployment rates on the aggregate unemployment rate and measures of cohort size. Absolute t-statistics in parentheses.

[2] Residual-based tests of the null hypothesis of non-cointegration: t-statistics in ρ in the ADF regression involving the residuals from the cointegrating regressions, $\Delta u_t = \rho \cdot u_{t-1} + \theta \cdot \Delta u_{t-1} + e_t$. The 5% critical value is -4.72.

[3] The 5% critical value is -4.43.

[4] The coefficient θ was set to 0, since its absolute t-statistic is smaller than 1.96.

[5] Regressions of first-differenced age-specific unemployment rates on own lagged differences and the lagged residuals of the corresponding cointegrating regression. Absolute t-statistics in parentheses. Each F-test tests the restricted ECM against the alternative of a complete ECM that also includes lagged differences of the aggregate unemployment rate and of the cohort size measures among the regressors. Critical 5% value for this test in parentheses.

Table 9.3. *Unemployment rates and cohort sizes (men)*

Age group	15–19	20–24	25–34	35–44	45–54	55–59	60–64
Cointegrating regressions[1]:							
Constant	−4.058	−2.324	−13.35	−9.612	−3.974	−15.49	3.617
	(1.08)	(0.32)	(2.87)	(3.77)	(2.51)	(2.18)	(1.55)
Trend	−0.044	−0.091	−0.061	0.014	−0.050	0.164	0.002
	(0.78)	(1.05)	(3.48)	(0.46)	(1.79)	(1.21)	(0.02)
Aggregate UR	1.050	1.523	1.251	0.790	0.572	0.757	1.022
	(11.2)	(16.6)	(25.2)	(18.1)	(19.5)	(5.57)	(4.64)
Adjacent younger cohort	—	0.472	0.552	0.209	−0.087	0.457	0.374
	—	(2.01)	(3.64)	(3.73)	(3.23)	(1.11)	(1.60)
Own cohort	0.505	−0.017	0.115	0.068	0.345	0.743	−0.493
	(5.60)	(0.04)	(1.46)	(1.25)	(4.06)	(3.75)	(2.02)
Adjacent older cohort	−0.150	−0.120	0.195	0.172	0.130	0.368	—
	(0.39)	(0.61)	(2.82)	(2.16)	(2.64)	(2.56)	—
DW	1.084	0.944	1.285	1.261	0.840	1.328	1.340
Adjusted R-squared	0.958	0.982	0.997	0.996	0.996	0.975	0.887
ADF[2]	−4.27[3]	−4.28	−4.39[4]	−4.04	−2.27[4]	−7.09	−4.32[3]
Error correction models[5]:							
Constant	0.028	0.093	0.122	0.207	0.147	0.229	0.005
	(0.13)	(0.35)	(0.56)	(1.70)	(1.78)	(1.45)	(0.02)
Equilibrium error$_{t-1}$	−1.625	−1.446	0.006	−3.019	−3.211	−1.046	−1.103
	(2.14)	(1.70)	(0.00)	(3.19)	(4.54)	(4.17)	(2.74)
Δ age-specific UR_{t-1}	0.966	0.757	0.489	0.219	0.267	0.511	0.553
	(3.16)	(3.48)	(2.16)	(1.19)	(1.82)	(3.43)	(2.07)
F-test	2.12	1.05	0.75	1.25	0.82	0.43	0.81
	(3.29)	(3.06)	(3.06)	(3.06)	(3.06)	(3.06)	(3.29)

DW	1.800	1.585	1.616	1.740	1.655	1.861	1.725
Adjusted R-squared	0.291	0.336	0.139	0.422	0.605	0.544	0.220

Notes: As Table 9.2.

Table 9.4. *Unemployment rates and cohort sizes (women)*

Age group	15–19	20–24	25–34	35–44	45–54	55–59	60–64
Cointegrating regressions[1]:							
Constant	-14.98	-30.66	18.74	-17.62	-19.82	-60.20	-6.805
	(4.05)	(3.87)	(2.84)	(8.09)	(7.71)	(10.3)	(1.08)
Trend	-0.367	-0.371	0.120	-0.051	0.013	0.376	0.523
	(4.56)	(4.70)	(2.21)	(3.18)	(0.77)	(5.76)	(3.22)
Aggregate *UR*	1.179	1.464	1.138	0.842	0.753	0.697	0.365
	(14.0)	(18.1)	(26.4)	(26.2)	(24.4)	(7.00)	(1.34)
Adjacent younger cohort	—	1.108	-0.575	0.354	-0.015	2.330	0.408
	—	(5.55)	(2.10)	(6.24)	(0.48)	(8.89)	(1.17)
Own cohort	0.530	1.040	-0.343	0.236	0.826	1.617	0.205
	(5.87)	(2.49)	(2.96)	(4.93)	(9.47)	(9.62)	(0.57)
Adjacent older cohort	1.128	0.490	-0.328	0.298	0.467	-0.074	—
	(2.65)	(2.38)	(3.47)	(7.50)	(7.51)	(0.56)	
DW	2.030	1.239	2.678	1.921	1.316	1.228	1.058
Adjusted *R*-squared	0.982	0.990	0.999	0.997	0.997	0.992	0.896
ADF[2]	-5.71[3,4]	-4.81	-8.37	-6.42	-3.47[4]	-3.80	-3.57[3]
Error correction models[5]:							
Constant	0.026	0.076	0.200	0.143	0.138	0.334	0.164
	(0.11)	(0.32)	(0.84)	(0.86)	(0.86)	(1.81)	(0.49)
Equilibrium error$_{t-1}$	-2.222	-0.967	-3.579	-2.512	-1.272	-0.913	-0.978
	(2.65)	(1.42)	(1.91)	(1.84)	(1.08)	(2.41)	(3.12)
Δ age-specific *UR*$_{t-1}$	0.892	0.650	0.544	0.552	0.550	0.519	0.495
	(3.54)	(3.65)	(2.65)	(2.38)	(2.43)	(3.03)	(2.14)
F-test	2.37	2.52	0.66	0.99	3.71	2.46	0.00
	(3.29)	(3.06)	(3.06)	(3.06)	(3.06)	(3.06)	(3.29)

DW	2.028	1.529	1.397	1.543	1.478	1.750	1.836
Adjusted R-squared	0.348	0.417	0.274	0.174	0.163	0.332	0.280

Notes: As Table 9.2.

pattern of the effects of (own) cohort size on relative unemployment experiences. One reason could be that wage adjustments play a larger role than presumed in the analysis. Some subsets of the labour force may influence the institutionalized wage-setting process in their favour. Others may affect their prospects by variations in their human capital investments. Finally, the estimations for women indicate that women in large cohorts might decide not to participate in the labour market. Thus, their unemployment rates will not respond to cohort size increases and they might even be lower for women in large cohorts. Nevertheless, the economic opportunities of the members of these cohorts would be negatively affected.

5   Ageing and unemployment: a re-evaluation

A changing age structure potentially alters the relative labour market outcomes for members of different age groups. Until now, most of the research on these effects has concentrated upon twists in the observed age-earnings profiles and upon unemployment experiences of the very young generated by the entry of baby boom cohorts into the US labour market in the early 1970s. In this paper it is argued that the problem is broader when European labour markets are under study. Using age-specific unemployment rates for Germany, it is investigated whether own and adjacent cohort sizes are important components in the long-term relationship between age-specific and aggregate unemployment rates.

The empirical analysis fails to establish such a clear relationship between the relative unemployment experience of an age group and its fraction in the population for a large subset of the sex-age groups considered. Nevertheless, for many of these groups a strong positive impact of own and adjacent cohort sizes can be observed. It appears that variations in the age structure will have an impact on relative labour market outcomes, but that these effects may at least partly be realized in terms of adjustments in outcomes other than unemployment. Therefore, further research has to investigate the impact of the age structure on wage and participation adjustments.

The results presented here already demonstrate, however, that unemployment effects of age structure variations might play an important role for teenagers as well as for adults in an economy characterized by a centralized wage-setting process involving a strong union movement. This pattern has significant consequences for an ageing society. As the results for the male and female age groups 55 to 59 demonstrate, large older cohorts might indeed experience a relatively high unemployment rate. Thus, government policy to reverse the trend to early retirement might alleviate the pressure on the system of social security, but lead to higher unemployment rates among the old.

If immigration of young (male) labour is used to solve the problems of labour force ageing, a relatively large share of unemployment is likely to be borne by the younger age groups, as demonstrated by the results for the male age group 25 to 34. Thus, although there is potentially a positive level effect of immigration, it will have distributional consequences in terms of unemployment. Government policy to counter population ageing should therefore contain provisions to mitigate the negative effects of generational crowding that could be created by such a policy.

NOTE

Previous versions of this paper have been presented at the Université Catolique de Louvain, Louvain-la-Neuve, and at the University of Konstanz. I thank Lutz Bellmann and Klaus F. Zimmermann for parts of the data material and Stefan Hochgürtel for his research assistance. The paper profited from comments by John Black, Horst Entorf, John Ermisch, René Garcia, Tim Guinnane, Paul Johnson and Klaus F. Zimmermann and from a stay at the Université de Montreal, Canada.

REFERENCES

Berger, M. C. (1985) 'The Effect of Cohort Size on Earnings Growth: A Reexamination of the Evidence', *Journal of Political Economy* 93, 561–73.

Bloom, D. E., R. B. Freeman and S. D. Korenman (1987) 'The Labour-Market Consequences of Generational Crowding', *European Journal of Population* 3, 131–76.

Börsch-Supan, A. (1991) 'Aging population: Problems and Policy Options in the US and Germany', *Economic Policy* 6, (12), 104–39.

Clark, R. L. (1989) 'Ageing Populations', in J. Eatwell, M. Milgate and P. Newman (eds.), *The New Palgrave: Social Economics*, New York, London: Norton, pp. 1–3.

Clark, R. L., J. Kreps and J. J. Spengler (1978) 'Economics of Aging: A Survey', *Journal of Economic Literature* 16, 919–62.

Connelly, R. (1986) 'A Framework for Analyzing the Impact of Cohort Size on Education and Labor Earnings', *Journal of Human Resources* 21, 543–62.

Dickey, D. A. and W. A. Fuller (1981) 'Likelihood Ratio Statistics for Autoregressive Time Series With a Unit Root', *Econometrica* 49, 1057–72.

Ehrenberg, R. G. (1980) 'The Demographic Structure of Unemployment Rates and Labor Market Transition Probabilities', *Research in Labor Economics* 3, 241–91.

Engle, R. F. and C. W. J. Granger (1987) 'Co-integration and Error Correction: Representation, Estimation, and Testing', *Econometrica* 55, 251–76.

Fair, R. C. and K. M. Dominguez (1991) 'Effects of the Changing U.S. Age Distribution on Macroeconomic Equations', *American Economic Review* 81, 1276–94.

Franz, W. (1987) 'Hysteresis, Persistence, and the NAIRU: An Empirical Analysis for the Federal Republic of Germany', in R. Layard and L. Calmfors (eds.), *The Fight Against Unemployment*; Cambridge, MA: MIT Press, pp. 93–122.

Freeman, R. B. (1979) 'The Effect of Demographic Factors on Age-Earnings Profiles', *Journal of Human Resources* **14**, 289–318.

Fuller, W. A. (1976) *Introduction to Statistical Time Series*, Ch. 8, New York: Wiley.

Hall, R. E. (1982) 'The Importance of Lifetime Jobs in the U.S. Economy', *American Economic Review* **72**, 716–24.

Hurd, M. D. (1990) 'Research on the Elderly: Economic Status, Retirement, and Consumption and Saving', *Journal of Economic Literature* **28**, 565–637.

Keyfitz, N. (1988) 'Some Demographic Properties of Transfer Schemes: How to Achieve Equity Between the Generations', in R. D. Lee, W. B. Arthur and G. Rodgers (eds.), *Economics of Changing Age Distributions in Developed Countries*, New York, pp. 92–105.

MacKinnon, J. G. (1991) 'Critical Values for Cointegration Tests', in R. F. Engle and C. W. J. Granger (eds.); *Long-run Economic Relationships*, Oxford: Oxford University Press, pp. 267–76.

Nelson, C. R. and C. I. Plosser (1982) 'Trends and Random Walks in Macroeconomic Time Series', *Journal of Monetary Economics* **10**, 129–62.

Perron, P. (1988) 'Trends and Random Walks in Macroeconomic Time Series. Further Evidence from a New Approach', *Journal of Economic Dynamics and Control* **12**, 297–332.

(1989) 'The Great Crash, the Oil Price Shock, and the Unit Root Hypothesis', *Econometrica* **57**, 1361–1401.

Schmidt, C. M. and K. F. Zimmermann (1992) 'Unemployment, Real Wages, and Union Membership', mimeo, University of Munich.

Welch, F. (1979) 'Effects of Cohort Size on Earnings: the Baby Boom Babies' Financial Bust', *Journal of Political Economy* **87**, S65–97.

Zimmermann, K. F. (1991) 'Ageing and the labor market', *Journal of Population Economics* **4**, 177–200.

Discussion

JOHN ERMISCH

In the spirit of the paper itself, my discussion will focus primarily on econometric issues. In terms of setting the framework for the econometrics, the monopoly union wage model is a nice way to motivate the analysis. The age-specific unemployment rates emerging from the model are *equilibrium* rates. They are not merely the result of sluggish relative wage adjustment, but would be maintained for a given sequence of cohort sizes and given demand conditions. This leads us to look for equilibrium relationships between cohort size and age-specific unemployment rates.

The main econometric issue concerns the inferences that we can make from the unit root tests, particularly in the small sample used here. I found it very odd that despite the fact that, for most cohort size series, a unit root is rejected (p. 234), the paper proceeds to treat all the cohort size series as integrated.

While the unemployment series do not produce ADF statistics below the stated critical value, these statistics are consistently around -3. In light of the low power of these tests when the series is stationary but exhibiting high autocorrelation, I would be cautious about accepting that they have a unit root. Additional evidence would be helpful, such as the correlogram. There is also a unit root test based on the Durbin-Watson statistic, but it is likely to fall in the inconclusive range.

The paper does not tell us the source of the critical values for the ADF tests. The exact critical values are strongly affected by unknown features of the process generating the data, particularly in small samples. The author must rely on tabulated values for a particular data-generating process, based on simulation methods; what is the source? I doubt that such tabulations have been done for such a small sample. These comments also apply to the cointegration tests that follow.

As Schmidt points out on p. 241, the properties of the variable series matter for at least two reasons. One is the validity of the *t*-tests, and the other is the issue of endogeneity of cohort size and the average unemployment rate when the individual series are stationary, as I suggest may be inferred from the above tests. This issue is addressed on p. 241, but it is not very clear what has been done. Have the cohort size variables been instrumented as well? Given the autocorrelation in the residuals, lagged dependent variables are unlikely to be valid instruments. Have instrumental variable estimates been computed for the specifications with adjacent cohort sizes?

There are some other good instrumental variables available to address this issue. In particular, births 20, 30, etc. years previously are exogenous and should capture the impact of birth fluctuations on cohort size. In addition, variables capturing economic conditions in the main countries from which German immigrants come may also be good instruments.

In light of the uncertainty about the critical values in small samples and the fairly 'healthy' ADF statistics in Tables 9.3 and 4, I think the author is too pessimistic about the main results of the paper. On p. 243, he offers reasons for a failure to establish long-term relationships for a large fraction of age-sex groups, but in my view there has not been a failure. The results in Tables 9.3 and 4 suggest quite strong and plausible effects of own and adjacent cohorts on age-specific unemployment rates.

It would, however, be more informative to see a further assessment of the quantitative importance of the cohort size effects. For instance, the biggest effects are at each end of the working life, but relatively few Germans are working at these ages. What pattern of unemployment rates over a person's life would the estimates imply for different cohorts, and how would the life cycle pattern of labour force participation mitigate these effects? It should not be difficult to simulate such patterns with the estimated relationships.

In sum, the analysis suggests that changes in the age distribution and migration have important impacts on the age pattern of unemployment rates in Germany.

10 Ageing, migration and labour mobility

RAINER WINKELMANN and
KLAUS F. ZIMMERMANN

1 Introduction

The substantial ageing of the European labour force will significantly alter the wage and employment structure. It will then also probably affect labour mobility, and with open borders, also induce immigration. In an equilibrium framework, labour markets tend to equalize real wages and labour productivity. If there are age-dependent productivities, there will be an adjustment of wages as soon as the age-composition of the labour force is altered. Although it has been found that the effect of age is marginal in comparison to other factors and that productivity variations within age groups are more significant than variations across age groups, there seems to be evidence that productivity increases over the work-life as, for instance, would be predicted by human capital theory. (See OECD, 1988, and the literature cited there.) However, the necessary adjustment relies on the flexibility of the labour force and may cause unemployment, at least in the short run.

It was argued that an increase in the age of the active population will reduce labour mobility and increase absenteeism and might adversely affect productivity also via the poorer health of older workers. (More detailed surveys of the arguments are given in OECD, 1988, and United Nations, 1988. See also for the effects on labour mobility Ashenfelter, 1982; Clark and Spengler, 1980.) Efficiency losses in the allocation of labour have to be expected if the aged labour force is less willing to change jobs, industries or regions. It would then be necessary to create specific labour market policies to maintain the perceived level of labour flexibility and to fight a potential increase in unemployment. There is also the fear that the duration of unemployment will increase, as older workers face a longer average duration of unemployment. It is also unclear to what extent older workers can replace younger workers, which will depend on the degree of substitutability and complementarity between the age groups. In any case

255

it is likely that the degree of mismatch between labour demand and supply will increase, either because of immobility, inappropriate skills, or the unwillingness of the old to accept wage cuts and take over the jobs of the young.

A larger amount of immigration might be a reasonable policy to account for the decline in the labour force and its ageing. Because of a positive selection process, migrants tend to be more mobile than natives. However, one has to account for the fact that these people also are ageing over time and that they may also adjust their flexibility to the level of the host country. A larger stock of foreign labour may also cause an increase of native unemployment.

There are two aspects of labour mobility that are of interest: the first issue is flexibility, the ability (and the willingness) to change jobs when there are economic gains from doing so; this is a virtue in a market system. The second is unemployment, which is related to the inflexibility of labour and is a bad in a market economy. This paper will study the frequency of direct job changes and the frequency of unemployment spells using a vast sample of German individual data. Central to our analysis will be how the age structure and the share of foreign labour in the sector affects both measures of labour mobility for natives and foreigners. Using *count data models* to account for the specific nature of the data, an econometric investigation provides the estimates for the quantitative relationships between the key variables. These estimates are then used to evaluate the effects in several simulations: What is the age-mobility profile? How is it affected by migration? What are the potential effects of labour force ageing as it is predicted for Germany and Europe up to the beginning of the next century?

Section 2 summarizes some stylized facts of ageing and migration in Europe and West Germany, stating that West Germany can serve as an important reference case because its labour force is ageing considerably and it has experienced a large inflow of immigrants in recent decades. Section 3 provides the theoretical background of the paper, outlining the equilibrium framework of the neoclassical labour market theory. Section 4 discusses data and econometric methodology, which is essentially robust Poisson regression. Section 5 contains a summary of the empirical results and their policy implications. Section 6 concludes.

2   Some stylized facts on ageing and migration

Population ageing in Europe is well documented in other papers of this volume. Concentrating on Western Europe, we provide some information on general trends only. Figure 10.1 summarizes population evolution in

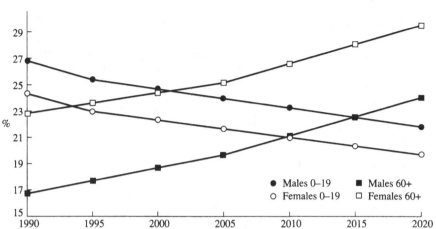

Figure 10.1 EC-12 male and female population aged 0–19 and 60 +, 1990–2020
Source: EUROSTAT, *Demographic Indicators of the Community*, p. 171.

the EC between 1990 and 2020 according to a recent EUROSTAT population projection (EUROSTAT 1991) for males and females in age groups 0–19 and 60 + . There will be already more old women than young women in Europe in 1995, and more old men than young men after 2015. In total, the decline of the younger age cohorts is combined with an even higher increase of the older age cohorts, leading to a decline of the total potential work force. Of course, this conclusion also depends on the degree of labour force participation and educational decisions, as well as retirement decisions.

Table 10.1 studies the potential labour force's age and how it develops if one compares the size of age groups 20–39 to the age groups 40–59. In all EC countries (excluding Greece for which no data is available), the age ratio 20–39/40–59 was well above 1 in 1990. In 2005, this ratio is already below 1, declining substantially if one relies again on the EUROSTAT predictions. It is interesting to see that the countries in Southern Europe (Italy, Spain and Portugal) are predicted to have the oldest labour force.

Migration affects the stock of labour in the immigration country, and it is of interest to what extent European countries presently rely on foreign labour. Table 10.2 provides an answer to this question. Columns 1–4 contain total population size, size of foreign population, total number of foreign workers, and number of workers from the EC countries. Columns 3–7 weight the last three statistics by total population size. Column 8 gives the share of foreign employment. West Germany, France and the United

Table 10.1. *Population structure: age groups 20–39/40–59, 1990–2020 (Ratio)*

	1990	1995	2000	2005	2010	2015	2020
Belgium	1.28	1.20	1.04	0.88	0.82	0.81	0.83
Denmark	1.18	1.11	1.03	0.92	0.86	0.84	0.87
West Germany	1.19	1.11	1.02	0.82	0.71	0.75	0.82
France	1.31	1.21	1.08	0.97	0.94	0.92	0.94
UK	1.27	1.22	1.11	0.96	0.90	0.91	0.99
Ireland	1.40	1.25	1.12	1.00	0.98	0.95	0.91
Italy	1.19	1.22	1.17	0.99	0.82	0.71	0.67
Luxemburg	1.27	1.16	1.02	0.89	0.83	0.86	0.91
Netherlands	1.37	1.26	1.10	0.94	0.85	0.83	0.89
Portugal	1.35	1.38	1.29	1.10	0.95	0.81	0.75
Spain	1.33	1.40	1.34	1.15	0.97	0.81	0.71
EC	1.25	1.22	1.12	0.97	0.86	0.82	0.83

Source: EUROSTAT, *Demographic Indicators of the Community*, 1991; own calculations. Data for Greece are missing.

Kingdom have the largest absolute numbers of foreigners and foreign workers. The picture changes if the numbers are weighted by population size. With respect to the share of foreigners in total population, the sequence is Luxemburg 25.8%, Belgium 8.6%, West Germany 7.3%, France 5.0%, The Netherlands 3.8%, United Kingdom 3.0%, Denmark 2.5%, Greece 1.9%, Portugal 0.9% and Spain 0.9%.

The more relevant countries with respect to foreign workers (their share of total population, see column 6 of Table 10.2) are Luxemburg 15.7%, West Germany 2.6%, France 2.1%, Belgium 1.9%, United Kingdom 1.4%, and The Netherlands 1.2%. Note also that West Germany has by far the largest stock of non-EC workers of all EC member countries: only 472.7 thousand out of 1.57 million foreign workers are from the EC. The share of foreign employment (column 8) provides the following order between the countries: Luxemburg (33.2%), West Germany (7.7%), France and Belgium (6.4%), United Kingdom (4.2%), The Netherlands (3.1%), Ireland (2.7%), Denmark (1.4%), Greece (0.9%), Portugal (0.5%) and Spain (0.2%).

The German situation has to be qualified for two different reasons: Unification has changed the picture somewhat, as East Germany had no significant immigration. On the other hand, a large part of immigration to West Germany after World War II was an inflow of East Germans or of people of German origin, who are not counted in Table 10.2, because foreign-born people are not considered as foreigners in this case.

Table 10.2. *Population size and foreigners in EC countries, 1988*

	Thousands		Workers		Per cent			
	Population (1)	Foreigners (2)	Foreign (3)	EC (4)	(2):(1)	(3):(1)	(4):(1)	Foreign employment
Belgium	9,884	853.2[b]	187.0	140.8	8.6	1.9	1.4	6.4
Denmark	5,130	128.3[b]	45.5	12.4	2.5	0.9	0.2	1.4
West Germany	61,451	4,489.1	1,577.1	472.7	7.3	2.6	0.8	7.7
France	55,884	2,785.0[a]	1,172.5	589.3	5.0	2.1	1.1	6.4
UK	57,065	1,736.0[c]	820.9	398.2	3.0	1.4	0.7	4.2
Greece	10,010	193.4[b]	24.9	6.6	1.9	0.3	0.1	0.9
Ireland	3,538	—	19.9	16.1	—	0.6	0.5	2.7
Italy	57,441	429.4[d]	57.0	14.0	0.8	0.1	0.0	—
Luxemburg	375	96.8[b]	58.8	55.9	25.8	15.7	14.9	33.2
Netherlands	14,760	568.0[b]	175.7	86.2	3.8	1.2	0.6	3.1
Portugal	10,305	89.8[b]	30.5	6.8	0.9	0.3	0.1	0.6
Spain	38,809	354.9	57.0	22.0	0.9	0.2	0.1	0.2

Notes:
[a] Statistische Bundesamt, *Länderbericht Frankreich*, 1989.
[b] 1987.
[c] 1985.
[d] 1981.

Sources: Population (middle of the year): OECD, *Main Economic Indicators*, 1991. Foreigners: Statistisches Bundesamt, *Statistisches Jahrbuch für das Ausland*, 1990. Foreign workers and EC workers: Statistisches Bundesamt, *Statistik des Auslands*, 1990. EURO-STAT, *Sozialporträt Europas*, Luxemburg, 1991.

Nevertheless, these are migrants who had to be integrated permanently in the German labour market. To obtain an approximate estimate about the potential size of the problem, consider the following calculation: from 1950–88, 4.8 million ethnic Germans came to West Germany, 3.2 million from the German Democratic Republic (GDR) and 1.6 million from Eastern Europe. (Before 1950, more than 12 million came, and in 1989–90 774 thousand came.) Of course, a substantial part of these immigrants had either died or retired by 1988. Nevertheless, the reported share of foreigners to population size for West Germany of 7.3% would have to be adjusted significantly above 10% if one wanted to account for these migrants.

Abowd and Freeman (1991, p. 4) report that the percentage of immigrants in the US labour force adjusted for undercounting due to illegal immigrants, was 7.3% in 1980. This reflection indicates that the German experience is comparable with the situation in the host country USA, because the reported share of foreign labour in Table 10.2 was 7.7% for West Germany and should probably be corrected upward because of immigrants of German origin. This justifies relying on German experience to answer relevant questions in this paper when EC data was not available.

It is of substantial importance for the evaluation of the effects of immigration to know in which industries migrants work. It is a common belief that immigrant workers tend to concentrate in different industries than native workers. In Table 10.3 this issue is investigated using industry data from West Germany and the USA. The American data treat non-natives as foreign-born (immigrants and refugees), whereas the German data on natives also include foreign-born if they were ethnic Germans. The first six columns report the shares of total, foreign, and native employment in each of eleven sectors in both countries. The next two columns study foreign employment as per cent of total sector employment for both countries, and the last column gives the percentage changes in the shares of foreign labour from 1982 to 1989 for West Germany. (For the US data see also Sehgal, 1985, and Collins, 1991).

In the USA, there were 109.1 million workers, and 7.97% of them were foreign-born. In 1982, West Germany had 20.5 million workers and 8.79% were foreigners. The distribution of total employment between the sectors is significantly different between West Germany and the US. In West Germany, the largest three sectors were manufacturing (39.6% of total employment, column 2 of Table 10.3), other services (17.9%) and retail trade (8.3%), whereas in the US the sequence was (column 1) other services (30.3%), manufacturing (19.6%), and retail trade (16.3%). These results are largely dominated by the distributions of the natives (see

Table 10.3. *Employment distribution by sector, USA and West Germany (D), 1982*

| | % of Total group employment | | | | | | Foreign[a] as % of total sector employment | | |
| | Total | | Foreign[a] | | Native | | 1982 | | % change 82–89 |
	USA	D	USA	D	USA	D	USA	D	D
Agriculture	3.4	1.1	3.6	1.0	3.4	1.1	8.4	7.9	− 15.2
Mining	0.9	2.4	0.7	2.0	1.0	2.4	5.7	7.3	− 1.4
Construction	5.9	7.8	4.7	9.9	6.0	7.6	6.4	11.3	− 11.5
Manufacturing	19.6	39.9	25.3	56.1	19.2	38.4	10.2	12.4	− 14.5
Transportation and public utilities	7.0	4.9	4.2	3.9	7.2	5.0	4.8	7.0	− 7.1
Wholesale trade	4.3	5.6	3.9	3.3	4.4	5.8	7.1	5.2	1.9
Retail trade	16.3	8.3	16.5	3.2	16.3	8.8	8.1	3.5	2.9
Finance, insurance, real estate	6.2	3.8	6.6	0.7	6.2	4.1	8.4	1.7	− 5.9
Private household	1.3	1.8	1.8	0.7	1.2	1.9	11.5	3.6	13.9
Other service	30.3	17.9	30.5	16.7	30.3	18.0	8.0	8.2	− 6.1
Public administration	4.7	6.6	2.4	2.6	4.9	7.0	4.1	3.4	0.0

Note: [a]USA: Foreign-born. Germany: Foreigners.

Source: Sehgal (1985); Statistisches Bundesamt, *Statistisches Jahrbuch*, 1990. USA: Foreign-born. Germany: Foreigners.

columns 5 and 6). In the US, foreign labour is distributed very similarly to total employment (column 3): agriculture 3.6%, mining 0.7%, construction 4.7%, manufacturing 25.3%, transportation and public utilities 4.2%, wholesale trade 3.9%, retail trade 16.5%, finance, insurance and real estate 6.6%, private households 1.8%, other service 30.5%, and public administration 2.4%. This implies that foreign labour is mainly in those sectors which are also dominated by the native workers. The most striking difference is manufacturing where the share of foreign workers of 25.3% is much larger than the 19.6% for total employment.

In West Germany, the distributions of native and foreign workers between the sectors differed much more (columns 4 and 6): 56.1% of the foreign workers were in manufacturing, whereas only 38.4% of the German workers were in this sector. The participation of foreign workers in the sector 'other services' was lower than by native workers (16.7% in comparison to 18.0%), and higher in construction (9.9% in comparison to 7.6%). The remaining sectors had a low foreign participation: agriculture 1.0%, mining 2.0%, transportation and public utilities 3.9%, wholesale trade 3.3%, retail trade 3.2%, finance, insurance, real estate 0.7%, private households 0.7%, and public administration 2.6%. It is further noticeable that the percentage of workers in the traded goods sector (manufacturing, mining, agriculture) was 23.9% (foreign-born labour 29.6%) for the US and 43.4% (foreign labour 59.1%) in West Germany.

Foreign labour as per cent of total sector employment is given in columns 7 and 8 of Table 10.3. Again, there are large differences between the US and West Germany. Foreign labour is more dominant in the US in the sectors agriculture, wholesale and retail trade, finance, insurance and real estate, private households, and public administration. The four sectors in the US with the largest share of foreign labour were private households (11.5%), manufacturing (10.2%) and agriculture and finance, insurance and real estate (both 8.4%). In West Germany, the ranking of the sectors were manufacturing 12.4%, construction 11.3%, other services 8.2%, agriculture 7.9%, mining 7.3%, transportation and public utilities 7.0%, wholesale trade 5.2%, private households 3.6%, retail trade 3.5%, public administration 3.4%, and finance, insurance and real estate 1.7%. The last column indicates that the share of foreign labour decreased in most German sectors between 1982 and 1989, but increased in wholesale and retail trade and private households.

One reason why the distribution of foreign and native workers are more different in Germany than in the US is that far more foreigners in West Germany are temporary workers, or 'guest workers', who may only eventually become permanent migrants. This is probably valid also for other European countries. It has to be expected that foreigners become more similar to native workers the longer they stay in the host country. The striking current differences in sector presence also indicate that foreign labour is more a complement than a substitute for German labour. Guest workers concentrate in sectors with less attractive jobs.

The paper attempts to study the relationship between population ageing and labour mobility, and how it is affected by immigration. Certainly, the ageing of the European labour force creates an incentive for immigration. Should it be allowed? At first, one could calculate the demand for foreign young labour that is needed to replace the missing young native population. Though this is an interesting question which was for instance studied by Coleman (1991), we will concentrate on other issues: using West Germany as a case study, we will try to quantify the potential effects of ageing on labour mobility and study how mobility as such could be affected by migration. Labour mobility is first considered to be the flexibility to change jobs, which is a virtue in a market system, or in contrast, the frequency of unemployment spells which is interpreted to be of negative value to society. The paper studies the effect of ageing and migration on both types of labour mobility.

3   Theoretical framework

The theory of production with multiple factor inputs is well described and applied to labour demand in Heckman and Sedlacek (1985), Hamermesh (1986) and Ermisch (1988a, 1988b), among others. Following this line of theorizing, it is easy to cover differences between natives and foreigners, older and younger workers, males and females, by allowing them to be separate production factors with potential differences in productivity. While this is easy to formalize, it is rather difficult to draw useful conclusions from it, and it is also not very convincing as a theoretical concept. Differences in productivity between natives and foreigners, old and young, or females and males occur because these groups exhibit characteristics with different qualities for production.

To simplify the analysis we will only distinguish between quantity of labour (Q) and quality of labour (H), where H refers to human capital, measured for instance by education or years of schooling. Denoting K for capital and assuming a standard neoclassical production function yields

$$Y_j = F^{(j)}(Q_j, H_j, K_j) \tag{1}$$

where j refers to the sector in which individual i is working. Without loss of generality we assume (1) to exhibit constant returns to scale. H_j is the quantity of human capital used in sector j, as Q_j and K_j are the stock of labour and the stock of capital, respectively.

After profit maximization under perfect competition, we obtain the marginal value product of each input equal to its real rate of return.

$$R_Q^{(j)} = F_Q^{(j)}(Q_j, H_j, K_j)$$

$$R_H^{(j)} = F_H^{(j)}(Q_j, H_j, K_j) \qquad (2)$$

$$R_K^{(j)} = F_H^{(j)}(Q_j, H_j, K_j)$$

Hence, individual i's wage in sector j, w_{ij}, is

$$w_{ij} = R_Q^{(j)} + R_H^{(j)} H_i \qquad (3)$$

where H_i is i's stock of human capital. H_i is a positive function of schooling (S_i) and experience (E_i):

$$H_i = H_i(S_i, E_i) \qquad (4)$$

Note that experience is usually measured by $Age_i - S_i - 6$, which enables us to study the effects of ageing in a natural way via the formation of human capital. (It is possible to separate the effects of sector-dependent experience from general labour market experience but this is neglected here for clarity of exposition.)

Equations (2) and (3) form the basis of an analysis of how a change in factor inputs will affect individual wages. Here the distinction between q-complements and q-substitutes in production as opposed to p-substitutes and p-complements is of value. Following Hicks (1970), inputs can be complements (q-complements) in the production of a variable output, although they are substitutes in the production of a given input (p-substitutes). Two factors are q-complements if $\partial R_X / \partial Z > 0$ and q-substitutes if $\partial R_X / \partial Z < 0$, and $X, Z = Q, H, K$ and $X \neq Z$. At least two factors have to be q-complements. Hence, if Q and H are q-complements, an increase in the stock of labour Q will increase the productivity of human capital H. Using equation (3), we obtain:

$$\frac{\partial w_{ij}}{\partial Q_j} = \frac{\partial R_Q^{(j)}}{\partial Q_j} + \frac{\partial R_H^{(j)}}{\partial Q_j} H_i \qquad (3')$$

$\partial w_{ij} / \partial Q_j > 0$ is the more likely the larger H_i is, but is unambiguously negative if H and Q are q-complements. Assume that there are two distinct groups in the labour market: the first group, let us call them natives, have a wage distribution following equation (3). The second, named migrants, have a zero stock of (usable) human capital. As a consequence an influx of migrants will lower the wages of less qualified natives, but may increase the wages of better educated natives.

Each period, individual i gets wage offers depending on his potential wage w_{ij}. The individual is assumed to receive more profitable offers the larger his productivity is, at least over some reasonable range of w_{ij}. The number of direct job changes (C_{ij}) of an individual is

$$C_{ij} = C_{ij}(w_{ij}, V_j) \tag{5}$$

with $\partial C_{ij}/\partial w_{ij} > 0$, where V_j represents transaction costs. Similarly, we assume that the frequency of unemployment depends negatively on the individual's potential wage ($\partial U_{ij}/\partial w_{ij} < 0$, at least over some range of w_{ij}) and transaction costs of employer and employee:

$$U_{ij} = U_{ij}(w_{ij}, V_j) \tag{6}$$

Equations (3)–(6) form the basic set of hypotheses that are investigated in the empirical section of this paper. To put it into practice, transaction costs must be discussed. To obtain measurable variables, we assume that transaction costs are covered to some extent by the micro data variables age, family status, trade union membership, and job type. This will be detailed in section 5. Here, we concentrate on the variable 'age'. A greater age often reflects a higher stock of firm-specific human capital, which is lost if the worker changes his employer. The older the worker is, the more likely he is to become unemployed again, indicating a bad risk. Hence, the number of direct job changes declines and the frequency of unemployment increases with rising age.

Also, the static framework does not account for structural change between industries that might affect job changes and unemployment. Growing industries create more jobs and hence more job changes are more likely, whereas declining industries exhibit the reverse pattern. This can be captured by an industry variable covering employment growth over the sample period.

The core of the model states (using equations (3) and (4)) that labour mobility is affected by schooling and age of the individual as by the level of factor inputs in the respective industries. Due to the lack of reliable data, the industry level variables will only be represented by the share of foreign labour in the various industries. By means of this variable, we compare differences in the size of uneducated labour as measured by foreign labour assuming that guest workers have a lower stock of (usable) human capital.

4   Data and methodology

The empirical study attempts to estimate the effects of individual characteristics and industry-level variables on labour mobility measured by the number of job changes during the ten-year period 1974–84 in West Germany. This period was characterized by two sharp recessions, in 1974 and 1981, in which the German unemployment rate rose from around 1% first to 4.5% and then to 9.1%. During the same period, the number of vacancies went down from 315,000 in 1974 to 88,000 in 1984. The individual data were taken from the Sozio-ökonomisches Panel, a large micro data set of West German households. Two variables contain the core information in our analysis, both based on retrospective questions asked in 1985 for the preceeding ten-year period: the individual number of employers and the number of unemployment spells a person had experienced during this period. We rejected the idea of using the information on job changes contained in the different panel waves since the observed variation in mobility is much smaller in the waves than in the retrospective question. Though the latter might be affected by measurement errors, the retrospective information is on a longer interval (there are 6 panel waves available) and thus gets closer to a measure of lifetime mobility. To ensure that all individuals were part of the labour force during the entire period, we excluded individuals whose age was less than 25 in 1974 and those more than 60 in 1984. Our analysis is based on 1,830 males, of whom 586 are foreigners. Females were excluded from the analysis to avoid the modeling of family formation.

Assuming that (i) people do not return to the same job after a spell of unemployment, and (ii) the individuals have been employed at the beginning of the period, the number of direct job changes between employers is equal to the total number of job changes minus the number of unemployment spells. We will follow the interpretation that spells of unemployment are involuntary, whereas direct job changes are voluntary, and study the number of direct job changes (or voluntary job changes), the number of unemployment spells (or involuntary job changes) and the total number of job changes for German and foreign workers separately. These variables can only take nonnegative integer values.

The appropriate statistical framework is an econometric model for discrete nonnegative variables. A genuine statistical model for counts is the *Poisson* distribution with probability function

$$P(Y = y) = f(y) = \frac{exp(-\lambda)\lambda^y}{y!}, \quad \lambda \in \mathbb{R}^+, y = 0, 1, 2, \ldots \quad (7)$$

where $E(Y) = Var(Y) = \lambda$. The equality of mean and variance is sometimes refered to as 'equidispersion'. To permit the identification of factors that explain the distribution of counts across individuals, observed heterogeneity is introduced by setting

$$ln(\lambda_i) = x_i\beta, \quad i = 1, \ldots, n \quad (8)$$

where x_i is a $(1 \times k)$ vector of non-stochastic covariates and β a conformable vector of coefficients. Equation (8) is called the *mean function* of the model.

The merits of this stochastic specification are manifold. It captures the discrete and nonnegative nature of the data, and allows inference to be drawn on the probability of event occurrence. It naturally accounts for the heteroscedastic and skewed distribution inherent in nonnegative data: the more the mean of the dependent variable approaches zero the more relevant this becomes. Only for large counts, the normality assumption might be a sufficient approximation. Finally, the Poisson regression model has a simple structure and can easily be estimated by the method of maximum likelihood. The log-likelihood is given by $log\, L = \Sigma_{i=1}^{n}$ $[y_i x_i \beta - log(y_i!)]$. The first-order conditions $\Sigma_{i=1}^{n}[x_i(exp(x_i\beta) - y_i)] = 0$ state, as in the linear model, that the residuals $e_i = y_i - E(Y_i|x_i)$ are orthogonal to the explanatory variables. The Hessian matrix $H = -\Sigma_{i=1}^{n} x_i' x_i\, exp(x_i\beta)$ is negative-definite and standard numerical algorithms converge to the unique maximum of the (log-) likelihood function.

The Poisson model yields efficient estimates provided that the assumed probability model is the true one. However, the Poisson assumption of equal conditional mean and variance is often not appropriate in practice, leading to overly high t-values in case of *overdispersion* (variance larger than mean) and to an underestimation of the t-values in case of *under-dispersion* (variance smaller than mean). We therefore review the robust-ness of the Poisson model when the mean function (8) is correctly specified, but the true data generating process is not Poisson. In this case, the Poisson log-likelihood $log\, L = \Sigma_{i=1}^{n}[y_i x_i\beta - exp(x_i\beta) - log(y_i!)]$ is a *quasi log-likelihood function*. Maximizing with respect to β yields a *quasi maximum likelihood estimator* (QMLE) $\hat{\beta}$ (called *pseudo maximum likelihood estima-tor* by Gourieroux et al., 1984). White (1982) shows that for the i.i.d. case

$$\sqrt{n}(\hat{\beta} - \beta^*) \sim N(0, A^{-1}BA^{-1}) \qquad (9)$$

β^* is the parameter vector which minimizes the expected difference between the log of the true distribution and the log of the underlying quasi-likelihood. The matrices $A(\beta)$ and $B(\beta)$ are defined as minus the expected value of the Hessian and the expected value of the outer product of the score vector respectively, where the expectation is taken with respect to the true density:

$$A(\beta) = \{ - E_0(\partial^2 log\, L(\beta; y, x)/\partial\beta\, \partial\beta') \}$$

$$B(\beta) = \{ - E_0(\partial\, log\, L(\beta; y, x)/\partial\beta \cdot \partial\, log\, L(\beta; y, x)/\partial\beta') \}$$

Both matrices are identical if the true probability function is chosen and give the Fisher information matrix. In case of misspecification, A and B diverge.

Gourieroux *et al.* (1984) derive that $\hat{\beta}$ is consistent for β_0, the parameters of the true mean function under two conditions: (i) The mean function is correctly specified. That is, there exists a $\beta_0 \in B$ s.t. $\lambda_0 = exp(x\beta_0)$. (ii) The quasi likelihood is a member of the linear exponential family (LEF) of distributions which are of the form (see McCullagh and Nelder, 1989, for instance)

$$f(y, \vartheta) = c(y) exp[\vartheta y - b(\vartheta)]$$

The Poisson distribution is a LEF with $c(y) = 1/y!$, $b(\vartheta) = exp(\vartheta)$, and $\lambda = b'(\vartheta) = exp(\vartheta)$. Thus, Poisson estimates are consistent also in the presence of overdispersion. (It should be noted that any other LEF, like for instance the normal, implying together with mean function (8) *nonlinear least squares*, or the gamma distribution, would do as well.) The intuition behind this result is that asymptotically, the empirical score converges to the expected score by the law of large numbers. For any distribution, the expected score is zero, but for LEFs only this condition reduces to the mean function that was assumed to be correctly specified in the first place. For the Poisson case:

$$E[x(exp(x\beta) - Y)] = 0 \quad \Leftrightarrow \quad E(Y|x) = exp(x\beta)$$

The previous results can be used to establish the asymptotic distribution of an estimator based on the Poisson likelihood if the true data generating process is not Poisson. Using the conditional distribution of Y, the corresponding matrices A and B for the Poisson model are given by:

$$\begin{aligned} A_{psn}(\beta) &= -n^{-1} E_y(-\Sigma_i x_i' x_i \, exp(x_i\beta)) \\ &= n^{-1} \Sigma_i x_i' x_i \, exp(x_i\beta)) \end{aligned} \tag{10}$$

$$\begin{aligned} B_{psn}(\beta) &= n^{-1} E_y(\Sigma_i x_i' (exp(x_i\beta) - y_i)^2 x_i) \\ &= n^{-1} \Sigma_i x_i' x_i \, Var(Y_i|x_i,\beta) \end{aligned} \tag{11}$$

$\hat{\beta}$ is approximately normal with mean β_0 and covariance matrix

$$Cov(\beta) = \left\{ \sum_i x_i' x_i \, exp(x_i\beta) \right\}^{-1} \left\{ \sum_i x_i' x_i \, Var(Y_i|x_i) \right\}$$

$$\times \left\{ \sum_i x_i' x_i \, exp(x_i\beta) \right\}^{-1} \tag{12}$$

The difference between the conventional covariance estimator (assuming that the Poisson distribution is the true model) and the appropriate covariance matrix for $\hat{\beta}$ is

$$A^{-1} - A^{-1}BA^{-1} = \left(\sum_i x_i' x_i \lambda_i\right)^{-1} \left\{\sum_i x_i' x_i \lambda_i\right.$$

$$\left. - \sum_i x_i' x_i \, Var(Y_i|x_i)\right\} \left(\sum_i x_i' x_i \lambda_i\right)^{-1} \quad (13)$$

This difference hinges upon

$$\sum_i x_i' x_i \lambda_i - \sum_i x_i' x_i \, Var(Y_i|x_i) = \sum_i [\lambda_i - Var(Y_i|x_i)] x_i' x_i \quad (14)$$

If there exists *sample* overdispersion, A^{-1} underestimates the true standard errors, the estimated t-values are upwardly biased. For *individual* overdispersion, the situation is less straightforward. If some individuals display under- and some overdispersion, and if $Var(Y_i|x_i)$ is unrelated to the explanatory variables x_i, then using A^{-1} to calculate standard errors might give satisfactory results. Of course, to calculate standard errors one first has to obtain estimates for $Var(Y_i|x_i)$. If no further information is available, $Var(Y_i|x_i)$ is replaced by its sample estimate $[y_i - exp(x_i\hat{\beta})]^2$. This is the most robust situation with the least restrictive assumptions.

Initiated by these theoretical developments, Monte Carlo studies have provided evidence on the small sample behaviour of the proposed methods, and thus guidance is available on which approach to choose in a specific situation. Winkelmann and Zimmermann (1992) study the behaviour of the Poisson QMLE using overdispersed data. The results indicate that already in small samples ($n = 100$), there is no bias in the estimated coefficients, but the covariance matrix calculated along (12) still leads to upwardly biased t-values, although the upward bias using the Poisson covariance matrix is much higher. For $n = 1,000$, the robust covariance matrix (12) gives the correct size of the test also for substantial degrees of overdispersion. In the empirical investigations, we rely on these findings avoiding the estimation of more general count data models (see Winkelmann and Zimmermann, 1991, for instance).

5 Econometric results and policy implications

Labour mobility is measured in this paper by the number of direct job changes and the frequency of unemployment within the period 1974-84. We also study the sum of both, the total number of job changes. It is a basic hypothesis that migrants are a special selection of people who tend to be more mobile, given the other characteristics describing individual behaviour. To investigate this hypothesis, we study the behaviour of Germans and foreigners separately, using samples of 1,244 natives and

586 guest workers. The set of control variables for foreigners is assumed to be the same except for nationality dummies and a variable *duration of stay*, which measures the number of years the foreign worker had spent before 1974 in the German labour market. If the foreigners in the German labour market are more mobile than Germans by nature, then there is a positive selection of mobile people, since only those individuals are sampled who changed their employer at least once when coming to Germany before 1974. The regression coefficient then measures if, and how fast, foreigners assimilate with respect to their labour market behaviour. Another interpretation rests on imperfect information about the productivity of the worker in the new environment. Mismatches will become less likely, the more time the worker has spent in the German labour market. We therefore expect a negative coefficient for this variable: if migrants are attracted to compensate for a decline of mobility of natives say because of ageing, then this effect will partially diminish over time.

The other central control variables are: *Age* is the key variable number one for this study and is measured at the time of the survey in 1985, and age-squared (*agesq*) is added to test for non-linear relationships. A reasonable hypothesis is that unemployment is lowest among the middle-aged and that people are less flexible with rising age. Migration, key variable number two, is evaluated at the industry level, making use of observations of the share of foreign labour in 34 industries in 1974 given in *Statistisches Jahrbuch 1976* (*migs*). A larger share of foreign labour reflects more competition and depresses wages because foreign labour has a tendency to work for lower wages. The likelihood of unemployment rises for natives and there are fewer direct changes of jobs, because jobs are less attractive after all. However, natives might be better motivated to change jobs under the competition of foreign labour so that the net effect on direct job changes is unclear.

We further included years of schooling (*school*) and schooling-squared (*schoolsq*), dummies for family status (*single*), membership in a trade union (*union*), the occupational status in the first job of the worker (reference group is the civil servant with an expected lower mobility) using the categories *ordinary blue*, *qualified blue*, *ordinary white* and *qualified white* collar workers, respectively, to account for individual heterogeneity. Differences in the sectoral employment trends are captured by a variable growth of employment 1974–84 in % (*growth*) on these sectoral levels. The latter variable is again from the *Statistisches Jahrbuch*. More highly educated workers are often expected to have a lower unemployment risk and be more mobile. Married individuals may be better motivated to work and experience a lower risk of unemployment. However, their moving costs are higher and hence direct job changes are less frequent. According to insider-outsider theories, membership of a trade union or a comparable professional organization should reduce mobility, since unions may raise firm's labour turnover costs. A higher growth rate of employment in the industries will tend to induce a lower frequency of unemployment and more direct job changes.

Table 10.4 summarizes means and variances of the variables used. German workers have a smaller mean and variance of direct job changes (0.34 and 0.60) than foreigners (0.63 and 2.33). Their average number of changes is only about half that for foreigners, and the variance is only one-quarter. Attracting foreigners therefore implies an increase in flexibility of the labour force. The average frequency of unemployment of foreigners is not substantially higher than of Germans (0.38 in comparison to 0.30), and its variance is substantially lower (0.80 in comparison to 1.20). Nevertheless, attracting migrants may also imply an increase in unemployment. The age distribution of Germans and foreigners is surprisingly similar (mean of 36.05 for Germans and 34.94 for migrants; variance of 48.57 for Germans and 41.70 for migrants). The sample weighted average of the sector shares of foreign labour is 14.9% for migrants and 10.8% for Germans, indicating that foreign workers are concentrated in different sectors than the natives. We do not detail the other findings in this table which we leave to the reader but draw attention to only one further result, namely that foreigners are all married in our sample.

Tables 10.5 and 6 contain the final estimates for frequency of unemployment, number of direct job changes and total number of jobs for both natives (Table 10.5) and foreigners (Table 10.6). The results for total job changes are for descriptive purposes only because we mostly expect different findings for unemployment and direct job changes. Asymptotic t-values are given for the ordinary Poisson in parentheses and for the robust Poisson in brackets. In many cases, the robust t-values are substantially smaller than for the ordinary Poisson, indicating that there is some overdispersion in the data, which makes inference on the basis of the latter statistics invalid. Noticing that the conclusions concerning the tested hypotheses are significantly different with both methods in many cases, we concentrate on the robust estimates.

We discuss the findings for Germans first (see Table 10.5). Frequency of unemployment is first declining and then rising with age, and schooling follows the same pattern. Singles are unemployed more frequently and trade union members are less. Unemployment is more relevant in those industries that have a larger share of foreign labour. The sectoral employment growth does not affect unemployment significantly. Ordinary and qualified blue collar workers are more frequently unemployed than civil servants. Direct job changes decline with age but are unaffected by the

Table 10.4. *Descriptive statistics*

Variance	Germans		Foreigners	
	Mean	Variance	Mean	Variance
Number of jobs changes 1974–84	0.52	1.22	0.90	3.16
Number of direct job changes	0.34	0.60	0.63	2.33
Number of unemployment spells	0.30	1.20	0.38	0.80
Years of schooling	11.60	6.71	10.05	0.17
Age	36.05	48.57	34.94	41.70
Industry share of foreign workers	10.82	37.18	14.91	23.66
Single (Yes = 1)	0.06	0.06	—	—
Union (Yes = 1)	0.47	0.25	0.48	0.25
Ordinary blue collar (Yes = 1)	0.14	0.12	0.62	0.24
Qualified blue collar (Yes = 1)	0.50	0.25	0.28	0.20
Ordinary white collar (Yes = 1)	0.06	0.06	0.02	0.02
Qualified white collar (Yes = 1)	0.19	0.15	0.02	0.02
Industry growth of labour force 1974-84	− 4.19	300.96	− 12.70	198.21
Years of stay in Germany before 1974			6.31	20.74
Sample size	1,244		586	

level of schooling, family status, the sectoral share of foreign labour, and are negatively related to union membership and increase with the sectoral employment growth. All workers are more mobile than civil servants. Results for foreigners (see Table 10.6) are much weaker. The frequency of unemployment is first decreasing and then increasing with age as was the case for natives. Again, trade union membership affects unemployment negatively. We also included dummy variables for different nationalities (Turks, Yugoslavs, Italians and Greeks, with Spaniards as the reference group) in the regressions, and some of the dummies have a significant impact on mobility. In particular, Turks and Yugoslavs are more frequently unemployed than the Spanish (the reference group), and Italians have less direct job changes than the Spanish.

All other variables are not significant, including the new variable, duration of stay. The latter finding indicates that migrants do not adjust their unemployment risks towards natives. In sum, unemployment is high, whatever the specific characteristics of the individuals and the sectors are. Similarly, the number of job changes is unaffected by most variables including age and duration of stay. The latter finding indicates that migrants do not become less flexible the longer they stay in Germany.

In the sequel, we study more carefully the effects of ageing and immigration of labour. Figure 10.2 contains the graphs of the isolated age effects on unemployment for natives and foreigners, given the sample means for all other exogenous variables, and Figure 10.3 the corresponding drawings for the frequency of direct job changes for natives and foreigners. Figure 10.2 indicates that the frequency of unemployment is at first higher for natives, but then declines faster and only increases slightly after about 42. The minimum for foreigners is about the age of 34 and unemployment risk is substantially higher after 44 than below 30. If guest workers stay, they may become a problem for unemployment policy programmes. Figure 10.3 demonstrates that the frequency of direct job changes declines drastically with age for Germans, whereas there is no effect for foreigners. What are the effects of an increased presence of migrants in the labour market on the mobility of natives? To answer this question we have increased the share of foreign labour in all sectors by factors 2 and 4, noticing that the estimated coefficient of this variable is hardly significant at conventional levels for direct job changes but is significant for frequency of unemployment. Results are shown in Figure 10.4 for the frequency of unemployment and in Figure 10.5 for the frequency of direct job changes. They indicate that, other things being equal, unemployment would rise substantially with migration, but direct job changes would be affected less. There are some costs of immigration.

What are the effects of the predicted ageing of the labour force in

Table 10.5. *Poisson regression results for Germans*[a]

	Unemployment			Direct job changes			Total job changes		
Constant	15.407	(5.901)	[3.252]	0.081	(0.176)	[0.138]	6.864	(3.747)	[2.288]
Age	−0.398	(−5.283)	[−2.240]	−0.061	(−7.922)	[−6.576]	−0.185	(−3.001)	[−2.198]
Agesq	0.483	(4.600)	[1.905]				0.157	(1.792)	[1.357]
School	−1.485	(−4.344)	[−2.871]	0.045	(2.005)	[1.393]	−0.586	(−2.626)	[−1.690]
Schoolsq	5.223	(4.207)	[2.800]				2.174	(2.710)	[1.791]
Single	0.898	(6.053)	[2.916]	−0.125	(−0.648)	[−0.495]	0.273	(2.051)	[1.220]
Union	−0.640	(−5.656)	[−3.210]	−0.459	(−4.450)	[−3.539]	−0.448	(−5.370)	[−3.789]
Migs	0.039	(2.926)	[1.790]	0.013	(1.108)	[0.961]	0.017	(1.836)	[1.415]
Growth	0.003	(0.668)	[0.454]	0.012	(2.908)	[2.484]	0.009	(2.639)	[2.266]
Ordinary blue	1.029	(3.277)	[1.896]	0.483	(1.894)	[1.614]	0.715	(3.323)	[2.728]
Qualified blue	0.849	(2.878)	[1.763]	0.645	(3.052)	[2.418]	0.800	(4.270)	[3.449]
Ordinary white	0.430	(1.177)	[0.738]	0.708	(2.690)	[2.378]	0.594	(2.514)	[2.201]
Qualified white	0.224	(0.746)	[0.512]	0.413	(1.998)	[1.711]	0.473	(2.571)	[2.131]

Log-likelihood	− 957.03	− 943.23	− 1,233.72
LRT baseline model	− 1,075.73	− 1,005.00	− 1,358.23
Sample size	1,244	1,244	1,244

Notes: [a] Asymptotic Poisson *t*-values in parentheses and asymptotic robust Poisson *t*-values in brackets. LRT is the likelihood-ratio test statistic of the estimated model in comparison to the baseline model that has an intercept only.

Table 10.6. Poisson regression results for foreigners[a]

	Unemployment		Direct job changes		Total job changes	
Constant	5.365		1.780		2.077	
	(2.004)	[1.773]	(0.924)	[0.903]	(1.105)	[0.838]
Age	-0.282		-0.003		-0.038	
	(-2.685)	[-2.347]	(-0.294)	[-0.208]	(-0.522)	[-0.344]
Agesq	0.402				0.049	
	(2.802)	[2.514]			(0.480)	[0.313]
School	-0.146		-0.235		-0.161	
	(-0.814)	[-0.738]	(-1.283)	[-1.339]	(-1.268)	[-1.145]
Union	-0.398		-0.016		-0.069	
	(-2.817)	[-2.179]	(-0.150)	[-0.087]	(-0.777)	[-0.459]
Migs	-0.003		0.029		0.021	
	(-0.132)	[-0.109]	(1.878)	[0.900]	(1.641)	[0.864]
Growth	0.011		0.015		0.015	
	(1.696)	[1.451]	(3.085)	[0.976]	(3.531)	[1.296]
Ordinary blue	-0.322		-0.102		-0.236	
	(-1.281)	[-1.001]	(-0.493)	[-0.255]	(-1.411)	[-0.804]
Qualified blue	-0.301		-0.061		-0.141	
	(-1.078)	[-0.823]	(-0.270)	[-0.146]	(-0.773)	[-0.451]
Ordinary white	-0.705		-1.000		-0.746	
	(-1.104)	[-0.671]	(-1.620)	[-1,273]	(-1.675)	[-1.180]
Qualified white	0.541		0.869		0.824	
	(1.329)	[0.839]	(2.692)	[1.367]	(3.152)	[1.455]
Duration of stay	0.005		-0.017		-0.012	
	(0.245)	[0.167]	(-1.165)	[-0.862]	(-1.029)	[-0.712]
Turk	0.672		0.712		0.397	
	(2.458)	[1.928]	(0.889)	[0.667]	(2.336)	[1.774]

Yugoslav	0.795	0.481	0.589
	(2.853) [2.030]	(2.459) [1.545]	(3.418) [2.311]
Italian	0.025	−0.642	−0.359
	(0.081) [0.067]	(−2.556) [−2.052]	(−1.718) [−1.390]
Greek	−0.122	0.130	0.151
	(−0.370) [−0.322]	(0.599) [0.444]	(0.779) [0.581]
Log-likelihood	−488.500	−726.341	−868.636
LRT baseline model	−517.346	−762.446	−918.907
Sample size	586	586	586

Note: "See Table 10.5 for explanations.

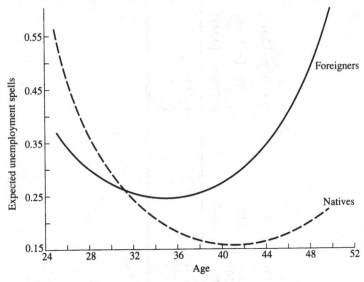

Figure 10.2 Age-unemployment profiles
Note: based on the Poisson regression results in Tables 10.5 and 6. All exogeneous
variables except for *age* are evaluated at their sample means. The vertical axis
gives the expected number of unemployment spells for an individual of given age
during the following ten years.

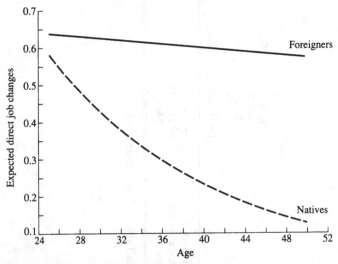

Figure 10.3 Age-direct job changes profiles
Note: see Figure 10.2. The vertical axis gives the expected number of direct job
changes for an individual of given age during the following ten years.

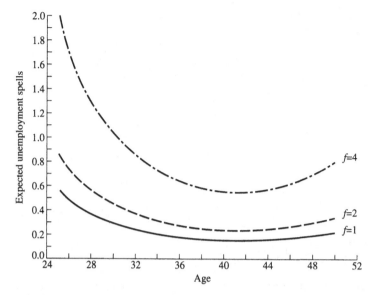

Figure 10.4 Age-unemployment profiles for varying foreign labour shares

Note: natives only. The share of foreigners is increased by factors 2 ($f=2$) and 4 ($f=4$) respectively.

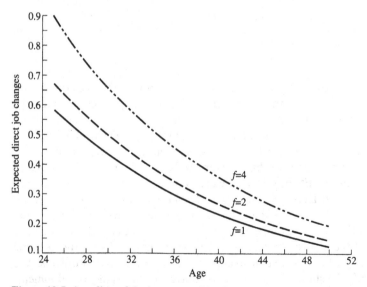

Figure 10.5 Age-direct job changes profiles for varying foreign labour shares

Note: see Figure 10.4.

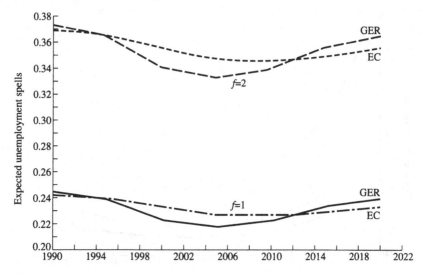

Figure 10.6 Age structure and expected frequency of unemployment of natives, 1990–2020

Notes: based on the EUROSTAT (1991) age distribution predictions for Germany and the EC. The lines depict the development of the marginal expected frequency of unemployment/direct job changes during a ten-year period. The values are obtained by weighting the estimated age-specific expected frequencies of unemployment/direct job changes by the predicted age distribution of the population. Two scenarios are used. For $f = 1$, the actual share of foreign labour is kept constant, and for $f = 2$ it is doubled.

Germany on the frequency of male unemployment and direct job changes? To obtain a rough guess of the likely partial effects consider the following procedure; conditional on our estimates for the natives from Table 10.5, the sample means for the variables, and the variables age and migration, we can generate Poisson distributions for the event counts. For comparative purposes we have taken the age distributions of males in Germany and the EC in 1990 as the predictions in five year intervals up to 2020 as given in EUROSTAT, *Demographic Indicators for the European Community*, 1991. We are then able to investigate the partial effects of the predicted German and European ageing on both types of labour mobility. In spite of the artificial nature of this experiment, it might indicate some tendencies as to what extent ageing will induce relevant problems. We also double the share of foreigners to control for this likely development. Drawings are given for frequency of unemployment (Figure 10.6) and for direct job changes (Figure 10.7). These results suggest that both types of

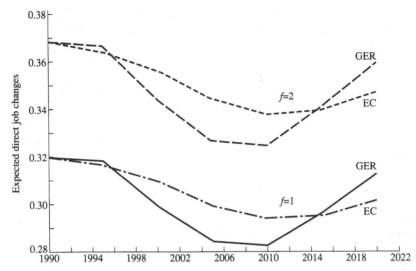

Figure 10.7 Age structure and expected frequency of direct job changes of natives, 1990–2020

Note: see Figure 10.6.

labour mobility would decline slightly with the population ageing as predicted and then increase after 2005–10, but the development is much more smooth for the predicted European age structure than for the German age structure. Again, an increase in the stock of migrants leads to a larger increase of the frequency of unemployment and to a smaller increase in flexibility, if at all.

6   Concluding remarks

This paper has studied the relationship between population ageing and labour mobility and its interaction with migration. Migrants can replace population losses in absolute size or in young workers. An older population might also have workers who are more frequently unemployed and less willing to change jobs. Are migrants of help here? Foreign labour is certainly more adaptable over changing jobs on average, but these workers are also more frequently unemployed, especially the older ones. Robust Poisson estimates have shown that there is a U-shaped relationship between age and frequency of unemployment for both German and foreign workers, and that foreigners have unemployment risks lower than natives in the early stages of their working lives and higher than natives in later stages. Direct job changes decline with age for natives but are unrelated to age and duration of stay in Germany for foreigners. The share of foreign labour affects only the unemployment frequency of Germans significantly, where the increase can be substantial. Simulations with the predicted age structures for Germany and the EC from 1995–2020 show that the age structure induces first a decrease and then an increase of both measures of labour mobility, but the EC structure leads to a flatter development. Hence, the adjustment processes in Germany will be more severe. Again, an increase in the stock of foreign labour will probably cause an increase in the frequency of unemployment which is not of negligible size.

NOTE

We wish to thank John Black, Gerd Ronning and conference participants for useful comments on earlier drafts.

REFERENCES

Abowd, J.M. and R.B. Freeman (1991) *Immigration, trade, and the labor market*, Chicago: The University of Chicago Press.
Ashenfelter, O. (1982) 'The economic impact of an older population: A brief survey', in A.J.J. Gilmore *et al.* (eds.), *Ageing: A challenge to science and society*, Oxford: Oxford University Press, 333–40.
Clark, R.L. and Spengler, J.J. (1980) *The economics of individual and population aging*, Cambridge: Cambridge University Press.
Coleman, D.A. (1991) 'Demographic projections: Is there a need for immigration?' mimeo.
Collins, S.M. (1991) 'Immigrants, labor market pressures, and the composition of the aggregate demand', in J.M. Abowd and R.B. Freeman (eds.), *Immigration, trade, and the labor market*, Chicago: The University of Chicago Press.
Ermisch, J. (1988a) 'Fortunes of birth', *Scottish Journal of Political Economy* **35**, 266–82.
   (1988b) 'British labour market responses to age distribution changes', in R.D. Lee, W.B. Arthur and G. Rodgers (eds.), *Economics of changing age distributions in developed countries*, Oxford: Clarendon Press.
Gourieroux, C., A. Monfort and A. Trognon (1984) 'Pseudo maximum likelihood methods: Theory', *Econometrica* **52**, 681–700.
Hamermesh, D.S. (1986) 'The demand for labor in the long run', in O.C. Ashenfelter and R. Layard (eds.), *Handbook of Labor Economics, Vol. 1*, Amsterdam: North-Holland.
Heckman, J.J. and G. Sedlacek (1985) 'Heterogeneity, aggregation, and market wage functions: An empirical model of self-selection in the labor market', *Journal of Political Economy* **93**, 1077–1125.
Hicks, J.R. (1970) 'Elasticity of substitution again: substitutes and complements', *Oxford Economic Papers* **22**, 289–96.
McCullagh, P. and J.A. Nelder (1989) *Generalized linear models*, 2nd ed., London: Chapman and Hall.

OECD (1988) *Ageing populations: The social policy implications*, Paris: OECD.

Sehgal, E. (1985) 'Foreign born in the US labor market: The results of a special survey', *Monthly Labor Review* **108**, 18–24.

United Nations (1988) 'Economic and social implications of population ageing', in *Proceedings of the international symposium on population structure and development, Tokyo 1987*, New York: United Nations.

White, H. (1982) 'Maximum likelihood estimation of misspecified models', *Econometrica* **50**, 1–25.

Winkelmann, R. and K.F. Zimmermann (1991) 'A new approach for modelling economic count data', *Economics Letters* **37**, 139–43.

(1992) 'Robust Poisson Regression', in L. Fahrmeir *et al.* (eds.), *Advances in GLIM and statistical modelling: proceedings of the GLIM92 and the 7th International Workshop on Statistical Modelling, Munich, 13–17 June 1992.* New York: Springer.

Discussion

GERD RONNING

Winkelmann and Zimmermann's paper (henceforth WZ) draws attention to the fact that immigration in general will alter the age structure and the volume and qualification structure of the working force. They use a data set from a German survey to analyse the impact on labour mobility within the country. Before I comment on the results of the paper I would like to make two general remarks:

(a) In a time of growing unification and harmonization of nations – at least in Central Europe – the paper provokes the question of the meaning of 'foreign' labour. Since immigration seems to be caused mainly by the search for a (better) job there is no clear distinction between (i) a German family moving from some less developed region to the industrialized area around Munich, (ii) a Turkish family coming to Germany or (iii) a British computer expert settling in Germany because of a better job. The authors apparently have in mind only low qualified immigrants when they write: '. . . which will lower wages of less qualified natives' (see section 3 'Theoretical Framework' of the paper). Clearly this group is responsible for the major part of immigration in the German case. But immigration of more highly qualified workers cannot be excluded *a priori*. The question then remains whether it is adequate to differentiate between 'natives' (native born) and 'foreigners' (foreign born people). Is a child of a foreigner when born in Germany ever a 'native'? And, will, say, a Dutch or Belgian worker not have adapted to the German life style within a few years, making him indistinguishable by socio-economic characteristics from a native German worker?

(b) The empirical part of the paper is based on *retrospective* questions from the 'Socio-Economic Panel' reaching back as far as ten years. The authors argue that this approach is more adequate than taking information from the different waves of the panel. Their main argument is that too little variation is observed in these waves. I do not know how carefully the information from these retrospective questions was checked by the interviewers. I suspect that the quality of data is not as good as if information were taken from the different waves of the panel (which so far covers a period of about 6 years). It might be an interesting exercise to compare the results from the two sources of data which both do not satisfy fully the econometrician's demands for good data.

All three comments are related to the design of the empirical study, the first remark being of a more general nature.

1   The design of the study

The study's main aim is to examine the influence of age on labour mobility. Ideally one would use individual records over total lifetime (typically censored from the right) to analyse this question. This would provide us with information about the sequences of direct job changes and/or unemployment spells and would additionally inform us about the duration of the different spells. Due to lack of better data, WZ use retrospective data which contain only the number of job changes (direct and via unemployment). Not only does this exclude the possibility of testing the transition behaviour by, for example, Markov chain models, but also the problem arises that different age cohorts are analysed jointly. However, due to the coarse nature of the data the latter is of no concern: Using the individual's age in 1985 as an explanatory variable controls for the effect of this variable in what is actually a *cross-section* study exploiting only the number of job changes in the ten-year period.

It would be of interest to know how much variation is taken out of the sample of this study by considering only workers who were not younger than 25 in 1974 and not older than 60 in 1984. For low qualified immigrants, in particular, working life starts already much earlier. The upper limit might be of less importance since highly qualified men

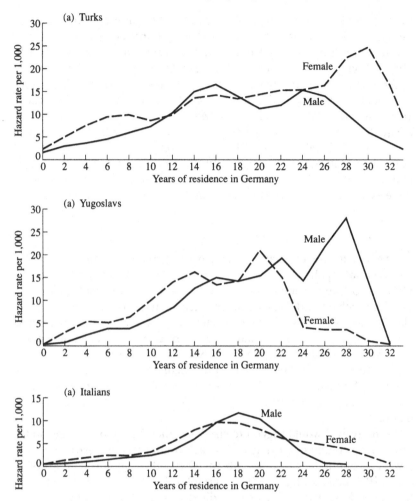

Figure 10A.1 Hazard rates of remigration for three nationalities of immigrants to the FRG

Source: adapted from Brecht and Michels (1991).

typically continue work until about the age of 65 but do not often switch their job at that age.

Finally, the nationality of foreign workers could be relevant: There have been several waves of immigration after World War II. The first groups to enter Germany were the Italians and Spanish workers, the Yugoslavs followed and finally Turkish workers moved into Germany. Therefore, the age profile of different nationalities should be different. More importantly, the *re*migration behaviour of these groups seems to differ quite substantially as is apparent from estimation results in Brecht and Michels (1991). Figure 10A.1 shows hazard rates for three nationalities which differ substantially in shape. Therefore, dummy variables indicating nationality should be added to the list of explanatory variables. Table 10.6 shows how this improves the fit. Maybe these variables are even more adequate than the duration of stay which is probably highly correlated with age and therefore causes the coefficients of both age and duration not to be significant (or less significant than in the case of natives). Such multicollinearity effects are more severe than in other instances since these estimates are the basis of simulations where only age is varied.

2   The dependent variables

I have noted already that the data do not allow the analysis of the sequence of spells such as CCCCCCC (only direct job changes), UUUUUU (only unemployment spells between employment spells) and mixtures such as CUUCUCC. In fact such an analysis might reveal more clearly that those who have never been unemployed have socio-economic characteristics differing from those experiencing unemployment. However, it would be possible to analyse the counts of U and C jointly, leading to a *bivariate* Poisson model if explanatory variables were added as before. Since standard software is not available a bivariate probit with at least three categories (0, 1, more than 1) should be used as an approximation.

Alternatively, I would suggest to check whether the double hurdle model provides a better fit of the data (using each count variable separately). The low average number of direct job changes and unemployment spells in Table 10.4 indicates that for both variables the zero count has very high frequency. In such cases the Poisson distribution, even when corrected for covariates, is no longer adequate. However, the pseudo-maximum likelihood estimates from the Poisson model in this study take care of this kind of misspecification.

3   The problem of industry-related and time-dependent variables

The authors try to capture some of the employment structure of the different industries by using the ten-year-growth of employment and the share of foreign workers in 1974 in these industries as explanatory variables. Not surprisingly, this adds explanatory power only in case of native workers when considering direct job changes (see Table 10.5):

sMany workers, in particular foreigners and those with unemployment pells, will have switched from one industry to another within the ten-year interval. This is not captured by the two industry-related variables.

WZ also use the qualification of each worker at the beginning of the period (1974). Many may have moved higher up to other qualification categories. Again this is not captured by the specification used, although in this case the specification seems more meaningful than in the case of industry-related variables mentioned before. A problem remains because of the normalization of the qualification dummies: the reference category is civil servant status, for which the phenomenon of job change is not clearly defined. On the other hand no qualification structure has been used for these workers. It might be better to use two variables, one indicating civil servant status and the other the level of qualification. Maybe this will change some of the implausible signs of the qualification variables for foreign workers (Table 10.6). In particular, the positive influence of white collar high qualification on the number of unemployment spells contradicts everybody's *a priori* expectations.

4   Concluding remarks

The paper also uses the estimated model for simulations based on projections of the age structure for Germany and the European Community. Of course, it is a matter of personal judgment whether one trusts in these age projections and the forecasts using these projections in the (estimated) Poisson regression model. I would only like to stress the empirical fact that growing age implies both higher unemployment risk (in particular duration of unemployment) and lower probability of losing one's job because of social security laws. The latter at least cannot be incorporated into the simulation approach.

REFERENCES

Brecht, B. and P. Michels (1991) 'Anwendung nichtparametrischer Schätzverfahren für die Hazardfunktion bei zensierten Daten auf die Aufenthaltsdauer von Gastarbeitern in der Bundesrepublik'. Discussion paper SFB 178 II – 137, April 1991, University of Konstanz.

Index